95

582534

MARKET OWNERSHIP

MARKET OWNERSHIP

The Art & Science of Becoming #1

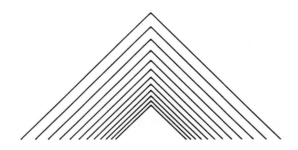

William A. Sherden

amacom
American Management Association

New York • Atlanta • Boston • Chicago • Kansas City • San Francisco • Washington, D.C.
Brussels • Mexico City • Tokyo • Toronto

This publication is designed to provide accurate and authoritative
information in regard to the subject matter covered. It is sold with
the understanding that the publisher is not engaged in rendering
legal, accounting, or other professional service. If legal advice or
other expert assistance is required, the services of a competent
professional person should be sought.

Library of Congress Cataloging-in-Publication Data

Sherden, William A.
    Market ownership : the art & science of becoming #1 / William A.
Sherden.
        p.   cm.
    Includes index.
    ISBN 0-8144-0258-5
    1. Marketing—Management.   I. Title.
HF5415.13.S515 1994
658.8—dc20   94-27809
                                                       CIP

Printing number

10   9   8   7   6   5   4   3   2   1

To
Molly,
Nathaniel,
and
Christian

Contents

Preface

One of the most profitable things your business can do is to "own" a market, that is, to become the preferred supplier within a defined market to the point where you have some immunity from the competition.

Although the concept of owning a market is occasionally mentioned in the business literature, it is largely overlooked as an opportunity and almost completely undeveloped as a concept. Yet there are, in fact, a number of companies in a variety of industries that, to various degrees, own their markets, usually within specific areas of large markets. These companies have enormous advantages over their competitors in selling and retaining customers and in the economics of their businesses.

The idea for this book came from my fifteen years of consulting experience. I became more and more intrigued by a number of companies in different industries that successfully operated as if they owned their markets—usually well-defined segments of broader markets. These companies were not necessarily the biggest or best known in their industries. However, they were, in many respects, the best because they had a powerful presence in their chosen market, immunity from price competition, excellent management principles, and superior profitability and operating economics.

Further analysis of these companies indicated that they shared several common themes in the way their managements had chosen to run their businesses. In all cases, these companies had focused on a chosen market and determined exactly what customers they wanted in the segment they valued. They ran their businesses in such a way as to maximize customer value and build an unusually high degree of trust between customers and prospects.

It became clear to me that if I were to incorporate these common operating themes into a blueprint for developing strategies for owning a market, the result would be valuable to any management that wanted to dramatically improve the long-term competitive sustainability and performance of its business.

I also wanted to write this book because of a growing concern. There are currently two isolated camps offering advice to management: the quantitatively oriented strategists and the subjectively oriented advisers who deal with quality and related topics. The strategist views the world much like an economist, focusing on concepts such as low-cost production, learning curves, and economies of scale. Typically, the strategist has great difficulty recognizing the relevance and importance of topics such as quality, customer relationships, and employee satisfaction. In contrast, the quality camp lacks the strategist's bottom-line orientation and often promotes a vision that management cannot implement. Many companies, for example, have great difficulty implementing a total quality program because they are too unfocused; they try to be all things to all customers. They may also waste resources in servicing unprofitable customers and thus lack the financial capacity to invest in quality.

Having conducted hundreds of studies involving both strategy and quality, I began to realize that while these two camps are, individually, severely deficient, each has a valuable principle and their concepts should be tied together. The market ownership concept and implementation frameworks thoroughly integrate the quantitative and strategy concepts with the qualitative, customer-oriented ones. For instance, I have provided a detailed model explaining how subjective phenomena such as market affinity lead to bottom-line impacts. There is also a model for linking quality with the broader concept of customer value (e.g., customer tradeoffs between price and quality).

Market ownershp represents a special relationship, a strong bond that a company has created through superior strategy and execution aimed at a particular market. In its highest form, it is analogous to becoming the sponsor of an affinity group, for example, the American Automobile Association (AAA), in which members (customers) and potential members (prospects) have common needs or interests and grant the affinity group sponsor (AAA) special status for fulfilling their needs in an especially focused way.

The market ownership concept is a unique way to gain formidable competitive advantages. These advantages are longer lasting than those effected by other general strategies—and, given the escalating pace of change and competitive intensity on what is virtually a global scale, having such advantages is an increasingly important consideration. Today, proprietary products are quickly rendered obsolete by technological advances; virtually instant copying by competitors shrinks the life span of previously unique products, rendering them mere commodities. Competing on price alone is a strategy that can lead to earnings problems and cause businesses to come unraveled. Even companies seeking scale advantages through expansion may end up trying to be all things to all markets; such companies may find their unit costs increasing sharply because of product proliferation and their books of business comprising marginal--or even unprofitable--customers.

There are many strategies that sustain market ownership; I explore all of them in depth in this book. The most important element, however, the main support of the company that owns its market, is its affinity with customers and prospects in a clearly defined market. Once developed, this market will continue as long as the company stays focused and reasonably current with competitive developments.

Acknowledgments

There are a number of people I wish to acknowledge as key contributors to this book. The first is Sandra Moore, an independent editor, who assisted me with all stages of the project from the original proposal to the final draft, providing guidance, encouragement, and critical feedback. I would also like to thank Andrea Pedolsky, my original acquisitions editor at AMACOM, for providing important insights regarding the ultimate reader of this book.

I especially want to thank various individuals and their companies for providing interviews and information that enriched the case studies and concepts presented in this book. This includes:

Diversified Investment Advisors:	Jack Boyce, assistant vice president; and Chris Cumming, vice president of marketing
Donnelly Corporation:	Don Auch, vice president of marketing and sales; and Maryam Komejan, corporate secretary
DPIC:	Paula Crisler, communications manager; the late Peter Hawes, president; and Jeanne Hotchkiss, director of corporate communications

Hewlett-Packard: Alan Bickell, head of geographic
                                       operations; Jim Christensen,
                                       manager, press/industry
                                       consultant relations; and
                                       Laurie Nichol, press relations
                                       representative
The Moorings: Charlie Cary, chairman; and Jean
                                       Larroux, vice president of
                                       investor relations
Sun Life Assurance Company of   Ian Kennedy, vice president of
   Canada: individual customer services;
                                       and the staff of the Sun Life
                                       Annuity Service Center
USAA: John Walmsley, media relations
                                       specialist

Finally, I want to thank my wife, Molly, for her assistance in negotiating the contract for this book and providing advice regarding intellectual property law and the publishing business in general.

MARKET OWNERSHIP

Chapter 1

A Different
Way to Compete

While companies that own their markets exist on a continuum of weak to strong, every one is distinguished by a number of marketplace characteristics in customer and prospect behavior. If, within a tightly defined marketplace, a company exhibits many of the characteristics listed in Exhibit 1-1, then the company has some form of market ownership.

In its prospect world, the company that owns its market is often the first to be considered, the logical choice at the outset of the purchase process. This is the company that's usually short-listed for a particular product or service or for solving a specific problem. The GhostBuster criterion—"Who you gonna call?"—applies here. If a particular company is clearly the answer, then it owns its market.

The company, having developed a strong image, dominates its chosen market. Depending on the maturity of its market ownership strategies, the company will experience either very rapid growth or very high market shares. Although a company that owns its market may have only a small percentage (perhaps only a single-digit share) of the overall product/service category, its "ownership" of its chosen market segment may be 50 to 90 percent.

In time, the originally small company may, if it chooses to do so, become a large and significant player. However, companies with strong market ownership restrain their solicitation outside their chosen markets and are very picky about which segments they will serve. They deliberately stick with the clearly defined

Exhibit 1-1. Indicators of market ownership.

Prospect World (Competitive Marketplace)
- Is a logical or most favored supplier at the outset of a purchase decision.
- Has dominant market share or the most rapid growth in narrowly defined markets.
- Is very selective in bid participation in seeking new business.
- Has strong, positive brand equity.
- Is perceived as the quality leader.
- Constitutes a safe purchase—has built trust that company follows through on promises.

Customer World
- Is seen as the best company to be with.
- Enjoys very high customer retention relative to industry norms.
- Benefits from large purchases of the company's products or services.
- Has high cross-sell ratios of new products to existing customers.
- Has high customer referral rate.
- Attracts best distributors (a type of customer).
- Benefits from customers' willingness to wait for new product introductions.
- Benefits from a "halo effect."

---

market focus and strategy rather than accept business outside their chosen markets. They do not seek growth or size as objectives.

Throughout the sales/service process, competitors have a long way to go to overcome the initial credibility of the company that owns its market. Although the company clearly has strong brand equity, it has much more than just brand awareness. While the company may in fact spend quite lavishly on advertising, it uses advertising to enhance its success model, not as the key to gaining an advantage. In general, this company usually spends far less on advertising per dollar of sales than does its average competitor. It can do so because it carries an image of trust, the perception of being a safe purchase. This company is not merely the best known.

In head-to-head competition, a larger company will often

lose out to the smaller company that owns its market. Larger competitors are likely to overlook the company as insignificant in the broader market and even to dismiss it as a niche player that does nothing particularly special. Through complacency (and perhaps arrogance), larger competitors fail to see the underlying success model and therefore don't feel threatened by it. This can be a major mistake. There may not appear to be a problem if the competitive arena represents a small submarket; nevertheless, at some point bigger competitors will start to recognize that the company that once owned a small piece of the market has begun to dominate a larger share of the market. Often, the company with market ownership dominates highly profitable and attractive market segments, leaving the larger companies to compete for the less attractive segments and to do so on the basis of price competition.

There are many quantifiable indicators of market ownership within a company's customer base, the most important of which is customer retention. A company with exceptional customer retention probably has a strong market ownership. Even in highly volatile, price-sensitive markets, where average customer defection rates may be as high as 20 percent per year, the company that owns its market may lose only 5 percent of its customers annually.

This high degree of customer loyalty and trust manifests itself in other ways. The company with market ownership often has deeper relationships that generate both larger sales for existing products and high cross-sell ratios for new ones. While competitors dream up new cross-selling strategies and have only mixed success, the company with market ownership appears to cross-sell effortlessly. Its strategies succeed when most of the industry has written off the cross-sell strategy as a flawed concept.

Another evidence of market ownership is a high referral rate from existing clients. When a company receives a significantly higher proportion of its business from referrals than do its competitors, market ownership is quite likely at work. Referral business is highly attractive; the referred customer is a buyer who is strongly predisposed to select the company and undoubtedly believes that he or she is buying the best.

Much of a company's success in furthering customer relationships is attributable to the "halo effect," which grants the company's new strategies and product introductions the same credibility and trust earned by the original strategies or products. This "self-endorsement" has a big impact: Clients who believe they have received high value and reliability in the past expect that new products will deliver the same. In addition, the company with market ownership need not be the industry innovator. Customers are willing to wait for its new product releases, and, once those products are introduced, sales are likely to surpass those achieved by the original product innovators.

The halo effect also extends to the company's perceived quality of service. A number of client studies I have conducted show that the customers of a company that owns its market often believe that the company's capabilities are stronger than they may actually be. Although it is doing many of the right things in the right areas, the company may not be as strong in all aspects of product or service delivery as its customers believe it to be. (This can be very frustrating to those competitors who can prove to themselves, through benchmarking internal performance, that they are doing better in some areas, even though they score lower in some of the same areas as the company that owns the market. More often than not, they dismiss any contrary customer research as being invalid in some way.)

Where the goal is to become the chosen company in a chosen market, the market ownership concept offers a different way to compete. Its strategy, which is firmly linked to providing higher value to the customer, requires carefully defining the business and chosen market; knowing the market better; focusing resources on maximizing customer value; and pursuing appropriately aggressive marketing strategies to penetrate the market deeply and to ensure customer satisfaction and loyalty. The success model is quite simple. It can be replicated by companies with insightful leaders who are willing to focus on select market segments and to deliver exceptional value to customers.

Although the concept can accommodate other strategic frameworks, it is the master blueprint for executives who seek to "own" a market. Whether used as a vision or a blueprint, it offers significant advantages over existing management prescriptions, which tend to deal with isolated ideas such as quality, culture, and reengineering.

As a vision, the market ownership concept sets higher goals for the company than mere incremental improvements to operations, and it can provide tremendous advantages that are hard to replicate in any other way. As a blueprint, it provides a more complete view of the business and ties together many otherwise excellent, but disparate, management ideas.

An underlying thesis of this book is that management people are overloaded with ideas on how to improve their business but that it is virtually impossible for managements to copy best-case companies and even harder for them to integrate successfully good ideas into their operations. Each individual company's situation is too different to allow it to copy another's success readily. As a master strategy, the market ownership concept does not attempt to invalidate the current base of management advice; nor does it overlook other important strategies. Rather, it draws on many excellent management concepts, introducing them as a holistic vision of the company and a game plan for developing a market ownership strategy.

This book constructs a practical framework for applying the market ownership concept and provides instructions for "getting there." Thus, it goes beyond setting a vision for corporate improvement or providing a well-organized list of best-practice ideas and case studies.

The market ownership concept applies equally well to large or small, strong or weak companies; its application, however, varies for different situations. Since achieving market ownership is a multiyear undertaking, the concept is most useful to those managements that are oriented toward building their businesses incrementally through a long-term vision. It is least useful to those seeking rapid growth or a quick-fix success story. In particular, the market ownership concept has little bearing on growth through acquisition, which in many cases works against the internally built approach that underlies market ownership.

Chapter 2
How Market Ownership Works

Although companies that own their markets come from many different industries and differ in many respects, they share a number of distinct business practices that are key to developing and maintaining their market ownership. Looking closely at these companies, you find nine common themes that reflect management philosophy, strategy, and operations, characteristics that drive their success (see Exhibit 2-1).

Each of these nine characteristics is critical to building a market ownership strategy. No one alone has much impact; each one interacts synergistically with the other eight. The first three factors are strategic concepts; the remaining six require a superior vision of the company. (As you will see later, sound strategies and superior vision are essential to owning a market.)

These nine characteristics can be summed up in the word *focus* and its corollaries *consistency* and *connectivity*.

Sharp focus starts with a clear vision of business definition and target customers. Companies that own their markets know precisely what businesses they are in, and they have a highly developed focus on all aspects of their operations. Their focus covers every aspect of the business's operations, from organizational goals, incentives, and operating practices and policies across the corporate spectrum to product manufacturing and delivery systems. These companies know precisely who their chosen customers are and what their customers value. They connect with their customers by knowing how to serve them

Exhibit 2-1. Common management characteristics of companies that own their markets.

- A clear vision of the profitable, or potentially profitable, customer
- An emphasis on maximizing value of the product/service to customer
- A focused, coherent business model
- Integrity throughout all aspects of the organization
- A strong commitment to employees
- Aggressive and shrewd marketing combined with an appropriate, relationship-oriented solicitation style
- Superior customer information
- Management bias in favor of financial stability and against growth for growth's sake
- Discipline sufficient to keep the company on course, yet swift-moving enough to keep pace with competitive developments

exceptionally well, and they know how to earn superior profits by doing so. In other words, focus takes in every detail of the business, and does so with consistency and connectivity.

The Market Ownership Model

The nine factors listed in Exhibit 2-1 have complex interrelated effects. The way they work together to create market ownership is described in the following three-step model:

1. The clear vision of, and operational focus on, serving a defined customer in a defined way promotes operating efficiency and creates an affinity with customers and prospects in the target market (see Exhibit 2-2).
2. Market affinity engenders further operational efficiencies that significantly improve both profitability and the company's competitive advantage in the market. This tends to be a self-perpetuating cycle.
3. Improved profits are (at least in part) reinvested in further enhancing value to the customer via product or service improvements or increased operational efficiency.

Exhibit 2-2. The impact of affinity with key constituents on the company's profitability.

Results of Affinity	Revenue Enhancement			Cost Reduction			
	Sales	Price	Cost per Sale	Channel Development	Promotion	Production	R & D
With Prospects							
Favored Bidder	High bid inclusion	Less sensitive	Higher hit rate	Attract more and better distributors	Less promotion required		More knowledge from existing customers
Referrals	Additional source of sales	Less sensitive	Presold				
With Customers							
Retention	Higher net growth	Insulation from price competition	Greater amortization of up-front costs			Lower costs due to learning curve	
Cross-sell	Additional source of sales	Less sensitive	Reduced sales cost				
Willing to wait	Sales less affected by new competitive offerings	Maintain prices for existing products	Reduced need to placate customers	Retain existing distributors loyalty		Restraint on product/feature proliferation	Can be a successful follower with proven new products
With Distributors	More loyalty Bigger share of their business	Insulation from price competition	Reduced cost/sale	Attract more and better distribution Retain them longer	More willing to cooperate in joint promotions	Greater feedback on operations	Source of ideas
With the Salesforce	More sales production Higher customer retention	More able to sustain price levels	Less turnover More level compensation				
With Production Employees	Higher customer retention					Higher customer retention High productivity and quality More qualified applicants	
With Suppliers						Collaboration in maximizing customer value	Source of ideas— sharing technology

Step 1: From a Clear Vision to Market Affinity

The nine characteristics listed in Exhibit 2-1 combine to enable companies to grow to "own" their markets. Together they can lead to improved efficiency and create market affinity, the second part of the model.

Focus on a Defined Customer

The first and most important characteristic of companies that own their markets is a clear vision of the attractive (that is, profitable) customer. Any business built on this concept is off to a good start, whether or not it actively seeks to own its market. This focused definition of the customer is where building market affinity starts; it concentrates the company's marketing resources on a much smaller prospect world, creating in the most efficient manner possible a presence in the market. The target customer gets much more exposure to the company than if the company were to spend its scarce marketing resources attacking a broader market. (Conversely, lacking this focus, even an enlightened business will squander its resources by serving a diverse customer base. The result will be mixed profitability, and management will probably be too constrained to make the necessary investments to own a market.) The focus on a defined customer does a number of things to the company's operations:

- It narrows down the company's prospect list, which creates efficiencies in sales and marketing.
- It creates a more homogeneous customer base with common needs. The company can focus on serving these needs, thus eliminating the proliferation of product features that can greatly increase a company's cost structure.
- R&D needs are similarly reduced, since the company can focus on the evolving needs of a focused customer base rather than on the whole market.
- A tightly defined customer base ensures that the company will have more consistent profitability. This avoids the typical scenario for most companies, in which 20 percent of the

clients produce the high profits that are then frittered away
serving the other, lower-profit 80 percent.

- Finally, customer focus promotes clarity in communicating
the company's strategy and vision to all employees. This
creates efficiencies because employees know what is important and thus are able to avoid duplicative and inconsistent
efforts in any of the company's operations.

Companies that own their markets have a focus on one or
more defined segments. For example, Apple Computer initially
focused on educational institutions by providing affordable computers to students and faculty. Later, as students moved into the
workplace, they were likely to retain their loyalty to Apple, even
though many worked for IBM-oriented companies. Although it is
a relatively young company, Paychex successfully competes with
ADP, the long-dominant company in the payroll processing market, because it has targeted smaller businesses and their distinct
needs. Paychex now virtually owns this market. Wal-Mart built
its market ownership by focusing on rural marketplaces where
customers were served by low-volume, high-cost retailers. This
focus has been so successful that in the space of ten years, Wal-
Mart grew from a small retailer to a major corporation and
overtook the longtime leader, Sears, in both revenue and profits.

Emphasis on Maximizing Value to the Customer

The second characteristic, maximizing value to the customer,
represents the company's desire to know better than its competitors what its chosen customers value most in terms of product
and service features, quality, and price. The company's efforts
are directed toward making sure that its strategies, organization,
and resource allocation are optimally aligned to deliver value.

The success of Lexus, for example, clearly demonstrates that
buyers of luxury cars value more than prestige. By offering a car
similar in quality to BMW or Mercedes but at substantially lower
prices, Lexus has achieved, in a very short time, an enviable niche
in the luxury automobile market.

The focus on customer value ultimately drives the company
toward becoming a high-quality company and a low-cost pro-

ducer. It provides a strong framework and the discipline for ensuring, to the greatest extent possible, that the company is allocating its resources effectively—that it is focusing on those product features or services that are valued most highly by its customers and ignoring those that are not as desired or that may not be needed at all. This discipline extends to reducing unneeded overhead, restructuring (if and as necessary) the company's existing operations, and making prudent investments for the future.

As a result of this customer-oriented philosophy, the customer develops trust in the company, clearly viewing the company's product or service as the best deal to be obtained in the market. This trust is reinforced when the company continues to focus on improving the value of existing products and extends that value to those new products or services it introduces.

Devising a Focused Business Model

The third characteristic, a focused, coherent business model, involves developing a tight-knit, streamlined strategy and organization for serving the client. Once it is armed with a defined target market and a knowledge of what customers value, the company picks an optimal way to attract, serve, and retain chosen customers. (This, in turn, maximizes the value of the customer to the company.)

This focused system requires consistency and connectivity in all aspects of the company's operations. It starts with the customer, continues through distribution channels, production, and client servicing units and includes all managerial and support functions. It demands coherency in communicating strategy and an alignment of internal values and policies with a single vision of how to deliver maximum customer value.

IBM's once-strong market ownership was built on an exceptionally coherent business plan. IBM created first-rate, locally deployed sales and service teams to help customers use their high-priced, complex mainframe computers effectively and efficiently. In those days, the local IBM team was as much a part of the product as the hardware. Dell Computer, on the other hand, has built a focused business model around selling deeply discounted personal computer equipment. Dell utilizes a very low-cost direct-response service capability and tight management on all cost items.

Wal-Mart has developed a coherent business aimed at reducing costs at all levels of the product delivery system, from product manufacturer to the retail store, which supports its strategy of providing deeply discounted merchandise.

The focused business model greatly simplifies a company's operations. It streamlines distribution systems and provides a strong degree of consistency and connection between all operating aspects. Since redundancies and inconsistencies are either reduced or eliminated, there are fewer components to manage within the business, and the company can therefore direct its quality delivery better.

Focusing also promotes clearer communication internally and constrains the company from adding new channels or ventures that can dilute its strategy or drain its resources. The company sends consistent messages to the market in terms of what business it is in, thus reinforcing the company's presence and credibility in its targeted market.

What the customer experiences is a consistent way of doing business at every level, from initial purchase to follow-up interactions. Simply put, the company becomes easy to do business with. This translates into credibility and a perception of quality by customers and prospects.

Integrity

The fourth characteristic, integrity in all aspects of its organization, refers to the company's policy on following through on commitments to customers, distributors, employees, suppliers, investors, the community, and any other relevant stakeholding party. Integrity sometimes costs more in the short term, but it pays off in the long term. While integrity is important in any business, it is essential to market ownership; it promotes the efficiencies that come from improved quality—doing things right the first time rather than taking the shortcuts that will require reworking or some other payment or cost in the future.

Integrity is critical to building affinity with customers and prospects because it creates the trust in the company that sets it apart from most of its competitors. Ratings of institutional credibility done by the Gallup polling firm and other researchers strongly suggest that the average customer has limited trust in most institutions, including (perhaps even especially) businesses. Most consumers, for example, are highly suspicious of whether their insurance companies, when and if they are needed, will ultimately pay their claims. Some insurance companies do not, in fact, come through. On the other hand, one insurance company, Chubb, has a corporate philosophy that roughly states, "We are in the business of paying claims." This element of its mission is communicated broadly throughout the company; it is the major drive behind Chubb's superior customer satisfaction ratings.

Integrity is vital to maintaining market ownership. Although customers usually grant companies that own their markets some leeway in the competitiveness of their products, it doesn't take long for a serious conflict or a series of conflicting actions on the part of the company to erode credibility and affinity. Thus, when several contaminated bottles of Tylenol were found in stores in 1986 and a customer died after using the product, it was a wise move on the part of Johnson & Johnson to pull its entire line of Tylenol off the market even though only a few containers of the drug were found to contain poison. This was a relatively inexpensive move, however, compared with the cost of ruining customer affinity had the company acted otherwise. Perrier made a similarly intelligent move in pulling its entire line of the beverage temporarily off the shelves in 1990 when some bottles were found to contain potentially harmful chemicals.

Integrity also pays off in building relationships with suppliers. It becomes increasingly important for the company that owns its market to develop trustful relationships with suppliers, since the suppliers then become more willing to establish favorable terms with the company than they do for other of the company's competitors.

Integrity has a significant impact on employees' loyalty and morale and on their commitment to producing quality work. This has a truly impressive payoff, because the company retains employees longer and the employees are more productive.

582534

Commitment to Employees

Concern for and commitment to the employee, the fifth characteristic, directly reflects the value the company places on all its employees at all levels. The company that owns its market acknowledges that its employees, because of their direct contact, are the critical resource in delivering value to the customer. The impressions and relationships employees create and their impact on productivity, quality, and product innovation are critical to success.

It is very unlikely that any company can own a market without being employee-oriented. A study conducted by *Inc.* magazine (November 1992) found that, among those businesses that the magazine tracked, the companies that consistently proved successful were those that had a strong orientation toward employee satisfaction.

Being employee-oriented provides many benefits operationally, as well as in the marketplace. As I have noted, companies that own their markets view employees as a critical resource. They invest heavily in screening to recruit the best employees and then in training and developing the new employees far better than do their competitors. These steps develop unusually strong bonds between management and employees, and the employees generally stay with the company much longer than is typical for the industry they are in.

Such a commitment also gives the company a reputation for being a superior place to work, greatly reducing recruiting costs while increasing the size and quality of the applicant pool. The image of being a superior place to work clearly improves a company's ability to retain employees; workers feel they work for the best employer and that to go somewhere else would be a big step down. Obviously, the company's ability to hire better people, train them better, and keep them much longer has enormous productivity payoffs.

The reward for building customer affinity shows up in at least two ways: (1) Because they deal with more competent staff, the customer and prospect perceive that the company itself is highly competent, and (2) customers believe that the company delivers higher quality service. This further builds trust in the company and its image and reputation in the market.

Employee retention also drives customer retention, especially for those businesses where it is desirable to assign specific employees to work wth specific customers. When employees leave, customers are likely to feel they have lost some continuity, that part of the product is gone, that they'll have to start over and build a new relationship with the company's representative. At this point, customers are inclined to leave the company out of frustration and the perception that they have less to lose by switching suppliers. Finally, nothing degrades a company's credibility quicker than having a reputation for high employee turnover.

Aggressive Marketing

Aggressive, shrewd marketing combined with an appropriate relationship-oriented selling style is required for the company to be heard in the market and for its market ownership to catch on. The goal is to become the dominant, best-known player with the highest quality reputation in the industry. Effective sale channels and promotion are required if the company is to go beyond being just an outfit with a superior offering.

Companies that own their markets are usually shrewd, aggressive marketers, but they're also cautious about their solicitation style, which starts when the company develops high-quality sales channels that provide value to the client through mutually beneficial, needs-based selling. These companies espouse a philosophy that takes a long-term view of the customer (rather than a one-sided sales effort to make any sale at any cost) and that has a strong positive impact on the company's reputation and post-sales customer satisfaction and retention. The company is also likely to market to existing clients just as much as it does to new ones, thus promoting client penetration (cross-selling new products, for instance) and customer retention.

Because it is armed with a focused customer, the company is able to target specific clients with specific needs at the specific times when those needs emerge and to do so with the right product offering. From the customer's perspective, this is appropriate solicitation; the company is reaching them when they are most open to sales, rather than continually bombarding them indiscriminately with sales offerings. From the company's perspective this is efficient marketing in terms of cost per sale and because it minimizes damage that might occur through inappropriate solicitation.

Finally, the company has its capabilities, track record, and reputation in place before it boasts its wares via sales promotions. It does not promise things it cannot deliver. This is both efficient and appropriate, because the advertising message is more likely to be heard and believed when it is consistent with the company's reputation. This also separates the company from others in its industry who promise anything and can't support their claims, and so builds even more customer trust in the company.

Fidelity, which owns a segment of the mutual funds business, is often referred to as a "jazzy marketer." Lacking a sales force, Fidelity spends a lot of money on direct response advertising and backs it up with a superior telephone-based customer service system. Fidelity also does extensive mailings to existing customers, much of which provides valuable consumer information that applies far beyond the product offering. Fidelity's customer service representatives are trained to provide quality service and, at the same time, to sell products in an appropriate way. It is not unusual for inbound callers seeking information to walk away with one of Fidelity's products. However, Fidelity avoids making outbound sales calls, which would annoy customers and erode the goodwill that underlies its market ownership.

Superior Customer Information

The seventh "must-have," superior customer information, points to the company's unique ability to create and use information to understand better its clients' needs and preferences and to service them in a higher-quality and much more efficient way than its competitors. For example, when customer service workers are armed with complete information, they can function faster and more efficiently. They can serve customers' needs better because they see a more complete picture of the existing relationship and have all the information necessary for them to understand the client. Because it can provide speedier and more accurate servicing, the company reduces time spent correcting mistakes, further improves its efficiency, and provides higher-quality service than its competitors.

Customer information is essential for relationship marketing and to support efforts such as cross-selling and customer retention. (Cross-selling, for example, is a complete gamble, very inefficient unless the company has superior customer information.) Finally, superior information on clients' needs is essential if the company is to succeed in developing new products; it greatly reduces the high failure rate companies normally experience when introducing new products.

Customers perceive a level of service that is as welcome as it is unexpected. They quickly come to understand that the company takes a holistic view of its relationship with its clients and that the company is invested in maintaining the vital information necessary to service the customer's account. This perception goes a long way to augment the company's image.

Superior customer information also helps the company avoid costly mistakes that damage customer relationships. A not uncommon example is the customer who has several product relationships with the same bank, such as checking, savings, and one or more loans. Let's say the customer has a problem relating to one product—such as a late payment on a loan—and the bank takes strong action, such as subjecting the customer to a threatening collections process. The customer may have thousands of dollars on deposit with the bank, many times more than the loan payment. If the bank had taken into account the full customer relationship—if it had used the full information available in its customer records—it might have used a less drastic means of dealing with the late payment; for example, a bank customer service representative might have inquired whether the customer might want to meet the payment from a checking or savings account.

L. L. Bean, for instance, maintains its market ownership in the mail-order business by using highly sophisticated customer databases that enable it to understand each customer better in terms of product preferences and purchase behavior. This helps L. L. Bean provide high-quality service to the people who call its service centers and aids it in managing and targeting its direct-mail merchandise catalogues.

Wal-Mart has successfully employed bar-code technology to collect data on customer purchases at the point of sale, enabling it to know immediately which products are selling. Wal-Mart thus avoids shortages while keeping inventory low and has the means to understand its customers' changing buying patterns better.

Bias toward Financial Stability: Disciplined Management

The final two characteristics require discipline on the part of the company's leaders:

1. Management must have a bias for financial stability over unrestrained growth. The emphasis must be on long-term, consistent financial health and on avoiding growth for growth's sake.
2. Management must also have the discipline to stay on course, to stick with the strategy and vision of the company and not allow itself to be distracted by every new opportunity that emerges. At the same time, management must be alert to real changes taking place in the industry and must respond to them swiftly and appropriately.

These disciplines are critical. They hold all the other themes together and enable the company to build and maintain its market ownership for the long term.

Management's long-term view of the business and its preference for profitability and stability over growth helps the company avoid overreacting to periods of price competition. Although growth may suffer in the short term, the discipline of maintaining price levels enables the company to continue to earn healthy profits during good times and bad. A management that is less interested in growth for growth's sake is also less likely to make other serious mistakes, such as making a poor acquisition, extending sales channels beyond what it can control well, introducing products that are flawed or untested, or discounting prices. All of these actions can be very costly and can cause the company to experience long periods of poor earnings.

It is during industry downturns that the company with market ownership shines. As other companies are forced to cope with poor earnings and to correct their past mistakes, the company's disciplined, long-term focus on profitability will usually enable it to sustain good earnings. And while the competition is preoccupied, often with slashing staff and making drastic cuts in spending, the company that owns its market will continue to maintain its quality of service and will invest in further improving value to the customer.

Consistent weathering of industry downturns and of tricky shifts in the market further add to the company's credibility. The company stands out as an exception, adroit at avoiding industry-wide problems that have beset others.

Management discipline is essential to keeping the organization focused on the strategy and vision that contribute to sustaining market ownership, while at the same time keeping pace with important changes in the industry. This in itself enhances the company's productivity, since resources are not wasted on every new industry fad or on the multitude of potential opportunities that emerges. Discipline also enables management to communicate the company's strategy and values by consistently doing what it says it plans to do, thus building the company's credibility and assurance with customers and prospects.

Each of the nine characteristics I describe is integral to building and sustaining a market ownership. As I noted earlier in the chapter, the characteristics interact synergistically; if a company lacks one or more, it will have great difficulty in owning a market:

1. Without a clear vision of its customer, the company will try to be all things to all customers. The company will lose its distinctive image in the marketplace and will very likely become a high-cost producer.
2. Without a focus on maximizing value to the customer, the company's products and services will inevitably appear to be undistinguished—or even unattractive—to customers. This perception will remain no matter how much is spent on sales efforts to convince customers otherwise.
3. Without a focused, coherent business system, the com-

pany can become too cumbersome and inefficient to provide valuable products and services.

4. Without integrity, the company cannot gain the trust of
its customers and prospects; it will therefore become impossible for clients to build an affinity with the company.

5. Without a strong commitment to employees, the company
will not retain the loyal staff that is so critical to providing
good service, retaining customers, and developing truly
efficient operations.

6. Without aggressive, shrewd marketing, the company cannot build sufficient presence in its target market for market ownership to catch on.

7. Without superior information on its customers, the company will find it very difficult to understand its customers
and prospects better than do its competitors. Nor will the
company be able to provide the good service that is based
on having a complete picture of the client's relationship
with the company.

8. Without a bias for financial stability over unrestrained
growth, the company can fall victim to periods of financial
distress. Such periods would force it to cut back on its
strengths, lose credibility in the market, and substantially
depreciate its market ownership.

9. Without astuteness in assessing developments in its markets, the company may involve itself in activities that will
dilute its strength and ultimately weaken its market ownership.

These characteristics promote operational efficiency and lead
to the second part of the model—market affinity.

Step 2: Affinity with the Market
And Other Constituents

Strong market affinity is clearly manifested in the company's
superior results in terms of:

- Favored bidder status
- A high referral rate

- Ability to attract more-profitable customers
- Customer retention
- Cross-selling success and customer penetration
- A willingness by customers and prospects to wait for product innovation

As I have noted, these characteristics build affinity with other key constituents, such as employees, distributors, and suppliers. In this section I describe how affinity with customers and other constituents has a favorable impact on the company's profitability.

The company that achieves a favored-bidder status has a highly prized position. The company will be included in more sales opportunities than its competitors, opportunities that combine growth potential with reduced expenditures on sales calls and advertising. The company is also more likely to have a higher "win rate," which means that the dollars spent on proposal development will produce higher paybacks. Both of these factors lower the company's cost of sales, usually a major component of unit costs. The favored bidder is also likely to retain healthy profit margins during the competitive bid situation because the prospective client will pay more for the psychological assurance that the favored-bidder company offers.

Just as the favored bidder has many sales advantages, so do the distributors and salespeople that align themselves with it. By offering greater growth potential rather than higher compensation, the company is able to attract and retain high-quality, productive salespeople and outside distributors. In almost every industry, the stronger the company's bidder status and market affinity, the lower the need to pay high incentive compensation. The reverse is also true; the lower the bidder status of the company, the more likely that it will have to pay a premium to influence aggressive sale efforts.

This is a win-win situation for the salesforce, the company, and the client. The company's salespeople have an easier job of selling and are more productive and better received by new prospects; because their higher productivity more than offsets their lower rate of compensation, they may earn more money than their counterparts at other companies. The company gets a lower sales compensation rate, one that is more likely to remain flat and stable. The client gets a lower-priced product provided by a higher-quality company representative who is not greedy or desperate and who is willing to spend their time to better understand and meet its needs.

Referral sales have many advantages. Like the favored bidder, the prospective customer comes to the company strongly predisposed to buy its product; the customer has already done the homework by drawing on contacts to narrow down the field of suppliers and trusts this process far more than advertising or dealing with an unknown sales representative. As a result, referrals shorten the sales cycle, greatly improve the company's success rate, and insulate the company (to a degree) from price competition. Referred customers are more likely to stay with the company, in part because they are motivated by having found a good company rather than having to seek out the best deal.

Perhaps the most significant indication of market affinity is a customer base that is more consistently profitable than that of the average company. It is not unusual, for example, for 30 percent of the average company's customers to be profitable, 40 percent about breakeven, and the remaining 30 percent money-losers. This situation, which at best results in mediocre profitability, is one that most managements are unaware of. The company that owns its market may have some unprofitable customers, but that portion may account for only 10 percent of the total customer base, rather than 30 percent.

The difference is partly a direct result of the disciplined focus on a known and tightly targeted client segment. It is also attributable to the fact that the company that owns its market usually attracts better, more profitable customers. This is true if for no other reason than that its customers are cautious about picking their suppliers and tend to stick with the companies they choose. They go to greater lengths to seek out the most reputable companies—the ones that are known for integrity, quality, and competence—and they rely heavily on reputation, referrals, and comparative studies such as those found in *Consumer Reports*. These buyers usually make great customers with favorable profit characteristics. They seek a longer-term relationship and therefore have good retention rates; they value more than price and thus are not as likely to force the company to negotiate prices to unprofitable levels; they value the supplier as a critical resource—given the original investment made to find the best—and treat the organization with respect; that is, they do not try to cut corners or exact concessions from the company outside the original contract.

This can work in reverse, too; companies with mixed reputations—those with "iffy" credibility—often attract the bottom of the barrel in terms of unprofitable clients, clients who seem to be attracted to suppliers that a reputable company will not deal with. (It may simply refuse to bid on the business.) The prospective customer organization ultimately deals with suppliers, who, on average, may have no market presence and perhaps even a poor reputation. There is a natural alignment of good and bad customers with good and bad companies. The same also applies to the quality of distributors.

Retention is another major factor in net growth. A company with high customer retention does not have to devote as much in resources to selling to new customers to achieve the same growth rate as does a company with lower retention. In fact, in some industries with high customer turnover, the growth companies are often those with the highest customer retention and not necessarily those organizations with the highest new-sales rates.

Customer affinity grows as the company and the customer establish a longer-term, deeper relationship. The operating costs are lower for serving a well-established, longtime customer whose needs are well known to the company, because the company is well along the learning curve in serving that client. Increased affinity can also lead to higher penetration of the client's business, more cross-selling of new products, and a decreased focus on competitive pricing, all of which keep earnings healthy and more stable. Finally, high retention has many of the same benefits accruing to the favored bidder, specifically, the securing of stronger ties to sales channels, which also benefit economically when the company retains its customers longer.

As customers gain trust in the company and in the value of its products, they become much more receptive to purchasing additional products. Cross-selling new products to existing customers has many advantages. When the response from customers is strong, the cost per sale diminishes, time is saved by avoiding lengthy prospecting and competitive bidding processes, and the payoff per dollar in direct mail advertising is greater. Altogether, the company that owns its market often can successfully cross-sell to its clients while reducing the cost per sale by about 80 percent. The company also avoids competitive pressures on the prices for cross-sold products, thus maintaining healthy margins.

Cross-selling also has an impact on market affinity and customer relationships. In particular, customer retention improves with the number of product relationships the company has with the customer. Multiple product relationships intensify the customer's involvement with the company and make it much more difficult to switch to one or more new providers. And, like favored bidder and customer retention attributes, the ability to successfully cross-sell new products to existing customers helps make the company's sales force and distributors much more successful, which strengthens the company's bond with them.

It is important to note, however, that many of the advantages in cross-selling do not apply so readily if customers do not feel any particular affinity for the company. Without the affinity, the customer will probably see the cross-selling effort as no different from any other solicitation, and the economics are the same as if the company were selling the new product to a completely new customer.

The customer's willingness to wait for the company to respond to new product releases or other competitive events in the market provides the company with an invaluable asset. Few, if any, companies, are always the first to the market with the latest product innovation, let alone one that always turns out to be a success. More often than not, companies find themselves responding to changes in the market rather than being proactive. However, time is becoming more and more critical as product life cycles shorten. To the extent that a company has market affinity, customers are willing to grant the company more time to respond to competition, helping the company both to avoid losing sales to companies that are selling the latest product innovation and to maintain prices on older product lines for a longer time.

A good case on this point is Apple Computer's late entry into the portable (laptop) computer market. Companies such as

Compaq introduced these products in the mid-1980s; by the early 1990s, the market for laptops was starting to expand rapidly. However, given customers' strong affinity with Apple and its products, Apple was able to maintain sales and prices for its maturing Macintosh product line while creating a portable product of its own. Apple had the advantage of knowing that the market was there, armed with a knowledge of Apple's existing products, and that customers were willing to wait for its new laptop to come out. Called PowerBook, it was a tremendous success in terms of sales and product design and was named "Product of the Year, 1991" by *Business Week.*

The company that owns its market can also avoid making costly investments in unknown and unproven products and markets. To the extent that the company can succeed in being a reasonably quick second-to-the-market, it can observe the market's response to new products and focus development on the areas that appear to be the most promising. The company does not have to have a strategy based on the premise of always being the industry leader in innovation; this is a very costly and, over the long run, a very questionable strategy in terms of its sustainability.

The same economic advantages of customer affinity work for the company's affinity with other key constituents, particularly its distributors and sales force, employees, and suppliers.

Affinity with distributors enables the company to retain its relationship with them for much longer and prevents them from being recruited by competitors. When the company loses a distributor, it often loses more than its investment in recruiting and developing that distributor. When a distributor leaves, he inevitably takes with him as many of his client relationships as he can, and the former employer experiences a quick decline in sales. The same story applies to salespeople, who tend to operate independently, often with little loyalty to the company. When successful salespeople leave, they take a piece of the business with them.

The economics of employee affinity and retention are quite similar to that for retaining clients: The company has a large up-front investment in recruiting, training, and transitioning new employees. The longer the employee stays, the longer the time period over which this investment can be spread.

More important, however, is the higher productivity and quality of work that comes from long-time employees, especially those who feel some affinity with their employer. Like satisfied customers, employees can provide the company with referrals, which can be a high quality, pre-sold source of new hires.

Managements are coming to see suppliers not as the "vendor" to be kicked around but as a potential strategic partner in everything from developing new products to improving quality to creating highly efficient manufacturing systems. Furthermore, the supplier's trust in, and affinity with, the company means that it will be willing to grant the company special concessions, invest in joint initiatives, share technology, and give the company favorable treatment during crises (for instance, by providing supplies and raw materials that are in short supply in the industry).

Step 3: Reinvesting in Market Ownership

The interactions described in steps 1 and 2 create many operating efficiencies that produce the bottom-line advantages shown in Exhibit 2-3. The net effect of these interactions is to produce superior company economics and high profits that can be paid out to shareholders and reinvested in the business to further

Exhibit 2-3. Summary of economic advantages of market ownership.

- A more homogeneous book of business with consistent profitability across customers
- Lower selling costs for existing and new products
- Lower promotional costs per sales dollar
- Lower costs to produce products and services
- Lower R&D costs per dollar of revenue
- Ability to maintain price levels when faced with price competition and industry discounting

enhance capabilities and maximize the value provided to its customers. The reinvestment that is an integral part of step 3 again strengthens the company's market ownership, which in itself creates further affinity and other advantages (steps 1 and 2), and the cycle repeats itself.

Given all these economic benefits, it's easy to understand that a major hallmark of companies that own their markets is that they have superior earnings performance, in terms of both higher and more stable profit margins, than other companies in their industries.

A second, and more subtle, hallmark of companies that own their markets is the fact that they have the resource capacity to reinvest continually in their businesses and thus maintain their superior operations. Resource capacity is an important strategic asset; having it enables the company to invest in programs to gain a further competitive edge, while not having it forces the company to retrench or to defer indefinitely various critical needs or improvements, thus causing it to depreciate what competitive assets it had. It is a fact of life that all companies operating in competitive markets experience constant pressures on their prices, profits, and expense budgets. Therefore, all companies that are not shielded from competition are resource-constrained to varying degrees. Long-term success in an industry can hinge on how constrained the company is at any time and how much flexibility it has in making selective investments.

Let's look at a model of the importance of resource capacity. First, favorable economics produces higher profits, of which part are distributed to the company's shareholders and part are—or can be—reinvested in the company's operations, thus creating capacity and freedom to make strategic moves. A company that seeks to strengthen is market ownership would invest the available, otherwise unused, resources in programs that improve customer affinity (for instance, adding important new product features, improving operational efficiency and quality, and lowering products' cost and price). In time these investments create further economic benefits and the cycle repeats itself, strengthening the company and its market ownership and setting it apart from its competitors.

Given the ability of companies that own their markets to

reinvest continually in the business, it is not surprising that the third hallmark of such companies is that they often rank among the lowest in costs and the highest in quality in their industries. This is about as strong a competitive advantage as you can imagine. It also mocks a seriously entrenched myth among many U.S. businesses, the one that says that high quality costs more to produce, when in fact the opposite is true—for companies that own their markets. But these companies are not driven by cost or quality goals and programs; they have instead a broader vision of their customers and what they value most. Low costs and high quality are the results of the market ownership model, not key inputs to it.

A Case Study—USAA

One of the best and most complete examples of a company with a strong market ownership is USAA, which started out in 1922 as a provider of automobile insurance to U.S. Army officers and later expanded to include officers in all services. Over the years, USAA has broadened its array of offerings to include most types of financial services, consumer products, and services such as travel programs.

Though USAA is often cited as a leading case study for quality, it is best described as a company that owns its market in a broader context. USAA exhibits nearly all of the characteristics listed in Exhibit 2-1 and discussed in this chapter. This is evident from its uniquely strong position in a highly volatile, price-competitive automobile insurance market, which is its core business. In this market USAA has:

- A 90 percent penetration of its target market, which is identified as current and former officers of the armed services and their families
- A 98.7 percent customer retention rate versus an industry average of about 75 to 80 percent
- A high rate of penetration in cross-selling new products to its customer base (75 percent of its auto insurance customers have bought one or more other USAA products)
- A consistently high ranking in *Consumer Reports* studies of customer satisfaction

- A consistent growth rate over many years—6 percent real growth compared with the industry norm of 1 or 2 percent
- Dramatic increases in market share of the auto insurance market

Clearly, USAA is focused on serving a carefully defined customer that it knows more intimately than does any other competitor. Although it extends product sales to family members of people now or formerly officers in the armed services (an extension that includes numerous U.S. citizens), it still insists on this connection as the way to define its market.

Being a USAA member carries an aura of privilege or exclusivity. Furthermore, USAA has invested over several decades in understanding the needs and behaviors of its targeted market, factors that are not generally known to its competitors.

USAA started up its business with the goal of providing a low-cost, high-quality product. USAA was well aware that an auto insurance product was (and is) little more than a piece of paper and a promise to pay future claims that the customer may or may not have. To maximize value to the customer, USAA has placed strong emphasis on claims payment, ensuring that when problems do occur, claims are paid promptly and without corners cut—a major consumer criticism of the industry. As a result, USAA ranks among the highest in *Consumer Reports* studies on claims payment satisfaction.

From the outset the company has concentrated on reducing its operating expenses by developing a low-cost distribution system and by continually seeking ways to improve its operational efficiency. This has enabled USAA to enhance customer value by using much of each dollar saved to control the price of its products.

USAA created a coherent business definition from the very first, with low-cost, high-quality service provided out of one of the largest facilities in the United States, located in San Antonio, Texas. This large concentration of employees enables USAA to achieve enormous economies of scale and thus lower its unit costs.

Another facet of its coherent business definition is its distribution network, built around a superior direct-response system that uses both mail and telephone service. This form of distribution is dramatically cheaper than the typical, agent-based distribution channels employed by the majority of its competitors. USAA's sales and marketing costs are 1.7 percent of sales (premiums), compared to 13 percent for its chief competitors. More to the point, it provides a savings to the consumer of 10 to 15 percent on their premiums.

The distribution system also enables USAA to have direct contact with its customers and prospects, giving management control over the nature and the quality of interactions with the market. Competitors who are dealing with a large, geographically dispersed network of agents find it very hard to maintain similar control.

Thus, USAA created a simple business model where there is only one way to sell to and serve clients.

USAA's integrity is clearly evidenced in its level of claims satisfaction, which, as I mentioned, is very high. In an industry generally noted for its suspicious nature, USAA honors its contractual commitments in full, with a bias toward trusting customers rather than toward questioning their case. The goal of USAA claims adjusters is to satisfy the customer, not to pay out as little as they can get away with.

USAA values its employees and has exceptionally high employee satisfaction and loyalty; employee turnover is about 6 percent per year, compared to 12.6 percent or more for similar service businesses. USAA is perceived as a prestigious place to work within its local labor market and receives twenty external applications for every new job position. It carefully selects the very best candidates for full-time employment and so has an enormous advantage in terms of service capability.

Employees are highly trained for their work (one full-time trainer for every one hundred employees). They are completely supported with leading technology. USAA excels in providing employee benefits. It has a four-day work week; provides 100 percent reimbursement for job- or business-related college education, which is available from four colleges that teach courses at USAA's facilities; has on-site restaurants and shops; and provides wellness programs. In exchange, USAA expects and gets a lot from its employees in terms of productivity and quality of work.

Although USAA has grown largely through reputation and word-of-mouth referrals, it clearly demonstrates its "know the customer" marketing style in its targeted advertising in military-related literature and in its extensive communications with existing clients, to whom USAA provides general information on safety and other helpful matters as well as information on new products. In particular, USAA employs a sophisticated life-cycle approach to meeting its members needs, using cues—for instance, a change in family status such as a birth, a marriage, or a home purchase—to trigger information aimed at emerging insurance and financial services needs. These mailings reach the consumer at the right time with the right offering and use an unobtrusive product solicitation; they are accorded much higher credibility by consumers than are the vast majority of mail solicitations.

While it may send substantial product information via the mail, USAA never engages in the outbound telephone solicitation that consumers find increasingly disruptive. This is yet another example of USAA's appropriate solicitation style.

For many years USAA has been a leading company in using information technology to support its strategy. This is all the more important since USAA must rely on remote direct-response connections to the market. USAA routinely supplements its customer information files, conducting extra market research studies to profile its customers more carefully. Examples of these supplementary data on customers include:

- Surveying one fifth of all members each year to update personal information
- Conducting an annual satisfaction survey of a sample of customers
- Conducting a periodic survey of competitors' customers' satisfaction
- Sending a survey of customer satisfaction to a sample of customers that calls in for some form of service

The use of these data is particularly evident in the customer service area. An inbound caller is served by a representative armed with virtually complete information about that customer and his or her relationship with the company. By obtaining the customer's name or number, the service representative can answer most of the caller's questions and make any necessary changes or transactions without the usual routing around various departments that handle only one type of transaction. To treat the customer as a relationship rather than a product sale requires a superior information system and the integration of many databases that can be accessed immediately by the USAA representative.

USAA has a carefully crafted charter aimed at serving its members by providing valued products and services. USAA has demonstrated management discipline in sticking with this strategy over the years. It has sought neither to expand greatly its target customer base nor to follow in the path of many other insurers by broadening out into financial services that are not closely linked. Although it now provides many financial services, it does so by aiming at the same customers with the same distribution system and with the same value premise that it offered in automotive insurance. Unlike many other insurers, it developed broader financial services internally, in a controlled way. It did not branch out into wholly new markets with multiple acquisitions, the strategy that created so many problems for most large insurers and other financial services companies in the 1980s.

The positive results of USAA's strategy are clearly evident in its current competitive position and financial results and in the affinity it has with its customers. Most strikingly, USAA is a leading low-cost producer with one of the highest quality ratings in terms of customer satisfaction. It defies the notion that quality must come at a high cost, that high-quality companies are likely to be high-cost producers. USAA ranks only twenty-first in the industry; yet many others that are bigger rank much lower in terms of unit costs and quality ratings. Instead, USAA employs many of the common characteristics of the company that owns its market, and these characteristics combine to produce superior operating performance and strong market affinity.

In terms of financial performance, USAA produces consistently better results in the profitability of its auto insurance business than does the overall industry. Its profit margins over the five years from 1988 to 1992 averaged 3.2 percent in an industry that lost .53 percent over the same period.

A testimonial to USAA's strong customer affinity shows in its mutual fund business. Although not the largest seller of mutual funds, USAA enjoys a significant penetration of its customer base and an unusually high degree of customer loyalty, as evidenced during the stock market crash of November 1987. In the space of a week, equity prices on the New York Stock Exchange dropped 30 percent, the biggest drop since the depression of the 1930s. Among the hardest hit were the mutual fund companies, whose equity products quickly lost their value as investments. Customers clogged phone lines as they attempted to withdraw their funds, and, perhaps setting a customer defection record, most mutual fund companies lost 30 percent of their investors overnight.

USAA however, lost only 5 percent of customers in the quarter during which the crash occurred, which was typical of its low redemption (cancellation) rate before the crash. A senior executive at USAA explained the phenomenon this way: "We found that the redemption rate was the same as it was before the crash, and additional investments to existing accounts continued. This is where you see things happening when you are taking in those people who want to do business with you. We felt that if we put our members first and made all of our ventures the same quality and price that they've come to expect in the sixty or so years that we have had auto insurance, then they will help us out, they will trust us, they'll remain loyal. They will still believe that we're the company that they want to do business with five years and ten years and twenty years from now."

I have often used USAA as an example of what can be achieved by market ownership. And often the response has been that USAA is an unusual case, the exception, not a real business, more like an association or an affinity group. This misses the point entirely. USAA started out after World War I as a tiny company—with no special help or special relationships—to serve as an alternative supplier of auto insurance. Management focused exclusively on U.S. military officers, whom they believed were underserved by existing insurers. After many years of working in a specific target market, coming to know it better and better, focusing operations to deliver maximum customer value in terms of high quality and low costs while competing in one of the most price-competitive markets in the United States, USAA has achieved true affinity group status—and thus they are a nearly perfect example of the market ownership concept.

Chapter 3
Building A
Focused Business

Owning a market is clearly an attractive way to run a business. The main question at this point is how to go about achieving it. But if every company operates in a completely different business environment, then owning a market is not a simple matter of copying companies that have achieved this status. Where do you start? Is there a logical sequence? In this chapter I outline the answers to those questions.

This chapter has two objectives: to discuss the staged process of building a highly focused company and—equally important—to provide a rationale for the elements of the market ownership strategy discussed later in this book. You will read why these elements are important and how they need to be linked together into a carefully thought-out concept of the company and the business.

The list of common characteristic of companies that own markets indicates that *focus* is the starting point (see Figure 2-1). So we start with a three-stage framework for building a focused business:

1. *Developing a coherent business model.* To begin with, management develops a clear definition of the business and a coherent model of what is required for success in the business.
2. *Focusing resources.* Next, management builds a framework

for focusing the company's resources on the right elements.

3. *Building a connected organization.* Finally, management creates a unified and highly coordinated organizational culture that ensures that the company stays focused.

Whether it is seeking to improve quality or pursuing a new program, management inevitably runs into the "everybody is busy" syndrome, where everyone in the company is stretched to the limit and there are no resources to spare for doing new things. On closer inspection, however, the problem often turns out to be that employees are performing activities that contribute little of value either to the profitable customers or toward strengthening the company. Although the employees can be very efficient and may even be working very hard, they are wasting a lot of their time serving unprofitable clients. The fact is that they are doing the wrong things—to a large extent because they do not know what the right things are. Peter Drucker, in his book *Management*, distinguishes between efficiency and effectiveness. He defines *efficiency* as how well a company does the things it does, whereas *effectiveness* refers to whether the company is doing the right things to start with.

Developing a Coherent Model

The first step in building a highly focused company is for management to develop a coherent model of its business (or businesses) that provides a clear, complete picture of what will allow the company to maximize its success.

Developing the model requires management to (1) define the scope of the business by applying stringent criteria to distinguish it from other businesses that may seem similar but are fundamentally different and (2) design a consistent model of how the distinct business needs to function to be successful.

Although it seems logical to first define a distinct business and then determine a coherent model for it, the logic works the other way, too. The characteristics of a coherent business model—

the things that drive success in the business—provide the most incisive criteria for determining what truly constitutes a distinct business. In other words, the distinct business is defined by what it needs to be in order to be successful.

Thus, the best way to apply these concepts is to use them together. A simple way to do this is to:

1. Use the key criteria outlined later on in Exhibit 3-1 to make a "first pass" at defining a distinct business. Put particular emphasis on customer segmentation, needs, and values.
2. Determine a coherent model for the business. In other words, define what the business needs to be.
3. Use the elements of the model as criteria for reassessing and tightening the definition of the coherent business.

Two examples illustrate this suggested approach. In the first, suppose you are analyzing the personal computer (PC) industry and defining it as a distinct business. To begin, you define selling low-cost PCs as a business distinct from other aspects of the PC industry. Next, you develop a coherent model of what it takes to be successful in selling low-cost PCs. Elements in the model will indicate that the company must have a structure and a way of operating that make low cost possible, such as selling the PCs via mail order instead of through stores or a sales force. It is those elements of the business model that then redefine the "low-cost PC business" more distinctly and coherently as the "mail-order PC business." This is very different from the PC business that sells through stores, because it sells to customers who value low-cost products and are comfortable in obtaining a computer via this no-frills channel.

The second example involves health maintenance organizations (HMOs), where our first-pass definition of a distinct business might be "prepaid health care" (customers pay the HMO a flat fee to take care of all their health care needs for the year).

However, a coherent model of the HMO business makes the definition much clearer. HMOs are formed first by signing up networks of local doctors and hospitals, then selling these services to local people via their employers.

Key to the success of an HMO is local market share, which

provides leverage in negotiating the fee discounts and efficient medical practices that lower medical costs and give the HMO a lower price in its market. For an HMO chain, each metropolitan area is a distinct business; being the dominant HMO in one city means nothing when the HMO goes on to compete in the next. Even large chains with tremendous resources—US Healthcare, for instance—must acknowledge that they are entering a new, distinct business every time they enter a new metropolitan area. Thus, the local-share aspect of the coherent model significantly refines the definition of this distinct business as "prepaid health care in a specific metropolitan market."

Defining the Business

In defining the scope of the business, management needs to recognize what distinct business (or businesses) its company is involved in. This task is more subtle than it may sound, and it has a significant impact on the company's success. It is as if you were playing a game. If you do not know what game you are playing, it is very hard—impossible?—to know which are the right things to do, the best moves to make.

It is not at all unusual for a company or a division to view itself as part of a single business when in fact it may be involved in several. For example, the retail division of a securities firm is usually considered as a distinct business that sells stocks and bonds to individuals. However, one insightful executive new to the retail division of his securities firm observed that, given all the combinations of different products and customer types that his brokers were selling, his company was, in effect, in more than fifty different businesses, with all the attendant problems of supporting all of them.

A distinct business should be defined by the key criteria listed in Exhibit 3-1. These are the characteristics that most often distinguish one business from another. The questions posed should be carefully answered, and the answers should be applied stringently.

Distinct businesses are always defined by who the targeted customer is. For example, Mercedes and Toyota are both engaged in the manufacture of automobiles, but they are actually in two

Exhibit 3-1. Key criteria for defining distinct businesses.

Customer segment:	What is the targeted customer group? How does it vary from those served by other distinct businesses?
Product/service:	What is the scope of the company's product line?
Needs and values:	What needs/values is the customer fulfilling by purchasing the company's products and services?
Channel:	How is the product sold? What value is added through the sales process?
Functions:	What functions does the business perform in providing the ultimate products or services?
Geography:	What is the geographic scope of the business? How does geographic involvement affect the company's competitive position?

different businesses. They serve two different customer segments, segments that vary in socioeconomics, demographics, and psychographics (i.e., needs, beliefs, and behaviors). They compete with different companies on different appeals to targeted customers. And they have different product design and manufacturing requirements.

Delineation of a distinct business around customer segments can be further complicated by what customer needs and values the company is actually fulfilling. Utility aside, what is the customer really looking for? What needs must be satisfied, what values addressed?

Take the customer who needs a car. While it is clear that Toyota is not in the same market as Mercedes, it is less clear whether Lexus and Mercedes are in different businesses, even though they both sell what the auto industry refers to as the luxury car market. The answer is that one sells value while the other sells prestige.

The same is true with Fidelity and Merrill Lynch mutual funds. The former has customers who are comfortable buying by telephone and by mail, whereas the latter's customers prefer dealing with a stockbroker.

Two stores on the same block selling somewhat the same goods—for example, a convenience store and a grocery store—can also be in two distinct businesses.

Geography can sometimes be an important dimension in defining a distinct business, especially where local sales, service, and/or manufacturing capabilities are required. For example, as I explained, geography is a critical dimension of the HMO industry.

Function is another factor. Distinct businesses may be defined by who performs which role, from sales to product design to manufacturing to post-sales servicing. In many industries, distinct businesses are defined by providing one or a few of the components of the full value chain. In manufacturing industries, companies represent the entire spectrum—and combinations within the spectrum—of functions, from parts suppliers, to technology companies that only license their intellectual property, to manufacturers' representatives, to value-added resellers who take original equipment and create turnkey packages for specific applications, to totally integrated companies. In financial services there are mortgage originators (sellers), mortgage servicers, mortgage financers, and mortgage packagers for the secondary market, among other providers. Each of these companies operates in a distinct business, even though it is operating in part of a previously vertically integrated business.

In the future, trends such as outsourcing will create even more distinct businesses. Many companies are already questioning whether they need—or should even be involved in—peripheral activities such as systems development, telecommunications, mail distribution, and just about any other noncore function. Similarly, technology spawns many businesses where there was once just one. This is especially true in computers, which grew from the single-mainframe-computer business with fully integrated manufacturers to the perhaps hundreds of distinct businesses that exist today.

A final criterion for identifying a distinct business is that it should be able to stand on its own (although maybe with some rearranging of functions), even though it may be buried deep within a large company's operations. In fact, it may function better standing alone than it would lost among the company's other businesses and operations.

Developing a Model for the Business

The next critical step that management must take is to develop the elements that describe what the business (and all of its components) needs to be successful. Too often, managements view their businesses too simplistically, as merely making and selling widgets. In fact, even the simplest business has numerous subtle interdependencies, characteristics, and underlying economics that make it tick. Unless management understands what these subtleties are, it is difficult to understand what the right things are for the company to be doing.

An effective model of the business should address fundamental questions regarding the company's strategic focus and its operations and management: What price levels and unit costs are required to succeed? Given service and cost per sale requirements, who should sell the product? Given product life cycles, how strong must the company be in research and development? Once defined, those fundamentals should become part of a consistent business plan.

Retail stores are a good example of the need for a coherent, consistent business model. On the surface, most people view retail stores as places to buy the things they need. A store is just a store, a facility that houses merchandise procured from outside vendors. This perception does in fact aptly describe the typical retail store. Yet masters of retailing envision a store quite differently. They see a tightly integrated concept that starts with a sense of who the typical customer should be and what need the store is fulfilling for that customer. This concept drives all considerations for tactical decisions, such as store location, appearance, advertising messages, and merchandise. It is carried all the way to the management principles required to make that particular store successful.

In retailing, this business model is called "retail concept," connoting an overarching vision that directs all the pieces and holds them together in a consistent business model. The greater the vision and the clarity of the retail concept, the greater the likelihood that the store will be not just any store but a highly successful enterprise that owns its market.

As an example of retail concept, consider convenience stores. The retail concept for convenience stores is very different from that for a major grocery store in terms of who shops there and why, the types of items carried, and the underlying economics. These specialized stores fulfill a particular need for consumers who wish quickly and conveniently to obtain a few food and household necessities without making a time-consuming shopping trip. The retail concept of the convenience store model goes like this:

- The convenience store's mission is to provide shoppers with quick local access to popular items. It is not the place to stock up for the week.
- The stores are conveniently located near customers' homes or adjacent to roads frequently traveled. Since they are often located in high-rent areas, the store usually must be much smaller in size than a full-line grocery store.
- Given the (usually) small space, and since it cannot afford the space to inventory slower-moving items, the convenience store must have very high product turnover.
- To succeed, the store needs to have up-to-the-minute sales and inventory records to determine which products are moving quickly, which may fluctuate seasonally or with changes in taste, and how new product introductions fare.

Using the logic of the model, the convenience store must have a keen insight into who the store's customer is, why he or she buys particular items, and a keen sense for what will move quickly off the shelves.

The 7-Eleven chain of stores is a good example of the conveience-store retail concept. The chain started in the 1940s and grew to several thousand stores that were mostly owned by franchisers. Over the years, the franchise chain foundered, and it eventually ended in Chapter 11. It was rescued by a $450-million cash infusion by the Japanese company Ito-Yokado. By reshaping itself around a consistent business model, 7-Eleven promises to become one of the hottest retailers in the United States and Japan.

One of the many things that 7-Eleven Japan did was to install a sophisticated sales and inventory control system that gave it daily access to information on what people were purchasing. As a result of this system and other programs, it increased inventory turnover threefold.

In assessing the old 7-Eleven store network, an executive from the new parent company commented in a *Business Week* article, "They forgot what a convenience store is supposed to be."

Discount stores need a business model that will enable them to provide the very lowest merchandise prices available in their market area. Wal-Mart has been especially innovative in building a model that has squeezed the cost out of many aspects of the business, in particular by narrowing the number of suppliers and forming closely integrated operations. This has enabled Wal-Mart to eliminate suppliers' sales force costs by dealing directly company-to-company, dictating where suppliers locate plants and distribution centers, negotiating prices down, and integrating inventory and reordering by linking purchase data from the cash registers to the suppliers so that they can immediately adjust manufacturing schedules. This linkage is characterized by the notion that when the cash register rings at a Wal-Mart store, it also rings on the supplier's factory floor.

There are many examples of business models in the business services (investment banking, auditing, consulting, and, increasingly, law) provided to multinational clients. For all of these services, multinational clients need research and analysis done on site at their local operations, including their many offices in foreign countries. The service provider must have the capability to conduct local analyses in numerous countries around the world and then to link everything together to provide a consistent and global picture of the customer's situation.

An effective business model for serving multinational clients has two key elements: on-site competence in all the major countries and continents and the ability to deliver a seamless service to the client company worldwide. Thus, the successful business-service company needs ways to manage global competence and to operate as a single company across multiple remote offices.

In the 1980s many commercial banks tried, with mixed success, to enter into the global investment/merchant banking business, which, on the surface, looks similar to commercial banking. Actually, it comprises many distinct businesses and is very different from commercial banking. Bankers Trust succeeded in transforming itself into a global merchant bank, however, because it recognized that it needed a very different business model if it was to operate as a merchant banker. It knew it had to have the most up-to-date investment technology to develop new products such as derivatives, advanced information technology, and a strong global network of offices. To implement this new business model required a complete revamping of existing staff, compensation and recruiting practices, and performance measurement and a fast-moving, results-oriented culture. Bankers Trust changed from having many people with average compensation to employing fewer, more highly paid staff. It also put in place a threefold increase in information technology.

Reassessing the Definition of the Coherent Business

Given the numerous interdependencies among the components of a business, it is often hard to figure out where to start and how to proceed in developing a coherent model of the business. Nevertheless, there is a logical flow of components, starting with a definition of customer requirements and proceeding with the things the company has to do to fulfill them. This framework is illustrated in Exhibit 3-2 (which also outlines the sequence for the remaining chapters in this book).

1. *Envisioning the right customer.* Developing the business model begins with a vision of who the customer is. Surprisingly, many companies have only a vague notion of who their current customers are and an even vaguer idea of who they should—and should not—be. This gap in their knowledge doesn't seem to bother the managements of these companies even as they embark on customer retention, total quality management (TQM), or other programs that should be driven by a tight definition of who the customers are and what they value.

Even worse, the investment made in these programs is wasted on customer segments that the company should not even

Exhibit 3-2. Building a focused business.

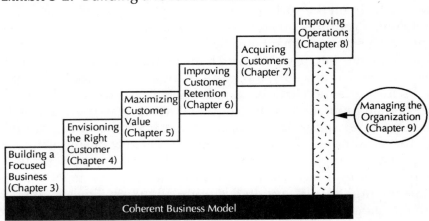

be involved with. One company, for instance, focused on the transaction-intensive small-business segment of its operations, spending millions of dollars and a lot of time automating its transactions processes. Years later, the company discovered that it was impossible to make money selling to small businesses— with or without automation. The definition of the customer is, therefore, the foundation of the model and it drives most of the other elements of the business as shown in Exhibit 3-2.

2. *Maximizing customer value.* Once the customer segment is defined, then it is possible to focus in on what that customer values. Understanding those values provides a strong picture of which areas the company needs to emphasize in order to gain a competitive advantage—for instance, required pricing and service levels, desired product features and options, and all the many other factors that influence customer value. These elements of the model in turn indicate what the company needs to do about its unit cost structure, distribution system, product manufacturing or service delivery, and all the other detailed specifications necessary for the business.

3. *Improving customer retention.* Once the company determines what customers value, it can develop a good sense of how to retain them long after the initial sale. Customer retention

dictates many other operational components of the business, sales in particular—for how a company sells to its customers has a lot to do with how long it retains them. It also influences other aspects of the business, such as quality of service, relationship building, and pricing methods.

4. *Acquiring customers.* Who the targeted customers are, what they value, and what is required to retain them determines the type of distribution system that is required to establish and build customer relationships at a reasonable cost per sale. These factors also dictate such things as the role the distribution system is expected to play in product delivery and post-sale servicing.

5. *Improving operations.* The previous steps indicate what the company's operations will have to do to be successful in terms of product cost, functionality, delivery time frames, and other requirements. In building highly effective operations, management must consider the following important issues:

- Are economies of scale an important driver of unit costs?
- How can processes be improved dramatically to make a breakthrough in maximizing customer value?
- Does the company need to make all components of the product or service, or should it purchase key components and technologies?
- What are the low-value elements of the product or service that can be eliminated or priced separately, thus streamlining product manufacturing and lowering costs and prices in the market?
- What process technologies must be employed to deliver targeted unit costs and quality standards?
- How important is innovation with respect to product obsolescence and life cycles? What R&D capabilities are required?
- What is required to service the customer, and how is this best done? Is local presence needed? Can this function be outsourced?

6. *Managing the organization.* All the foregoing steps show which organizational skills are required and how the business

needs to be managed to keep it focused. These indicators in turn dictate requirements for senior management to provide proper leadership and management style.

7. *Using strategic information.* Each of the preceeding steps has some information component that is critical to running the business, so employing information is the last step. Information is required to understand targeted clients and their needs better than do competitors, as well as to enhance the company's products and to build information bridges with clients. It is needed to assess customer satisfaction and to manage retention; to better manage employees; and to exchange knowledge to build staff capabilities.

Two Industry Case Studies

Managements that are able to look at their evolving markets and operations, recognize distinct businesses, and develop effective models for them are well positioned to lead their companies in the right directions. This is the heart of strategic planning. Despite the wealth of literature on the subject of strategy, there are still no off-the-shelf methodologies that provide strategic answers for all businesses, in all situations, and for all points of time. However, if management can acquire skill in seeing distinct businesses and then determine either what makes them tick as a coherent model or what is needed for them to be successful, then it has mastered much of the art of strategic planning.

As you will see in the following two case studies, this skill is particularly important in businesses that tend to evolve into new, distinct businesses and where rapid change causes distinct businesses to emerge, merge, and decline.

Strategic skills are important to keep track of the company's scope of activities as it evolves over time. If management is not paying attention, then companies tend to drift into new distinct businesses. One small, new opportunity leads to the next, and before too long the company may find itself in new businesses that drain its resources and weaken its core business. The company may unwittingly drift into businesses that it cannot easily develop, or the businesses may require operating economics different from the company's core business. Either of these scenarios usually leads to losses that sap the company's strength.

An Insurance Brokerage

Our first example is a commercial insurance brokerage company whose primary business is assessing clients' risks and arranging for appropriate insurance programs. While the global industry includes several billion-dollar companies, it is made up mostly of thousands of regional companies whose primary role is to fulfill the business insurance needs of mid-size companies. This is clearly a distinct business, one that regional brokers are well equipped to handle. However, the nature of this business inherently lures management into new distinct businesses, too often at great cost to the company.

As in the convenience store business, it is easy for management at the regional broker's office to get distracted and to forget what a regional broker needs to be to serve mid-size regional companies. The first problem is that although the company may exist to service mid-size businesses, it often ends up serving companies of all sizes. A unique sales opportunity might, for example, enable the company to bring in a large account with complex, international requirements that extend beyond the local brokers' capability.

At the other end of the spectrum, the company may acquire numerous small-business customers that are attracted to it by way of referrals, its local advertising, or its prominence in the local market. Before too long, the company has a client base that mirrors the local economy, 80 percent small accounts, many mid-size clients, and one or two large companies.

Other "apparent" opportunities may emerge when a client expresses frustration over the need to run its employee benefits program and requests that the company make a proposal to handle it. Soon after, clients will inevitably ask the broker to insure partnership-related risks, handling the life insurance program for owners and key executives. Then comes the next apparent opportunity—solving the personal insurance problems of clients' management and staff, including insuring their homes, cars, small businesses owned by relatives, and other assets.

While these opportunities may sound attractive, they pose the potential problem of dragging the company unwittingly into new distinct businesses, each with a different business model. In this scenario, the insurance broker company may become involved in as many as eight different, distinct businesses. On the one hand, doing business with large corporations requires global servicing with on-site visits to the company's foreign operations. On the other hand, the businesses that generate low fees (small businesses and individuals) require efficient service operations and low-cost distribution channels.

Trouble begins when the company's involvement in each one of these areas grows and the management of the brokerage company fails to perceive these eight sales "opportunities" as distinct businesses. Management is likely to take a "one-size-fits-all" approach to servicing the eight businesses, providing a high-cost service for some businesses that generate low revenues (such as small businesses and individuals with auto and homeowners insurance) and underserving other distinct businesses that stretch the company's capability to the limit (such as multinational companies with international service requirements). The insurance brokerage soon finds itself in a quagmire in which all employees are working very hard and seem productive—yet profit margins continue to shrink.

The only way out of this dilemma is for management to define its distinct businesses (which are quite probably, by now, spread throughout the company), focus on those that are profitable, and draw on its key competitive strengths. It should exit or downsize all other peripheral businesses.

This type of restructuring can involve painful changes. It is better to avoid the problem from the start, keeping close scrutiny over the scope of the company's business involvements, especially those that ever so subtly lead the company into new businesses.

The Computer Industry: IBM vs. Hewlett-Packard

The computer industry provides a second example of how rapid change can cause distinct businesses to emerge, merge, or decline quickly. Since the 1980s, perhaps no other industry has experienced more change in less time than the computer industry. The survival of a computer company can depend on its management's ability to recognize these distinct businesses and to develop new business models for each one. The industry's initial distinct business, mainframes, has proliferated into many new businesses, each requiring a different business model.

The computer industry started out as a single distinct business with what were then called mainframe computers, big expensive machines invented by UNIVAC and built by IBM that few buyers could afford. IBM succeeded famously in this new business, in part because it saw it as a distinct business apart from its traditional core business of making tabulators, punchcards, and other mechanical devices and focused on it. As former IBM CEO Thomas J. Watson,

Jr., commented in an interview for *Datamation* (March 15, 1991), "We put everything we had into it. We were solely focused on applying computing machines to customers. And we had nothing else to divert us. So from 1952 on, we were just pressing computers."

IBM also developed the most powerful business model in the industry. Recognizing the difficulty customers encountered in buying, using, and maintaining the complex machines and the urgency of keeping them running, IBM built one of the most impressive sales and service organizations of the twentieth century. IBM service was known for its integrity and was inseparable from customers' operations. IBM also controlled quality and reliability by making every component of the mainframe, from the internal electronics to the software that ran the machine, and by performing every role from initial sales to maintenance.

For three decades, IBM owned the mainframe computer business. The notion that "you won't lose your job if you buy IBM" was widespread throughout MIS departments in big corporations. In fact, the U.S. Justice Department thought IBM was too successful. It filed an antitrust suit in 1975 which lasted until 1985, by which time the computer business had changed and the government's claim became irrelevant.

IBM's downfall in the 1980s can be directly attributed to its failure to see the computer business blossom into numerous distinct businesses. This evolution was clearly evident as far back as the early 1970s when Digital Equipment Corporation and others started introducing the smaller, cheaper minicomputers. Every year since then the computer business has been on a path of inexorable change that spawns new distinct businesses.

Driven by the decline in the price of computing power, known as the price/performance ratio, the computer business is more volatile than any other industry. The same performance that cost $1,000 in the 1960s today costs pennies. The cost of computers and peripheral equipment drops dramatically each year. If the same gain in productivity occurred in the auto industry, for example, cars today would cost less than one dollar.

Today, the computer industry comprises perhaps hundreds of distinct businesses, each requiring different business models. The upper end continues to grow from supercomputers to massively parallel ones, while the bottom end continues to shrink from minicomputers to micros to desktops to laptops to palmtops. The way corporations configure integrated corporatewide systems has changed from mainframe to networks of PCs, file servers, and groupware software that connects all the users. A similar explosion in the growth of distinct businesses has occurred in all of the functional aspects of computing, from integrated circuit design and manufacture to operating and application software to sales and service.

Each of these distinct businesses emerges and overlaps with other distinct businesses. Sometimes quick to decline or disappear, these businesses create very narrow windows of opportunity.

To succeed in the computer business today, a company needs to recognize emerging distinct businesses (or even create them) and to determine the optimal business models for those distinct businesses they choose to enter. The business models may mean scrapping old ways of doing things fast, including changing distribution channels, outsourcing parts of the business—even to competitors—and pulling the plug on businesses that wane or become otherwise unattractive. In short, the right things in the computer business change rapidly, and staying on top of what they are is an essential skill for survival in the industry.

Against this background of tumultuous change, IBM failed to recognize that the computer industry now comprised many distinct businesses. It insisted on describing its operations as a single business in its 10-K reports, the required profiles of separate businesses. IBM stuck with its mainframe-oriented business model even as it was being overtaken by new rivals that recognized new, distinct businesses that needed wholly different business models.

IBM continued with its vertically integrated, proprietary product approach, applying the same mainframe practices and management principles to all its new product ventures. In many markets—for example, in selling low-end PCs, which cannot support a high sales and service cost allocation—IBM's sales and service organization became a liability. Successful companies like Dell, unlike IBM, sell their PCs through low-cost mail and telephone channels.

IBM withered even in areas where it had developed leading-edge technology. For example, it developed the RISC circuit design (reduced instruction set) that became a driving force in the workstation and file server markets—only to see Hewlett-Packard commercialize the technology with great success.

In contrast to IBM, Hewlett-Packard is perhaps the most successful broad-based player in today's computer industry, especially in the PC file server product configuration that is replacing mainframes. And HP is significantly different from IBM in its ability to see emerging distinct businesses and to develop successful business models flexibly and quickly, before competitors. As one HP executive stated, "We see the horizon and try to get there before competitors do." It manufactures products where it makes sense and licenses its proprietary technology to competitors when appropriate. It uses its strong sales organization where that works best and sells through stores and value-added resellers in other settings.

Yet HP and IBM are similar in many ways: They both have excellent research and development labs and sales and service organizations. Their corporate cultures are employee-oriented and are known for their integrity.

HP's success is in part attributable to a Darwinian evolutionary process that required HP to acquire the all-important skills of seeing distinct businesses and acting flexibly in each. HP always had IBM—and, later, DEC—as formidable competitors. As a main strategy, HP sought out niches in the computer industry that it could dominate, thereby avoiding head-on competition with the owners of the mainframe and the minicomputer markets. Meanwhile, others like Honeywell and Burroughs, which had tried to carve major niches, disappeared from the mainstream of the computing business.

As Alan Bickell, head of HP's Geographic Operations, noted in an interview with me, "IBM and DEC held strong traditional positions in the market. This encouraged new market opportunities where we could make a substantial contribution. We picked opportunities that we believed would clearly be pervasive in the future. Examples included our belief that distributed computing would lead to the client server business (to support PC networks) and that laser printing would become a major market once we were able to dramatically lower prices. We like to go around the competition, quietly."

Conversely, IBM had had comfortable ownership of the mainframe computer business for nearly three decades. It never needed to acquire the skills of seeing distinct businesses (or so management thought) or to act flexibly—until it was too late. Had IBM had more formidable competitors in the 1960s and 1970s, perhaps it would have acquired the necessary skills to succeed in the computer industry.

Ironically, as it moves out of niche markets into the mainstream markets, there are signs that HP is replacing IBM as the leading computer company. HP is often seen as the authority in helping companies rewire themselves by replacing IBM mainframes with HP-configured PC/file server configurations. As analyst David Wu of S. G. Warburg noted, "People are clearly looking to Hewlett . . . for leadership in the computer business."

Defining a distinct business and developing a coherent business model for it should determine what the right moves are for the company that aims to own a market. In the next section, we discuss a methodology for reshaping the company to focus its resources on these right things.

Focusing the Company's Resources

Sharply focused companies are very disciplined in how they handle allocation of resources such as capital, operational spending, and employee and management time. The companies' managements have a clear sense of a coherent business model and spend lavishly on the right things. These often include strategies such as hiring and developing the best people and selectively applying leading technology where it pays off the most. Beyond this, management of focused companies can be very stingy about spending money on anything they believe is superfluous to the company's mission, that does not add value to its clients or build its competitive strengths.

In contrast, the unfocused company squanders its scarce resources, in part because managements have no sense of what constitutes a distinct business, which ones they should be in, or how to define a coherent business model. Once management has resolved these issues, it is prepared to reshape its company by focusing resources on those aspects that contribute to owning the company's chosen distinct markets.

In the rest of this chapter I outline a methodology for restructuring your company's resources, thus enabling you to maximize the value of your products and services to your targeted customer. Essentially, restructuring means reallocating resources from superfluous, ineffective activities to those that make a significant impact. This includes redeploying capable employees to perform jobs that matter, stopping wasteful activities and curtailing losing businesses, and trimming the fat that inevitably resides in most companies.

The methodology includes six steps, beginning with a macro view of the company and a rationalization of the various businesses it supports. It then burrows deeper into each distinct business, outlining opportunities for further resource allocation.

1. *Focusing on viable, distinct businesses.* Once the company's distinct businesses are defined, management should take a hard look at the prospects for each one and decide whether to invest, build, fix, disinvest, or exit. Businesses that are unattractive and/ or in which the company has a weak competitive position are usually the biggest drain on the company's money, staff, and management-involvement resources. The company greatly benefits from exiting these businesses. Successful companies like General Electric, Hewlett-Packard, and Bankers Trust have a reputation for not wasting resources on losing businesses. They routinely use a disciplined approach to minimizing their commitments to businesses with limited potential.

Honeywell is another good example of this approach. Honeywell has always been a successful maker of sensors and controls for regulating industrial processes, controlling building temperatures, and supporting aviation and navigation applications. Yet for years Honeywell slugged it out with IBM in mainframes, even though it was generally viewed as an ineffective competitor. This "noncompetition" diverted Honeywell management's attention and took substantial resources away from its core businesses. Ultimately, Honeywell wised up, selling off its computer business to the French company Machine Bull in 1985.

By exiting the mainframe business Honeywell has been able to refocus management attention and resources on its traditional core businesses and is starting to reassert itself as a market leader. Reflecting on its past diversion into computers and the power of market ownership, Honeywell's CEO, James Renier, is quoted (*Fortune*, Spring/Summer 1991) as saying, "We learned from our past failures that winners make life miserable for those who trail."

The analysis of what do to with each distinct business should incorporate considerations of at least three important factors:

1. Business attractiveness: market growth rates, competitive intensity, the ability to differentiate products and services, competing technologies, and business obsolescence
2. The company's competitive position: market share, unique strengths, sustainable advantages, reputation, degree of market ownership

3. Financial attractiveness: projected return on investment required to sustain or grow the business

Assessing financial attractiveness is especially important for companies that have not segmented their distinct businesses and treated the company as a single financial entity. When a financial analysis of business units is done for the first time, management is often surprised to find that a number of its distinct businesses lose money, including some favored businesses that might have appeared attractive because they were seen as somehow enhancing the company's image. A further analysis often reveals that some of these businesses justify fixing, while others are destined to be losers and should be cut away.

Bankers Trust attributes much of its success in transforming itself into a highly successful merchant bank to its rigorous tracking of financial performance in its forty distinct businesses. Bankers Trust employs a financial measurement system called RAROC (risk adjusted return on capital), which measures return on equity adjusted for the riskiness of the business in which the equity is invested. Using this methodology has helped Bankers Trust to focus scarce capital funds (and other resources) on profitable businesses. The bank also maintains a policy of reviewing all of its businesses with a strict, three-option yardstick: invest, disinvest, or divest.

By eliminating unprofitable or marginally profitable businesses, a second opportunity arises: Management can now refocus resources by cutting back on the infrastructure and functions that had been required to support the exited businesses. These include items such as dedicated finance, human resources, information systems, and marketing. Management positions that were specific to these businesses no longer have a role and can be eliminated or redeployed.

2. *Reorganizing around business lines.* This step requires organizing the corporation around its distinct businesses, instead of functions, geography, or other dimensions of the business. This form of organization structure is generally referred to as strategic business units (SBUs). Its purpose is to focus the company's resources on its distinct businesses. Although fads in organiza-

tional trends come and go, the SBU structure is an enduring managerial concept and a commonsense way to organize a corporation.

The SBU structure addresses a common problem that afflicts many companies: Distinct businesses that could stand alone are shuffled in together in an organization that is functionally or geographically structured. In this environment, key functions of each distinct business are spread throughout the company and come together only at very high levels, often with the company's president. Instead of line management, committees are employed to direct each business unit. Work is fragmented among many different people and units; decision making is impeded by bureaucratic reviews and approvals; accountability for performance is limited; and resources are wasted on activities unrelated to the creation of value for either customers or shareholders.

As a general rule, each distinct business should control at least 80 percent of the functions needed to run the business and 80 percent of its total costs. Where possible, key functions should report directly to the SBU head, except where economies of scale exist or where a concentration of expertise is desirable. For example, it might be essential for multiple SBUs to share a common distribution system because of the costs involved in creating one for each individual SBU. These should be the exceptions, however. The SBU should still control shared services with strict performance agreements.

Organizing around distinct businesses produces the immediate benefit of focusing management's attention on each business in a way that was not possible when the businesses were combined. A second benefit is the identification of resources, functions, and positions that do not fit any of the businesses and thus are probably no longer needed. For example, companies that lack an SBU structure usually have coordinators who look after the various distinct businesses that are spread throughout the organization. These coordinators generally have little impact on the company's direction, serving more as cheerleaders or champions for the business. The elimination of superfluous functions such as these lowers costs without undermining competitive strength and may actually help to reduce needless interference and inefficiency that previously downgraded the company's performance.

3. *Restructuring the remaining business units.* Once the distinct businesses are housed in an SBU structure, there is an opportunity to restructure the various elements of each business. Now it is possible for management to focus the company's attention and resources on customer value and on those activities that contribute to the company's financial and competitive strength. These business elements include customer segments, product/service lines and features, distribution channels, and geographic markets and office locations. Like most things in business, the 80/20 rule applies to them as well: 20 percent of the business elements contributes 80 percent of the value provided to the customer or generates 80 percent of the company's profits.

The restructuring of these business elements should include four stages in the following order:

1. Pruning clients that do not fit the company's target market
2. Pruning or consolidating unprofitable business elements such as ancillary products, weak distribution systems, and geographic offices
3. Pruning features and options of core products and services that contribute little customer value
4. Pruning the functions that supported aspects of the business addressed in Stage 1, 2, and 3 and that are no longer needed

Stage 1. Pruning clients. The primary component of a coherent business model is the targeted client. Building a focused business requires the management discipline to prune customer segments that do not fit the targeted profile. Clients who are a poor fit significantly divert the company's strategic focus, are difficult to serve profitably, and are a substantial drain on the company's resources. Management must prune them out, then put new programs in place (repricing, for instance) to stop attracting new misfits.

Stage 2. Pruning business elements. The next opportunity is to restructure unprofitable business elements that drain resources.

Among the most resource-draining elements are ancillary products and services that are unimportant to the business unit, consume resources, and/or are unprofitable. These products creep into the business because somewhere along the line someone thought that they were essential. However, they inevitably (and sometimes almost invisibly) consume increasing amounts of management time and increasing amounts of critical sales resources and other costs in order to support and maintain themselves in the company's inventory. Nevertheless, product proliferation is common to most businesses, and management discipline is essential to prune out the unneeded elements and restrain future proliferation.

Pruning geographic markets is important and must happen where the company is losing ground or where there are markets that are hard to support and weak and unprofitable offices in unattractive locations. Few business models require a broad national or international presence. However, managements frequently take their companies into broad geographic markets for no strategic reason, before even covering home plate. This creates an enormous drain on resources, one that can needlessly weaken a business.

Some industries are global by their nature, but most are not. International expansion can be a major resource drain. Many managements have taken the concept of global economy too seriously. Like lemmings, they have driven their companies over the edge by entering into new countries for no apparent strategic reasons. This is especially illogical for companies that are weak domestic players, yet choose to expand internationally. Perhaps they think foreign markets will be less competitive and easier to succeed in. Why, for instance, an American company that does not dominate its market in the United States or that has failed as a player in Canada should think of entering European markets is a complete mystery.

Similarly, it is essential to consider pruning distribution channels. When companies develop focused business strategies, they typically find that some segment of their distributors or sales staff no longer fit the plan. Segments of distribution channels can also be a large resource drain. Again, the 80/20 rule applies: The top 20 percent brings in 80 percent of the profit, and a sizable portion of the other 80 percent creates sizable losses.

Stage 3. Pruning features of core products. Even after pruning businesses, customers, and unneeded products, there is much that can be done to eliminate superfluous features and options attached to core products. Product features, like product lines, tend to proliferate over time as engineers, marketers, salespeople, management, and others seek to improve products, often under the false notion that such improvements are desperately needed if the company is to stay competitive. The problem is that the customer may have little value for these added features; if they were priced separately, customers might not purchase them. Management needs to determine what the targeted customer values are and to refocus the company's product features to deliver that value. This may mean stopping the unnecessary things and rechanneling resources to bolster those aspects of the product that matter most.

Stage 4. Pruning unnecessary support. Completing Stages 1 through 3 eliminates the need for the ancillary support functions. These unneeded functions can include (1) regional management and support staff for areas the company plans to abandon wholly or in part and (2) all functions that support discontinued products such as sales, marketing, systems development, and production.

4. *Improving core operations.* The previous three steps laid out the right things (what Peter Drucker calls "effectiveness") the company must do to build a focused company. Successfully reaching this point makes a company far more focused and stronger than its run-of-the-mill competitors. To go further, the company must take an additional step: It must do the right things with a high degree of proficiency. This epitomizes what Drucker calls efficiency, "doing the right things exceptionally well."

5. *Restructuring overhead functions.* Now management must address the opportunities to restructure the overhead functions, the cost of which is allocated to business units by internal suppliers. The chronic complaint from heads of business units is that they get a large expense allocation and receive little value in return, that the internal suppliers are out of touch with the needs of the business. This complaint often has some justification, as it

is very hard for internal suppliers several steps removed from the action to know what their "right things" are.

The solution to this problem is to allow business units to deal with internal suppliers as they would with outside vendors. Each business unit should be able to decide for itself which services it needs and where it will obtain them, including using outside suppliers or re-creating the function within the business unit. Once given this power, individual units will make a variety of decisions, scaling back on purchased services, centralizing or decentralizing such services, outsourcing them to the external company, or establishing tough internal service contracts with unit cost, quality, and opt-out provisions. These decisions will inevitably lead to a restructuring of internal service providers. Thrust into a competitive environment, the providers of internal services will seek to enhance their efficiency and responsiveness in order to retain their previously captive internal customers.

6. *Rationalize management structure.* The final opportunity for restructuring is the rationalization of management structures. Following steps 1 through 5 will result in a very different type of organization, one that is leaner, more simplified, and better focused and that needs less management and fewer levels of hierarchy. This last step, the one that ties all the others together, is to rationalize and minimize the management structure within each business unit and throughout the corporation. By reducing layers of management, broadening spans of control, delegating more responsibility to teams, and creating a flatter, more responsive organization focused on key activities that add value to clients and improve profitability, the company can rechannel its resources away from superfluous management positions and toward value-adding ones.

These six steps for restructuring a company may seem like a lot of change, really heavy medicine for the organization. This is true. However, they are not overkill, especially for companies that have drifted afield and whose survival is at stake; such companies either make these changes or get put out of business by more-focused competitors.

In reality, all companies have only two options in restructuring: They can make the concept of the focused business part of management's philosophy and do incremental restructuring day by day as a matter of course, or they can ignore the small (but nonetheless difficult) decisions that lead the company astray. Certainly, the company can wait until competitors threaten its survival before taking this prescribed heavy medicine. Those managements that have survived the second option attest to the pain of the treatment, but they were lucky; they were the ones who could still speak about the future. Not surprising, many of these survivors have now become ardent supporters of option 1.

Building Organizational Connectivity

The final requirement in building a focused company is "organizational connectivity." This is defined as a corporate culture in which all employees in every function, business line, or geographic location work together as a single company with common goals and objectives. The connected company, even the one with a mediocre strategy, will overtake the disconnected company with better ideas, since the disconnected company wastes resources and makes the implementation of business strategy next to impossible.

The lack of organizational connectivity exists in most companies of any size and is the ultimate cause for the lack of focus I have discussed. These disconnections exist between the company and its customers and suppliers, across key functional departments, across levels in the organization, across geographic territories, and across divisions within corporations. They cause the company to be ignorant about the marketplace and keep the company from knowing what the right things to do are. Further, they impede the company's effectiveness in executing them.

Regardless of how successful the company may appear to be, it is vulnerable to a more focused competitor who is connected to the market and across elements of the company. This is what happens when Japanese competitors enter the U.S. market, searching for lumbering, disconnected companies in a wide variety of industries. The disconnected company may, for example, have an attractive profit margin supported by a few products with exceptionally high profitability, products that offset the company's wasted resources. When the focused company enters the market with better products for a fraction of the going prices, the disconnected company gets in deep trouble as it is forced to cut its prices.

This is not an extreme case study that applies only to the worst of bureaucracies. It is typical of most mid-size and large companies that operate as complex multiple societies existing within one corporation. It also includes highly successful entrepreneurial operations that started small and quickly grew too large for the old hands-off management approach to work any longer. As a general rule, once any company gets more than about fifty employees, it needs a whole new approach to managing a connected organization.

Even if the company has developed a coherent model to begin with and has aligned its resources to support it, the lack of cooperation in the disconnected company will hinder its success. Lack of focus and inefficiency will creep back in quickly. Thus, the third and final remedy is to build a connected organization, and this section provides a framework for instilling "connectivity" throughout the corporation.

Transforming a disconnected company into a single, cohesive company is extremely difficult. For most managements, the issue is one of effecting a basic change in the company's culture. This can't be done by management fiat. It takes several years of dedicated work led by senior management. There are many strategies that management can use to build a connected company, which will be addressed in Chapter 9, on managing the organization.

Chapter 4

Envisioning The Right Customer

Of all the decisions that management must make in order to own the market, envisioning its customer is foremost. The company with a superior understanding of who its customers are can focus its resources on doing the right things, thus giving itself a significant advantage over its competitors. In contrast, the company that lacks this knowledge will inevitably waste its resources trying to be all things to all clients. It will produce mediocre products and services that are suitable for the lowest common demoninator in the market.

This vision of the customer is not a new concept. However, it is one that needs continual reinforcement, since it seems to be lost on most businesses. In the words of Harvard Business School professor Raymond Corey (from Charles Ames and James D. Hlavacek, *Market Driven Management*):

> All else follows. Choice of market is a choice of the customer and of the competitive, technical, political, and social environments in which one elects to compete. It's not an easily reversed decision; having made the choice, the company develops skills and resources around the markets it has elected to serve.

The main problem for most companies is not choosing the wrong customer but choosing one at all. Many managements are blind to the subtle, but all-critical, variations in needs and behaviors across customer segments. They see clients as being interchangeable or even identical and believe that any sale is a good sale. They refer to their customers as "accounts," connoting faceless items in the company's accounting ledger. And they are vulnerable to their move savvy competitors, who take the best customers and leave behind the unprofitable, uninspiring, bottom end of the market.

This customer-blind group includes many adherents of quality management and being "close to the customer." Being close to the customer is great advice if management has a sound idea of who it is the company should get close to, but it is foolish to listen and respond to an undifferentiated group of clients. As Michael Schrage wrote in a provocative *Wall Street Journal* (October 5, 1991) article, "Contrary to popular belief, customer service doesn't begin with the customer's expectations of the business— it begins with the business's vision of the customer."

This chapter presents a seven-step process for envisioning the customer (see Exhibit 4-1). The first four steps define the dimensions and structure of the market. The remaining three steps focus on identifying smart customers within the various market segments.

Envisioning the Market First

Market ownership requires a broad vision of the customer in the context of the overall market and a clear idea of how the market may evolve over time. There are four important dimensions to consider in analyzing markets:

1. The segmentation of different types of markets
2. The logical geographical boundaries of the market
3. The likely evolution of the market
4. The existence of multiple customers

1. *Understanding types of markets.* There are three different types of markets for products and services: niche, multiniche, and mass markets. The three types, as well as the ways they differ in the customer values and needs that exist across customer

Exhibit 4-1. Framework for focusing on the right customers.

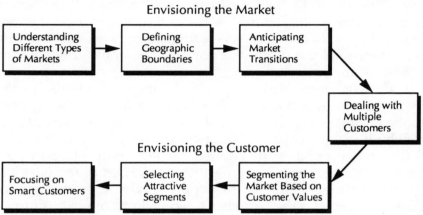

segments, the extent to which there are economies of scale in producing the product or providing the service, and the competitive strengths required to compete in each market are presented in Exhibit 4-2.

Niche markets exist where there is significant variation in needs and values among customer groups and where meeting these distinct needs is more important than whatever economies of scale may exist. In this type of market, companies can be successful by focusing on one or more distinct customer segments. This is a good strategy for both weak and strong competitors, as segment focus is more important than the company's relative economies of scale. It is very difficult to displace a company that owns its market segment in niche markets. (This usually happens only if the leader becomes complacent and fails to continually improve and tailor its product and services to meet the segment's needs.)

Niche markets can exist where there is plenty of customization and/or small unit volume, neither of which lends itself to economies of scale. A good example is the market for supercomputers. Cray Computers built a successful business in this area, one of the few niches that existed at a time when the computer business was dominated by IBM.

Niche markets exist for industrial products (e.g., machine

Exhibit 4-2. The different types of markets.

Market Type	Differences in Needs Across Segments	Economies of Scale in Product Manufacture	Required Competitive Strength
Niche	Highly differentiated	Minimal to moderate economies	Weak to strong position
Multiniche	Somewhat differentiated	Moderate to substantial economies	Moderate to dominant
Mass	Minimal differentiation	Significant economies	Dominant

tools) that are used very differently by different types of companies and industries. They also exist for many consumer goods, such as clothing and cosmetics, that appeal to different tastes and different customer segments.

The multiniche market is one in which obvious segments with distinct needs exist but these distinct needs are not quite as important as the economy of scale achieved in producing the product. Unlike a company seeking a niche market, a company operating in the multiniche market cannot just pick out a target segment and focus on it exclusively, because the economies of scale demand a much broader, multisegment approach in order to achieve sufficient volume.

Owning a multiniche market is not something that should be attempted by competitively weak companies, since significant size and resources are required to excel as a major player in the whole market. It is an ideal strategy, however, for competitively strong companies seeking to become a dominant factor in the industry. For the company that wants to enter the multiniche market, a good strategy involves selecting a number of sizable, attractive market segments with distinct needs and then tailoring the product or service to meet those needs far better than the competition does.

The mainframe, minicomputer, and client/server computer businesses are good examples of the multiniche market. The computer industry, in fact, refers to these multiniches as "vertical markets," meaning vertical slices of the overall market. These mainstream businesses have great economies of scale in production, yet their customers' characteristics, needs, and usage patterns vary significantly. For example, retail companies need to focus on purchasing and inventory control; banks need to excel at mistake-proof and efficient transaction processing; manufacturers need to control production processes. But these differences, as great as they are, do not affect the scale advantages required to develop and manufacture the state-of-the-art computers, software, and peripheral devices to support industry-specific applications.

This is why the leading companies in these businesses, notably IBM, Digital Equipment, and Hewlett-Packard, organize their sales and service functions around major industry groups with distinct computing needs. At the same time, they mass-produce the hardware components on a standardized basis to achieve economies of scale. Essentially, the field organization performs the necessary customization by configuring mass-produced hardware and software to fit specific, distinct needs.

Commercial banking is another multiniche market where the financing needs vary across industry segments. The financing needs of agricultural companies, for example, are seasonal; the cash flow patterns reflect the planting and harvesting cycles. But these industry variations do not outweigh the importance of the bank's scale of operations, such as maintaining a large branch network to service local businesses or perhaps having sufficient worldwide representation to service multinational clients.

The automotive market is a multiniche market with substantial economies of scale and tremendous variation in customer needs and tastes. Understanding the existence of the multiple segments is as much a key to success in the automotive business as mass production skills. The temptation to treat the business as a one-size-fits-all mass market was classically demonstrated by Henry Ford's insistence on mass-producing and selling cars of "any color as long as [they were] black." Even he had to cave in to market demand eventually. Today, the most successful auto makers produce cars aimed at many different segments. They gain economies of scale by sharing key components of the car, such as engines and frames.

At the other end of the spectrum is the mass market. Here, mass production and the lower prices that result from economies of scale far outweigh whatever minor variations in customer values and needs may exist in the market. Clearly, owning a mass market requires a company to be the dominant scale player. It must have superior production capabilities to allow for low prices and for the special distribution and marketing capabilities necessary to reach the mass market. Its products and services must provide the most value across an array of price and feature ranges.

Consider consumer electronics, which are dominated by large companies selling quality products at ever-decreasing prices. The PC market is a good example of a niche market that evolved into a multiniche and then into a mass market, driven by rapidly declining prices and sold through mass market channels—including the mail.

2. *Defining geographic boundaries.* Geography is an important dimension in analyzing a company's market. It affects how the company's resources need to be allocated and how its market might evolve over time. In general, the smaller the company's geographic market, the easier it is for the company to dominate it, because the company can focus and conserve its scarce resources.

Management needs to determine the geographic boundaries of competition, whether its company is operating in a local market or a broad market. In a local market, local dominance is sufficient to own and retain ownership of the market. In broad markets, competitive strength comes from participation in many geographic markets, and this strength can be used as leverage to enter new geographic markets. To determine whether a market is geographically local or broad, start by defining the characteristics of the broad market. Whether multiregional or global, broad geographic markets exist under one or more of three conditions:

1. Significant economies of scale exist that can be exploited by serving a large geographic market.

2. There is a need to provide local service for companies operating in many locations.
3. Networks provide a competitive advantage when expanded to a broad geographic area.

First, economies of scale commonly exist in product manufacturing, research and development, national advertising, and other aspects of a company where significant up-front costs are spread across a large base of clients. To capitalize on these economies, the company may have to sell to broad geographic markets to build sufficient volume. The market for computer chips, for example, is one that requires global participation to take advantage of economies of scale; it is becoming more and more important to sell successfully to major customers in Japan and other parts of Asia, as well as in Europe and North America.

Second, broad geographic markets are created by markets where customers are multiregional or global and need on-site local servicing. The major CPA companies (e.g., KPMG and Arthur Andersen) fit into this category because they need to service the local operations of multinational companies. Computer stores are becoming global because multinational companies need help to maintain the networks of PCs operating in their offices around the world.

Finally, broad markets are created by products and services with networks that can increase in strength when given broader geographic coverage. Federal Express, for example, has increased the value of its service through the addition of new geographic points to its delivery network. Yacht chartering is another example. As a charter company opens up new bases throughout the world, it creates new vacation options for its customers, thus enhancing its product.

A truly local market is one where dominance of the local market provides more advantages than any economies of scale offered by larger, multiregional companies. The competitive advantages that arise out of local dominance develop from strategies such as building a strong local service network or concentrating marketing and brand development efforts to become the best-known name in the local market. A modest advertising budget has a much higher impact when concentrated locally than if it were spread across the whole country.

As mentioned earlier, HMOs are truly local businesses that derive their strength from leveraging local market share to obtain better prices and conditions from health-care providers. Consumer banking is also local, appealing to consumers by offering the convenience of a dense branch system in a local market. In both examples, local strengths make it hard for new players from outside the area to enter the market, since strength in one location means nothing in the next.

Retail stores and restaurants are often local. The retailer's success depends on its brand image and on store convenience in a local market (although national purchasing has created economies of scale for some retailers, such as Wal-Mart). This is why it is smart to develop a national chain of retail outlets by dominating a single, local market first and then slowly branching into other areas where a similar build-and-dominate plan will succeed. The worst strategy is to enter multiple markets as a complete unknown. Dollars spent on building brand awareness are a drop in the bucket compared to what it costs to capture the attention of the local market.

3. *Anticipating market transitions.* A third consideration in envisioning the broader market context is to visualize how the market and customer segments may evolve over time. There are two important ways in which customers and markets can change: They can evolve from a niche business to a broader market, or vice versa, or they can evolve from local businesses to broader georgaphic markets, or vice versa.

Changes in the client's business, technology, intensifying competition, and many other major trends continually transform markets at an ever-increasing pace. To attain and sustain market ownership requires farsightedness regarding ways a company's markets are likely to evolve. In some industries, markets will change very little—but management should be especially wary of this possibility. The more successful the company, the greater the likelihood that someone is plotting an end-around strategy, changing the rules of the game by transforming one market type into another.

For example, it is quite possible for parts of a mass market with historically few variations across segments to become a niche business. Several things can happen to cause this. In one small corner, a group of customers might start to experience new trends that pose threats or opportunities that are critical and distinct from the broader market. The shrewd competitor can focus on this market segment and carve a niche market out of the mass. If this is done successfully, the competitor can take business away from more-established companies and own this market.

A good example of how trends have transformed a market is the commerical property/casualty insurance business, which is treated by most of the industry as a mass market. Yet, the rapid escalation of lawsuits filed against professionals (e.g., lawyers, doctors, accountants, architects, and engineers) has created new, distinct needs and enabled a few select firms to carve out a defensible niche in what had been a mass market.

One such company is DPIC Companies, which focuses on providing professional liability insurance for architects and de-sign engineers. Instead of just paying claims and raising prices, DPIC's approach is to help clients avoid litigation in the first place through ongoing liability awareness training and various other programs that target dispute avoidance and resolution.

Conversely, factors such as technology can transform a niche market into a mass market. Mass markets can evolve in a classic way: First, sales are made to early customers who pay a very high price for a crude product. At some point, a new technology or manufacturing approach enables a company to cut prices dramat-ically and to improve quality. The niche market then grows rapidly into the mainstream mass market. Owning an evolving mass market requires focusing current sales and support efforts on the early users while anticipating the end-game mass consum-ers and what it will take to win them.

Hewlett-Packard used this approach to own the high-quality computer printer market, which includes laser ink-jet printer technologies. HP's printer business is one of the rare instances in which a U.S. company has recaptured a market from Japanese manufacturers; HP now has a 65 percent share of the high-quality printer market, and there are waiting lists in computer stores for its inexpensive, high-quality printers. HP achieved its success by initially working with demanding customers such as Japanese consumers, who demand excellence in general and need dense, high-quality printing to handle their iconographic alphabet. At the same time HP envisioned the mass market consumer, figuring that everyone would want high-quality printing if it were affordable. So HP lowered the price of its laser printers to the point where they were comparable in cost to low-resolution dot matrix printers. By plowing profits back into the business, HP has been able to keep competitors at bay by lowering prices and adding new features such as color. As the CEO of ComputerLand Corp. commented in a *Wall Street Journal* (May 11, 1992) article, "Every time it appears someone is going to catch up, they move proactively with new price points or new engineering."

Mass markets rarely stay static. They are replaced by products based on new, superior technologies, as when lasers replaced dot matrix printers, and PC/LAN configurations replaced mainframe computers. Mass markets also tend to fragment over time, becoming susceptible to niche and multiniche segment strategies.

To sustain market ownership, a company must constantly review the mass market, envisioning and even creating new customers. It must find niches and exploit them before someone else gets a foothold. Where possible, it must employ a multiniche strategy, tailoring the product delivery to serve segments with slightly different needs.

Geography also has an important effect on market transitions. Markets can change from local to broad or even reverse themselves and go from broad to local. For example, when corporate clients expand geographically into multiple regions or internationally, their needs shift from having a local slant to requiring a broader geographic perspective. Suddenly clients expect their suppliers to be able to service them in many geographic locations, thus transforming a local business into a broadly defined geographic market. This is certainly the case for the computer, accounting, investment banking, and other industries that service multinational corporations.

Geographic markets can also go the other way. The selling of health insurance plans to major U.S. companies was once a national business. Insurers had to have some representation in every corner of the country to satisfy corporate buyers that their local servicing needs could be met. That changed with the emergence of HMOs, which depend on dominant local share and clout with health-care providers to control costs. This shift changed the market from national to local.

Local markets can also be affected by savvy multiregional competitors who have found new ways to build economies of scale into the equation, thereby overcoming the advantages of local players. McDonalds is a classic case. Million of dollars spent on building brand awareness has transformed the convenience food business from a local "Eat at Al's" affair to sticking with an internationally recognized brand. Wal-Mart represents a case in which a large national player obtained economies of scale by large-scale purchasing from suppliers and used the resulting favorable prices to defeat local retail stores.

4. Dealing with Multiple Customers. A complete vision of the customer must also include multiple customers, quasi-customers, and/or other parties that significantly influence the purchase decisions. The most common example of this is the selling of a company's product through an independent distribution channel. Because they can partially or completely determine which company's product gets sold, such channels are in effect a type of customer; the company must sell the distributor customer before its product can reach the end customer.

"Multiple" customers can be a subtle concept. It can, and often does, include the people who influence the ultimate purchase decision. To the extent that such people routinely play a significant role, they too need to be considered to be customers. This subtlety exists in, for instance, the building materials business, where potential customers may include both the developer and the ultimate property owner, the architect who specifies brands to be used, and the contractors (whenever they have the freedom to choose suppliers).

The existence of multiple customers usually causes an endless debate within companies over the real customer and whose needs should be met first, especially when the needs of the various customers are inconsistent. Conflicts are built in, for instance, over commissions paid to the intermediary; the more the intermediary is paid and given financial incentives, the higher the price of the product is to the end consumer—which lowers its value.

As long as there are multiple customers in the market, the company must deal with all of them as if they were the singular customer described throughout this chapter. Thus, a company must have a clear vision of whom the multiple customers need to be. It is every bit as important to segment the intermediary customers as it is to segment the end customer. Often, there is a close relationship between the two types of customer segments.

The company must also take a balanced approach to developing products and strategies that satisfy all of the customers equally well. Even companies that declare that the intermediary is the real customer must provide high-value products and services to satisfy the end customer. Otherwise, the intermediary customer will not have much to sell. The trick is to support the intermediary with product, compensation, and valued services, but not beyond the point where the total offering detracts from value provided to the end customer.

Envisioning the Customer

The second phase of envisioning the right customer is to identify the customer carefully within the broader market context. Defining the company's customer is a three-step process:

1. Segmenting the market around customer groups that have common needs and values
2. Picking the segments that the company can serve better than competitors and that are or can be made profitable
3. Ensuring that the chosen segment includes "smart customers" with high integrity and leading-edge qualities that can challenge your business and contribute to its intellectual growth

1. *Segmenting the market.* To own a market requires that you have a tighter definition and a deeper understanding of who the customer is than your competitors have. The challenge at this

Exhibit 4-3. Examples of factors that define need/value
                segments.

- Price sensitivity
- Preference for quality
- Desire for convenience
- Need for reliability in product delivery
- Need for quick turnaround
- Need for advice and counsel in using the product
- Need for prestige
- Need for customization
- Tolerance for risk
- Desire for one-stop shopping
- Importance of supplier relationship

point is to develop a far more creative and sophisticated way to segment the market around distinct groups of customers. It is not enough merely to decide to focus on (for instance) mid-size companies or wealthy individuals; virtually all competitors can get this far.

The need for creative segmentation is captured especially well by marketing professor Theodore Levitt in his book *The Marketing Imagination*: "To think segments means you have to think about what drives customers, customer groups, and the choices that are or might be available to them. To think segments means to think beyond what's obviously out there to see. If everybody sees segments as obviously consisting of certain demographics, industries, user groups, buying practices, certain influencing groups, and the like, then the thinking that gives real power is thinking that transcends the ordinary."

Although there are many ways to segment a market, the best way to do so is on the basis of what customers' needs and values will be satisfied by buying and using the company's product. This type of analysis yields segments that consist of groups of customers and prospects with common needs and values with respect to the product or service in question. Several items that often distinguish needs/values-based market segments are listed in Exhibit 4-3.

There is a simple two-step process for achieving needs/values-based segmentation:

1. Segment the market by broad demographic characteristics (e.g., age and income for individuals, and industry type and company size for businesses). These characteristics must represent basic differences in customer needs and values.
2. Further segment the market by differences in what customers need and value.

Two detailed case studies illustrating this two-step process are presented later in this chapter.

The first step of the process puts you in the ballpark. The second provides much greater insight on what various groups of customers need and on the ways what they value differs from what other groups value. As Levitt points out, this extra step enables management to "think beyond what's obviously out there to see."

A good example is the business of managing people's money, where nearly every player seeks to serve the affluent market because that is where the investments come from—and (not coincidentally) the most profit. Picking the affluent market as a first step is important—obviously, customers' investment needs vary by the amount of money they have to invest. Unfortunately, in this case, this form of segmentation is so obvious as to be clear to all competitors.

The first step, demographic segmentation, is good, but it does not go far enough. The second step addresses the fact that the "affluent" market has at least six subsegments, each of which has different needs and values in the investment advice and services they need and are willing to pay for. The market includes, for example, people who want little or no personal involvement in investment decisions because they do not feel confident about investment matters. Another group includes those who want to do it all themselves and who feel quite secure making their own choice of investments. The first group might be ideally suited for private banking; the latter might be attracted to discount brokerage services and market information products.

A product designed to serve both subsegments will satisfy neither.

One company making good use of the two-step segmentation process is the insurer DPIC Companies, which first defines its market demographically as consisting of architects and engineers and then, in the second, needs/values step, looks for companies with a strong appreciation for professional practices that can enable them to avoid lawsuits for malpractice. DPIC's CEO, Peter Hawes, commented on his firm's target market: "We are looking for the professional services firm that considers itself well managed, that shares our belief that liability risk can be managed, and that values our services."

In some cases, needs and values are not related to demographics. That is, some needs/values segments do not map to any particular industry or age/income demographic segments. In these cases, the market is best segmented by needs and values alone.

For example, the yacht charter business serves clients of all ages and within a wide range of income groups, yet the business serves a certain needs/values-based segment. Charlie Cary, chairman of The Moorings, a yacht charter company, envisions his customers as people who value sailing as a hobby. His customers include both younger clients who can not afford a boat and older customers who are former boat owners.

Similarly, Harley-Davidson sells to customers who value the look and feel of the more traditional heavy motorcycle and who constitute a needs/values segment that cuts across age and income groups. Another example is Tootsie Roll, whose target customer is defined by its special enjoyment (value) of orange-flavored chocolate. This definition also cuts across many demographic groups.

It is undoubtedly a lot easier to segment the market using factors that make prospects readily identifiable. But, as Levitt points out, "[doing so] does not transcend the ordinary." Any mediocre competitor can get this far. To go further requires creative thinking, segmenting the market on the basis of customer needs/values that are not readily apparent to competitors and enabling the company to focus its resources on meeting the homogeneous needs of the selected segment.

2. *Selecting attractive segments.* The next step in envisioning the customer is to evaluate the various segments for attractiveness and strategic fit. Judging the attractiveness of a market segment depends on criteria such as market size, growth, and profitability. There must also be a strategic fit. Management has to ask itself, "Does our company have the right capabilities and competitive strengths to become a truly dominant player in the segment?"

The first two criteria of attractiveness are very straightforward. All else being equal, the bigger the market, the greater the opportunity. And certainly a growing segment is more desirable than a declining one.

The third criterion, profitability, is equally obvious but actually so overlooked as to require special attention. For market ownership to work, the company must serve clients who are either inherently profitable or that the company can make profitable in some way. Unprofitable clients are a common blight that afflicts most companies, sapping their strength and substantially draining resources that could be spent on building the company's competitive strengths. The blight goes largely undetected, often until the company encounters serious problems and reassesses how and where it makes money.

The customer profitability problem is so widespread and acute that the conventional 80/20 rule should be amended to become the 80/20/30 rule: The top 20 percent of customers generate 80 percent of the company's profits, half of which is lost serving the bottom 30 percent of unprofitable customers (see Exhibit 4-4). This problem is common because companies usually lack accounting systems that track customer profitability. Lacking factual data, management is likely to view all customers as being profitable and all revenue as profitable revenue.

However attractive a segment may be, it is critical to consider whether the segment is a good strategic fit for the company. To assess fit, management must consider whether the company meets these criteria:

- The company has (or is confident that it can develop) the capabilities to meet customer requirements better than its competitors.
- The competition in the market is reasonably fragmented.

Exhibit 4-4. The 80/20/30 rule of customer profitability.

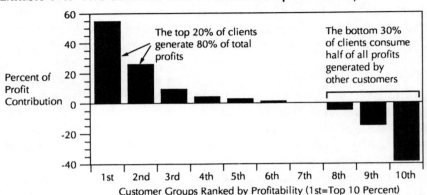

No company or companies dominate the market with substantial market share and sustainable strengths.

- The company has (or is confident that it can develop) a strong image in the market and is (or could be) perceived as a logical market leader.

If a company scores high in these three criteria, then it can probably devise an effective strategy for succeeding in the segment. Furthermore, it is much easier to become a significant player in a fragmented market segment than in one dominated by one of a few very strong companies.

It is also easier to succeed in market segments in which the company, for any number of reasons, does not have to overcome a significant image problem. Image is reality, and if the company's image is inconsistent with how it wishes customers in a particular segment to view it, then it will have real difficulties succeeding in the segment. The two case studies that follow illustrate the way that strategic fit can play a large part in a company's selection of a target market.

Two Case Studies

Diversified Investment Advisors—Part One

Diversified Investment Advisors sells an array of investment products and services to individuals and corporations for their pension plans.

In 1988 the company's new chairman was particularly interested in building Diversified's pension business, which was one of the firm's most profitable divisions. He was especially interested in the pension division's 401(k) business, which provided investment and administrative services for the fast-growing and increasingly popular 401 (k) pension plans.

Although Diversified enjoyed rapid growth, it grew at about the same rate as the overall 401(k) market; Diversified thus maintained its relatively small market share of less than 1 percent. In seeking to break out of this historical pattern and to increase its growth substantially, Diversified conducted a comprehensive strategic planning exercise with particular attention on where to focus its sales and product development efforts.

As a first pass, it made sense for Diversified to focus on the "middle market," consisting of companies with between one hundred and five thousand employees and product and service requirements that fitted well with Diversified's existing capabilities. This initial focus also enabled Diversified to avoid competing directly with larger rivals, such as Fidelity, which competed at the larger end of the corporate market. A second and less clear question was how to further segment this market so that Diversified could find one or more target markets around which a strategy could be built.

Although Diversified started out using a variety of approaches for segmenting the market, its use of an extensive survey of customers and prospects in this middle market finally provided the insight it was looking for. The survey inquired about respondents' needs, values, and buying/switching behavior for their 401(k) plans. It then analyzed the survey data, using a quantitative statistical method that identified clusters (or groups) of prospects with common needs, values, and behaviors. The analysis revealed that the market was made up of five distinct segments that shared common needs/values. These are summarized in Exhibit 4-5.

The names of the segments reveal the types of companies they contain. The companies in the first segment, "Clean and Simple," value simplicity above all else in purchasing 401(k) products and services; companies in the second segment value investment performance along with simplicity. The typical company in the third segment ("Customized") wants its 401(k) products and services tailored to its particular needs. Companies in the fourth segment want a lot of attention and good investment performance; companies in the fifth segment ("Cost-Sensitive") want to minimize the cost of their 401(k) pension plans. It is interesting to contrast the values of

Exhibit 4-5. Description of five needs/value-based segments.

Segment Name	Summary Description
1. Clean and Simple	Simple plan through single source. Supplier takes care of everything— not a burden on company staff. Reasonable range of investment options.
2. Investment-Oriented and Simple	Investment performance is key. No-frills plan with moderate range of investments. Internal staff will work with provider.
3. Customized	Tailored, sophisticated service and services. Experienced buyers.
4. High Touch/High Return	Investment performance and range of options are key. Provider takes care of everything with high levels of contact.
5. Cost-Sensitive	Low cost; simple plan

companies in the "Clean and Simple" and the "Customized" segments.

The motives of the "Clean and Simple" segment come through loud and clear: "We are not in business to provide 401(k) plans to our employees; we are very busy attending our core business. While we want to offer this important benefit to our employees, we want to minimize the amount of attention and time we spend on it." These companies want standard products that are simple to understand and offer few options. They want one-stop shopping in that all of the related services (e.g., investment and administration) are provided by one supplier. And they want their plan to be easy for employees, so they want 800 service and support lines and literature that describes the plan as simply as possible.

In contrast, the motives of the "Customized" segment can be stated as, "We do our own thing. We have our own corporate culture to maintain, and we go to great lengths to adapt employee benefit programs to suit our needs." Companies in this segment design their own plans' product features and reporting requirements and typically use different suppliers for investment and administrative services. They also demand dedicated service teams to handle their accounts.

The 401(k) pension market proved to be a multiniche market in which distinct segments with different needs and values existed, yet these distinct differences were too small to take advantage of economies of scale. Diversified responded appropriately by developing a multisegment strategy in which each segment would be addressed in a logical sequence according to its capabilities.

Diversified first decided to focus on the two "keep it simple" segments (segments one and two) for mid-size companies with fewer than one thousand employees and, after some success, to go after the "Customized" segment for companies with more than one thousand employees.

Diversified's initial segment focus was based on the following logic:

- Diversified was much stronger in the middle market where competition was fragmented and relatively weak. Diversified could avoid the mutual fund companies, which, while very strong, avoided the middle market.
- The two "keep it simple" segments demanded the capabilities that Diversified was best able to deliver: local presence to help install the plan and enroll employees.
- Combined, the two segments were the largest portion of the middle market.
- The "keep it simple" segments were more profitable than others that either demanded more service or were price-sensitive.
- The "keep it simple" segments were served primarily by regional banks, which viewed the 401(k) business as an afterthought and consequently had dissatisfied customers who were more likely to consider switching to Diversified.

Although the segmentation strategy made sense for Diversified, the company was frustrated to find that the targeted "keep it simple" segments did not readily map to common characteristics that would make them easy to find. First, the segments had no correlation with any particular industry; they were equally represented in all of the major industry groups. There was, however, some linkage to company size, as shown in Exhibit 4-6. Not surprisingly, the prevalence of the customized segment increased with company size, and there was a corresponding decrease in the prevalence of the two "keep it

Exhibit 4-6. Needs/value-based segments by size of company.

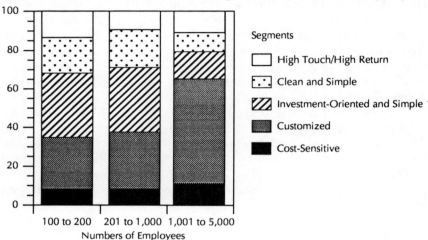

simple" segments. Other segments (e.g., "Cost-Sensitive" and "High Touch/High Return") varied little with company size.

Diversified readily addressed the problem of finding the targeted "keep it simple" market by training the sales organization to classify prospects quickly according to the five segments. This was accomplished by having the sales force ask a few easy questions similar to those in the original survey. It also tailored its communications programs, such as brochures, with the theme "Diversified Makes It Easy," which immediately appealed to the values of the targeted market.

Lexus—Part One

Toyota's entry into the luxury car market in 1987 is a good example of how to segment the market first by demographics and then by the subsegments of the broader market.

At the outset, Toyota set its sights on the upper-income level of the luxury car market, positioning itself against Mercedes, BMW, and Jaguar, rather than against Cadillac and Lincoln. This meant that it was going after a market it knew little about, given its primary involvement in the mass market.

In 1983 Toyota embarked on a two-year "brute force" qualitative market research effort. The research involved some thirty executives and designers who performed direct observations such as visiting dealerships, interviewing customers, and sitting in on focus groups. Their close involvement enabled them to develop deep insights into the image-intensive luxury car market, find an unexploited target segment, and develop a successful strategy.

The intensity, scope, and personal involvement of key company staff assigned to the project represents an unusual way of understanding the market. It paid off unusually well, especially considering that the luxury car market had been served by European manufacturers for many years.

Toyota's first discovery was that age was a major segmentation factor. Older luxury car owners valued prestige and defined prestige as a long-standing reputation—like that of Mercedes-Benz. As a totally new entrant into this market, Toyota could not pursue this market until it had become a well-recognized brand. This posed a chicken-and-egg dilemma, with dubious prospects for entering the prestige segment of the market.

Toyota's breakthrough came when it discovered a somewhat younger market that contained two subsegments with different values. The first group included "yuppies" (young urban professionals), who were also motivated similarly by prestige but who tended to buy BMWs rather than Mercedeses. Interestingly, Toyota decided to avoid this younger segment. Mr. Shiro Sasaki, executive vice president and the project leader, is noted to have counseled colleagues "not to be too much influenced by the opinions of yuppies" (*Automotive News*, September 28, 1992). His decision now appears to have been a piece of remarkable foresight, as many of these younger people experienced dramatic income declines with the 1987 stock market crash and the subsequent recession in the late 1980s and early 1990s.

The second group, however, was motivated more by making the best value purchase—the most intelligent purchase of a luxury car for the price. The value-oriented segment was pragmatic. It was willing to spend $10,000 more for a superior car but believed that paying $20,000 to $30,000 more than the cost of a Cadillac was wasteful. In describing this segment, Kazuo Okamoto, deputy chief engineer on the Lexus project, commented in *Automotive News* (September 28, 1992): "We realized that among wealthy Americans there is a fine line between 'buying something less expensive and being looked at as if you really haven't made it because you settled for less' and 'you know a good value and buying the best makes you look smart.'"

While the yuppie segment sought prestige by buying expensive, status-symbol cars, members of the value-oriented segment sought prestige by demonstrating that they were smart. Toyota found that the average customer in this segment was forty-seven years old and earned $170,000. To Toyota it seemed that the targeted group was "defined more by attitude and mind-set than by occupation and age, and that this group should be relatively recession-proof because of its practical orientation" (*Automotive News,* September 28, 1992).

Toyota ultimately decided to focus on this "smart-buyer" segment of the luxury car market. Toyota created a new division called Lexus and developed a car that offered record-breaking value to customers, especially in comparison to the expensive European luxury cars.

3. *Focusing on Smart Customers.* It is doubtful that a company can ever be better than its best customers, whether those customers are corporations or individuals. While the preceding section discussed focusing on attractive market segments, this section deals with finding "smart" customers within the market segment. Smart customers play a key role in helping the company develop and sustain its competitive strengths and market ownership.

The characteristics of the smart customer are listed in Exhibit 4-7. Although these characteristics are phrased in terms of corporate customers, they pertain to individual customers as well. Note that *smart* means more than leading-edge or sophisticated; smart customers know that good working relationships with

Exhibit 4-7. Profile of the smart customer.

- Is sophisticated, innovative, highly successful.
- Makes good use of purchased products and services.
- Sees supplier as a partner in product development and in improving operations.
- Has very high expectations of self, associates, and suppliers.
- Is driven by value, not price.
- Values relationships with all key constituents, including suppliers.
- Is seen as leading-edge and trend-setting in its own industry.
- Has high ethical standards and integrity.

---

suppliers are critical to their ability to satisfy their own customers with the goods and services they provide. Although smart customers may be demanding, they will be far more profitable than the customers who cut every corner and exploit suppliers every chance they can get.

It is unrealistic and restrictive to expect all of a company's customers to meet all of these stringent criteria. Instead, the company should strive to:

- Seek customers within the target market that generally conform to many of the business characteristics listed in Exhibit 4-7.
- Specifically target a set of known leading-edge customers as part of the company's strategy. These customers will stretch the company's product development and process improvement efforts, thereby making the company stronger.
- Avoid the bad customers who score poorly on the criteria listed in Exhibit 4-7, especially in the area of ethical considerations.

The smart customer is critical to the company's innovation in product development and process improvement. A corporate environment can be a very insular place, and one of the most important ways that companies learn is from their customers—and if the customer is a poor teacher then the company will be slow to learn. In fact, a study conducted by Professor Eric von Hippel of MIT and published in the book *The Sources of Innovation* found that users of technology-based products (i.e., the company's customers) are a major source of new technologies. In some industries customers are the major source; consider the scientific instrument business, for example, in which users develop 77 percent of all new technologies.

Clients who are good "teachers" are innovative, fast-paced, always looking for opportunities for improvement. They are very thoughtful about the goods and services they buy, and they put them to good use. Suppliers should carefully observe smart customers to learn how to improve their products and to develop new ones.

Smart customers see the supplier as a partner in integrating products and services into their operations. This gives the supplier invaluable firsthand experience in how its products are actually used day to day by the customer, a far more effective way to learn than through market research.

The good customer values supplier relationships and often narrows down the number of suppliers in order to forge deeper ties with fewer of them. This customer knows that there is more to buying goods and services than the actual purchase and that good supplier relationships mean more than repeatedly getting the lowest bid.

Good customers are demanding but in an important way, and with important effects for suppliers. They demand value and often define it in an innovative way. Instead of insisting on price discounts, for example, the good customer may demand prompt delivery, electronic linkages, quality control measures, and other considerations that make the supplier's product more valuable to the customer. Thus, the good customer stretches the supplier's capabilities, which often builds into the supplier's organization strengths that would not have been developed by less demanding clients.

However impenetrable Japanese markets may seem to be, Japanese customers are an unusually good source of good customers. And companies like Hewlett-Packard, Applied Materials, and Donnelly claim to have benefited from their Japanese clients.

HP learned leading-edge quality management from its Japanese subsidiary, Yokogawa-Hewlett-Packard Ltd., which won the Deming Prize in 1982 for its breakthrough quality improvement. The Japanese subsidiary served as inspiration and teacher for setting quantum-leap goals in quality and for applying quality management techniques widely used in Japanese industry.

Similarly, Applied Materials' Japanese customers helped it become and remain the leading supplier of equipment for making the silicon wafers used in producing integrated circuit chips, a global and intensely competitive industry. More than 40 percent of Applied Materials' revenues come from Japanese chip manufacturers, and an even higher share of ideas comes from them. Applied Materials CEO James C. Morgan was quoted in the *Los Angeles Times* (June 20, 1991) as saying, ''No question, we learn more from our Japanese customers than we do from our American ones. That's beginning to change, but much of our success in the rest of the world comes from what we learn from our best Japanese customers."

The Donnelly Corporation has had a similar experience in Japan, which has helped it maintain its ownership of the market for car mirrors and windows. When Japanese car makers started to make inroads in the market in the 1970s, Donnelly targeted these companies. "We've learned a lot from customers like Toyota, Nissan, and Honda. We had to learn a different way of doing business," recalls Kay Hubbard, advocate for Human Research Management Development at Donnelly. . . . "The Japanese companies we dealt with were very thorough. They didn't just want to talk to a salesperson; they wanted to meet quality control experts and engineers—they wanted to see the process, not just the product," says Dwayne Baumgardner, Donnelly's CEO and Chairman. . . . "Of course, not everyone was comfortable with it at first, but our corporate culture really changed at that point, from a focus on what we could do, to a focus on what our customers needed us to do, or learn how to do. It used to be enough just to keep General Motors happy, but we had to abandon that mind-set," says Hubbard. [From S. C. Biemesderfer's "On Demand," *Profiles*, the Magazine of Continental Airlines (June 1993).]

Smart customers are ethical and have high integrity. They prefer to have a trusting relationship with suppliers that enables both parties to function quickly and efficiently without having to run every transaction through their legal departments.

Finally, smart customers are seen as leaders in their industries. The rest of the industry frequently follows their actions and decisions. Thus, acquiring smart customers is perhaps one of the quickest ways to penetrate, and gain credibility within, a targeted segment.

For example, in targeting industry niches for its computer equipment, HP aims at companies that are demonstrated leaders in applying new technologies to transform their businesses. In selling its latest business server products, which automate via networked PCs, HP succeeded in penetrating the retail industry by acquiring as clients Wal-Mart, Home Depot, and 7-Eleven Japan, three of the most innovative, admired companies in the retail business. Not only will these companies stretch HP's capabilities and contribute to its intellectual capital, but they will no doubt open doors for HP throughout the rest of the industry.

Conversely, the unimaginative, unaggressive customer inspires no new ideas or opportunities. This customer sees little value in working closely with suppliers, either to help them help the company or to learn new things from them. Such customers reveal themselves by referring to suppliers as "vendors," as in little more than "street vendor." Relationships mean next to nothing; they extend only to the next competitive bid, by which time it will be a whole new ballgame. Whether the supplier may have helped the customer in the past will be irrelevant. This customer does not understand the concept of value and is motivated purely by lowest-price mentality. Supplier relationships are delegated to the purchasing department, which is instructed to select only the lowest bidders. Not surprisingly, these customers are usually unprofitable.

These customers are a drain on the company's intellectual capital, and a major impediment to developing staff capabilities. In this regard, Michael Schrage, the innovation journalist, counseled in *The Wall Street Journal* (October 5, 1991):

> While most companies wouldn't dream of letting their customers become financial deadbeats, they seem all too willing to let them become conceptual deadbeats. In particular, software designers, lawyers, consultants, advertising agencies, and other professional service companies invest too much time and effort in clients that neither demand nor inspire creativity.

There is a huge downside in dealing with customers who are unethical. They are always cutting corners and failing to keep commitments and usually wring more product out of the supplier while paying less money than agreed upon at the outset. Worse still, the unethical client can degrade the supplying company's integrity.

Given that customers are the foundation for the business, it is critical that the company acquire more than its share of the smart ones. There is a natural alignment of good customers and good suppliers. Good customers are attracted to good salespeople and independent distributors, all of whom are attracted to good companies with good people and run by good management. The logic works the other way as well. In many industries, getting the best employees requires having the best customers with the most challenging needs. Employees must have confidence in making the supplier's product a success in and for itself, and thus a success for the supplying company and its employees. This is obvious in creative businesses such as advertising and research and in related businesses like consulting and technology. In a more subtle way, it is true for many other industries as well.

It is also true that "bad" customers attract "bad" suppliers. Well-managed companies refuse to deal with bad prospects; thus, the bad customer is left in a desperate situation, forced to deal with suppliers for whom any sale is a good sale. And they deserve each other.

The company seeking to significantly upgrade its capabilities and performance is faced with a chicken-and-egg dilemma. It takes great clients to create a great company; yet it takes a great company to get great clients. At the very least, then, the looking-to-be-great company needs to tackle internal improvements while at the same time upgrading its clients. This means acquiring the very new best customers while pruning out the losers from the existing client base. To accomplish this, Schrage suggests that "these [bad] clients are dogs. They should be put out of your misery. The smartest thing most customer service-oriented companies could do today is lay off about 10 to 15 percent of their customers."

I have raised a lot of questions concerning the vision of the customer for today and in the future—questions about market types, logical geographic boundaries, attractive market segments, and smart customers. While these questions may seem to complicate matters, in reality, addressing them up-front greatly simplifies the development of a company's strategic focus and the decisions regarding spending scarce resources.

Chapter 5

Maximizing Customer Value

The bottom line for every company is not its profitability but the value it provides to its customers. A company's current profitability is merely ancient history; it reflects the results of the company's past strengths and decisions. The company that provides superior value will win in the markeplace and achieve great financial success. Why? Because customer value is a true bottom line, embracing all the salient aspects of the company's products—pricing, performance, quality—everything that matters to the customer.

Although the concept of customer value is often cited, it is greatly misunderstood. There are many misconceptions and, sometimes, dangerous conclusions. Furthermore, given the all-encompassing nature of the value concept, it is surprising to see managements getting caught up in single-minded initiatives such as total quality management, cost reduction, and profit improvement. As Peter Drucker notes in his book *Management*, "What is value to the customer? It may be the most important question, yet it is the one least often asked."

In Chapter 4, I discussed customer value in terms of defining a market segment on the basis of common needs/values. In this chapter I explore the customer value concept in depth and address two questions fundamental to market ownership: What is customer value? How can your company maximize it?

What Is Customer Value?

In the mind of the customer, value equals the sum of the perceived benefits minus the sum of the perceived costs, where benefits and costs extend beyond narrow boundaries and are highly subjective.

This basic definition of customer value can be simplified by viewing it as a value balance sheet. In Exhibit 5-1, the value a customer receives from any product or service equals the difference between the perceived benefits (on the left side of the chart) and the perceived costs (on the right side).

The higher the value of the product in comparision to competing ones, the larger the demand for it will be, and the greater the company's competitive advantage.

Price is an important item on the liability side of the balance sheet. Assume for the moment that it is the only liability or cost

Exhibit 5-1. The customer's value balance sheet.

Perceived Benefits *(Assets)*	*Perceived Costs* *(Liabilities)*
Economic:	*Economic:*
• Increased revenues	• Total purchase cost
• Decreased costs (including time and convenience)	• Price
• Expectation of enhanced assets	• Future prices
• Value of risk reduction	• Cost to install
• Expected product life and resale value	• Cost to use
	—Expected maintenance costs
	—Cost of downtime
Psychological:	*Psychological:*
• Fulfillment of self-image	• Uncertainty that value will be obtained
• Prestige	• Potential personal threats and embarrassment
• Entertainment	
• Ease of doing business	
• Health and personal safety	

Customer value = benefits minus costs.

to the customer. This implies that products that provide benefits significantly greater than their prices give high value to the customer. If there is no similarly high value for competing products, the costomer is willing to pay more to reap the benefits, thus putting the product in high demand.

To own a market requires providing higher value to the targeted market than does the competition. By examining both sides of the ledger, the value balance sheet helps to probe deeper into what determines value.

The elements of the value balance sheet have three key characteristics. First, note that on both sides of the chart there are two classes of items: perceived benefits and costs, and psychological rewards and costs. For the moment, consider them as the rational and the subjective; value is always driven by both the rational economic and the irrational, subjective psychological aspects of the product. On this point marketing professor Theodore Levitt notes in *The Marketing Imagination*, "A product is, to the potential buyer, a complex cluster of value satisfactions. The generic 'thing' or 'essence' is not itself the product."

Second, note that the economic items are tagged as "perceived," indicating that even "hard" items are seen through the hazy perspective of each customer and that no two customers view the same "hard" economics the same way. For example, any two individuals will place a different value on the same investment in terms of how they react to risk and how quickly they want to get their money back. Some investors prefer greater risks in hopes of greater returns, whereas others opt for safe investments with little risk and modest return. Some customers buy too much life insurance; others buy none. The hard facts are the same, yet the value tradeoffs are part of the customer's perception.

Third, customers' purchase decisions always involve a tradeoff based on their perceptions of benefits and costs. The purchase decision is made by determining which product or service has the highest value after each feature—benefits, cost, price, options, and so forth—is traded off against the others. Finally, as I explained in Chapter 4, values differ by customer segment; these perceived tradeoffs differ from customer to customer.

An examination of the items in the value balance sheet

provides further insight into the concept of value. For one thing, the list of economic benefits includes considerations that increase revenues, reduce costs, and/or improve future earnings capability. Value derived from enhancing clients' revenues can include such things as the advertising agency that creates a new program to boost sales; the company with a training program that offers to make the sales organization much more productive; or the machine that promises to improve the quality of the customers' products, thus enabling the company to increase both its prices and the demand for its products.

Even cardboard boxes can enhance clients' revenues. With the increasing popularity of discount houses that sell products by the boxload, a box manufacturer can increase both the manufacturers' and the sellers' revenues by printing catchy graphic displays on what otherwise would be a "plain vanilla" box. In an article in *Purchasing Magazine* (February 18, 1993), Tom Santelli of Georgia Pacific commented:

> Warehouse clubs are hot. They tend to receive and display full pallet loads of products. Units are not taken down (i.e., they are left in original shipping boxes). Good graphics are vital. A consumer takes only a few seconds to pass by an aisle. If he doesn't notice the package, he's probably not going to buy. [Reprinted from *Purchasing Magazine*. Copyright by Cahners Publishing Company.]

There are many ways that products can add value by reducing the customer's day-to-day operating costs, especially for industrial products. One currently popular value-enhancing service is to deliver goods and services "just in time" (JIT). By delivering supplies to the customer as needed, JIT saves the customer all the costs of maintaining an inventory, costs that include facilities and storage and that tie up operating capital that could be put to other uses.

Here is another example. Kingston Technology makes memory storage and processor components that supercharge PCs and sells these components through computer dealers. Kingston builds a product and ships it to the dealer on the same day the order is received, so that its customers do not have to maintain inventories.

In today's information age, newly introduced information services can reduce customers' costs. Emery Worldwide, an air freight carrier, has a service called "QuickSource," which centralizes the inventory tracking of equipment and spare parts. This service enables Emery to ship needed components door-to-door throughout the country on short notice, virtually eliminating customers' need to warehouse parts.

In the consumer world, the economics play a subtler role. Consider, for example, investment products that promise to produce a competitive return on investment, for instance, the many consumer products that are bought on the premise of reducing household costs, the products that save energy or prolong the life of expensive assets such as cars and houses.

In the consumer's mind, economics may be denominated more by time than by dollars; thus, convenience is a major value component of a consumer's value balance sheet. Depending on the customer, convenience and time savings may mean a lot. The harried business executive, perpetually short on time, is more than willing to pay full airfare to get the right flight at short notice, while the student long on time and short on money might opt for standby. Nike, the shoe manufacturer, will send a pair of shoes overnight via Federal Express if a customer cannot find his or her size in the store, saving the customer the time it would take to visit another store and enhancing the store's revenues by enabling it to make the sale where it otherwise might have lost the customer.

Risk reduction also has economic benefits. For businesses, risk reduction includes such things as using JIT to reduce inventories and exposure to downturns in business cycles; perhaps adopting new safety measures to reduce the risk of fire or workplace accidents; or avoiding exposure to environmentally related litigation by choosing raw materials that are nonpolluting. For consumers, risk reduction can mean minimizing threats to themselves and their families and to major assets like house and car. Thus, purchasing a smoke detection system or a car with a good safety record is of value to many consumers.

Finally, the expected life of the product and its resale price are major economic benefits for many products. That is why even a modest home in a desirable neighborhood sells for a premium. It is more likely to retain its value regardless of cycles in the real estate market. Since no one can know product life or resale price when making the original purchase, consumers use the product and company reputation as a surrogate measure.

The benefits of a product or service often go beyond tangible economics and can include psychological rewards, such as image-enhancing prestige. Psychological rewards accrue to business customers as well. The real human being who makes the purchase might want to get something personal out of the decision, such as being perceived as an intelligent decision maker making a wise purchase.

Many, if not most, consumer goods have important psychological benefits. This is especially true for personal items, such as clothes and cosmetics, the only benefits from which may be psychological. Even hard goods such as a home or car have large psychological components in terms of what messages are conveyed by the choice.

As Theodore Levitt comments in *The Marketing Imagination:*

> An automobile is not simply a tangible machine for movement, [that is] visibly or measurably differentiated by design, size, color, options, horsepower, or miles per gallon. It is also a complex symbol denoting status, taste, rank, achievement, aspiration, and, these days, being "smart"—that is, buying economy rather than display.

One major psychological benefit of both industrial and consumer products is "ease of doing business." This is a catchall phrase that refers to how responsive and courteous the supplier's people are in daily interactions. Whether the buyer is a private consumer or a corporate purchasing manager, it is human nature to seek out pleasant experiences and to avoid aggravation. Customers will pay more for products and services provided by companies that are easy and pleasant to deal with, and any smart company today has built this fact into all aspects of its operations that touch customers.

On the perceived cost side of the value balance sheet are

factors that detract from the value of the product or service. Like the benefit side of the ledger, the cost side is divided into perceived economic costs and psychological costs.

Note that costs include much more than what is on the price tag. The costs of acquiring a product can include installation and all the peripheral components that might be needed to use the product. Even perceived or expected future prices influence value. If the price of a product has a history of escalating, then customers expect that trend to continue. As a result, they may place less value on the product, especially if the initial purchase means committing to a technology that locks them into future purchases.

Other hidden costs are critical as well. These might include the cost of owning and using the product—maintenance and gas mileage for cars, property taxes for homes, and the need for extensive facilities to operate mainframe computers compared to desktop PCs. A June 1991 study of luxury car owners by the J. D. Power Co. noted that "BMW and Mercedes rate higher in status than they do as cars that people actually want to own. Among the reasons: They are more expensive to maintain than competing models from Japan."

Downtime caused by product failure is a significant economic cost, especially when it disrupts major business operations. For example, a bank incurs great economic costs when its central processing systems fail, causing the bank to curtail much of its operations. Forklift trucks are another good example. As noted in *Purchasing Magazine* (February 18, 1993), "To buyers of forklift trucks little else matters besides dependability and reliability. Downtime is a buyer's worst enemy." Product reliability and the supplier's ability to react quickly to product failures are therefore highly valued aspects of products and services.

The cost of switching—changing suppliers or using many suppliers—is especially important for the company that has to make a commitment to a particular technology that is incompatible with other technologies, for example, the business and individuals who must make the choice between PCs and Macintoshes. The cost of switching from, or interfacing between, one computer operating system and the other can be significant.

Value is also affected by perceived psychological costs, many of which are the flip side of psychological benefits. Perhaps the biggest psychological cost is the fear that the product will not live up to expectations built up at the time of the sale. This is why strong, positive brand image is so significant to the customer at the point of purchase.

Product assurance is especially important in the yacht chartering business. As The Moorings chairman Charlie Cary notes, "Imagine you plan a one- or two-week trip a year ahead, you put down deposits, and buy airline tickets, and if something goes wrong along the way you've lost a lot." Being sensitive to this perceived risk, The Moorings guarantees that if a client's boat has maintenance problems that take it out of use for more than four hours, the company will refund the cost of the time. It also arranges for all ground transportation and food and lodging upon arrival so that the client's trip isn't marred by a bad experience getting to the boat. As a result, The Moorings can command a 10 to 15 percent markup over other yacht charter services and still increase sales five times as fast as the overall market growth.

Image, trust, and integrity are vital to the success of a company's products because they directly affect the perceived psychological cost. Service guarantees that assure "100 percent satisfaction or your money back" can be effective in addressing risk.

Customer value is the difference between the product or service's perceived benefits and costs. The process of reaching a purchase decision through this mental subtraction no doubt involves a complex and often subconscious process of trading off the various items in the person's own value balance sheet.

Case Studies in High Value Delivery

The following case studies illustrate the concept of value. Each one shows how leading companies have created products and services that offer much higher value than do their competitors. Each one underscores the importance of maximizing customer value to market success.

Lexus—Part Two

Recognizing the challenge Toyota faced in entering the prestige-driven luxury car business, Dick Chitty, corporate manager parts service and customer relations, noted in a November 1989 speech: "To establish ourselves as a new entry in the upscale, luxury car market, Lexus has not only to match Mercedes-Benz, BMW, and Jaguar in features and quality, but to exceed them in all other areas. . . . We will achieve this goal with an excellent product, outstanding dealer networks, and by elevating the automotive experience to the Lexus buyer throughout his, or her, ownership lifetime. All for a base price [of] $35,000. [This is] value for the dollar."

The Lexus offers significant value in terms of economic benefits and cost. On the benefit side, it was designed with many safety features, including a driver's-side air bag and a body and a frame that were designed to be both rigid and energy-absorbing. Toyota also put considerable effort into extending the life of Lexus's interior and exterior. A spokesman for Lexus notes that "[The] LS 400 is designed to age gracefully. Its interior components benefit from a careful study of five- to six-year-old Toyotas in the U.S. that helped identify 96 items for anti-aging refinements. This anti-aging program will pay dividends to Lexus owners years after their initial purchase."

Lexus's value is further enhanced by minimizing items on the cost side of the balance sheet. First, the price of a Lexus is 25 percent lower than that of comparable European cars. Second, it includes many standard items, such as cruise control and leather interior, that are options on other brands. It is economical to use: It gets high gas mileage for a luxury car, mileage good enough that the buyer can avoid the "gas guzzler" tax. It offers free initial maintenance. Its product warranties extend up to seventy-two months for the power train.

J. D. Power Co. rated Lexus (along with Infiniti) best among forty-one brands in number of problems in the first ninety days of ownership. If a breakdown does occur, the company provides twenty-four-hour roadside assistance via an 800 number. If the problem cannot be fixed on the spot, the owner gets a free loaner car, and meals and lodging if he or she is stranded.

As Levitt notes in *The Marketing Imagination,* cars provide more than transportation; they also provide many psychological rewards. Lexus, given its strong reputation for economic value, offers the "smart buyer" prestige.

Lexus was also careful to emphasize ease of doing business with its dealer network. It chose its dealers carefully, expecting them to meet strict criteria. Lexus appointed only seventy-two dealers from the fifteen hundred who initially applied for a dealership. That this paid off was evident from the J. D. Power satisfaction ranking in

March 1991, which indicated that Lexus was first in customer satisfaction with dealer service.

Lexus gained significant advantages by providing customer value. In its first month, it outsold BMW. Within five months it had become the number one car in all categories included in *Car and Driver's 1990 Buyer Study*. Within three years Lexus had overtaken Mercedes and was the most sought-after luxury car in the United States.

Hewlett-Packard Business Servers

Business servers are powerful computers that link networks of PCs, terminals, workstations, corporate databases, and applications into a corporatewide integrated system. The networked system replaces the function of the old centralized mainframe while allowing workers to use their PCs or workstations independently.

HP entered the business server market in 1986 with the intention of becoming the dominant supplier by 1995. HP's plan was to position itself as a strategic partner with leading corporations as those companies sought to revamp their traditional computer processes, employing business server technology to replace centralized or mainframe configurations.

A number of things contributed to the value of HP's product. First, its price/performance ratio was substantially lower than its competitors'. It ranked high in the quality of its maintenance and service. HP minimized customers' "lock-in costs" by creating open systems that are built to industry standards and that can be integrated with competitors' products. HP also designed its products so that customers could upgrade their business servers along a continuum of products with different capacities. HP was also able to deliver leading-edge applications as references, thus assuring prospects that it could deliver performance results with the applications they want.

Because of this high-value offering, HP now is the leader in this market. According to the Aberdeen Group (February 1993), HP has 47 percent of the market, while its nearest competitor has only 16 percent. HP's sales increased 42 percent in 1992 and approximately 35 percent in 1993, two to three times the growth rate of the overall market.

Home Depot

Management Review (May 9, 1992) claims that "Home Depot may become the Wal-Mart of the home improvement market. Largely this can be attributed to Home Depot's high-value retail service."

Home Depot, which sells approximately thirty thousand items in its stores, offers convenience and one-stop shopping for supplies and materials. Mass purchasing enables it to obtain lower prices on merchandise, and it passes those price savings on to its customers. Home Depot guarantees that its prices are at least 5 percent lower than those at any competing store, and it routinely sends its employees into competing stores to ensure that this statement is true.

Home Depot employs about 175 customer service people per store. It also hires some employees from the building trades, people who really know all the details. These sales representatives greet customers by asking, "What project are you working on?" and they make sure the customer purchases everything needed for that project. They provide in-store demonstrations on how to install everything from electrical wiring to floor tiles. In addition, they conduct weekend seminars to educate customers on various do-it-yourself projects.

DPIC Companies

DPIC was capitalized by a group of concerned engineers in private practice. Its goal was to provide professional liability insurance and risk management services for professionals involved in construction projects. The company started out with a close affiliation with its target market; some six hundred design professionals participated in the company's initial public offering.

While most insurance companies view their business as spreading risk (across all their customers), DPIC views its business as risk avoidance—helping clients stay out of trouble in the first place. Peter Hawes, chief executive officer of DPIC, characterizes this philosophical difference as follows:

> There are two opposing views of what insurance is. The first is that it is a commodity that you buy without value considerations; it's just price and coverage. The other side of the coin—instead of insuring fires—is to not have fires in the first place. Some would view professional litigation as an arcane thing that only lawyers could deal with, while insurers just funded the game. DPIC's founder had a different idea to attack the root causes with preventive measures that could influence litigation and, when problems arise, to resolve them outside the litigation process.

The value of DPIC's product offering starts wtih its network of agents, who are carefully chosen and dedicated to DPIC. These agents are specialists in managing the risks that architects and engineers encounter. They are expected to understand clients' businesses and to serve as a chief adviser to the company's partners.

DPIC encourages its clients to take continuing education courses on avoiding liability claims and takes 10 percent off the premiums of those who take such courses. DPIC also reviews clients' contracts to identify ways to avoid future liabilities and reimburses clients for the cost of peer reviews to help them maintain high professional standards. Finally, should problems emerge, DPIC provides an "early warning system" that enables it to help clients resolve problems before they have to seek legal recourse. DPIC stresses the use of mediation as a lower-cost alternative to litigation and subsidizes the cost of arbitration.

The same programs that help clients avoid lawsuits also help DPIC's insurance rates to stay competitive. DPIC tries to keep rates low by focusing on design professionals with professional practices, who are less likely to have lawsuits. As a DPIC representative claims, "We'll continue to look for the best customers we can find, so the design professionals we insure become part of an exclusive club of practitioners with above-average performance records."

With this focus, DPIC has the highest customer satisfaction rating of its competitors, as determined by a survey done by the trade association American Institute of Architects: 79 percent of its customers claim to be very satisfied, twice the industry average. Its success is also evident in its high customer retention rates, which range between 90 and 100 percent, compared with an industry average of no more than 80 percent. DPIC found that on average it takes a 30 percent price differential before customers decide to defect to competitors, which is unusual for a market that is normally price-driven.

Intuit

Intuit is a software company that specializes in helping individuals and small businesses manage their finances, from writing checks to balancing accounts. It is known for its award-winning product Quicken. The company has invested enormous time and effort in making Quicken easy to use, even for the most unsophisticated users. Intuit has highly responsive technical support capability to help customers use the product. The support staff is guided by the management directive, "Intuit stands or falls with whatever happens in tech support. Do whatever you need to do to satisfy customers." With such a directive, it is not surprising that there are many heroic war stories about ways Intuit's service staff has gone to great lengths to help customers.

The product is inexpensive compared to almost any other type of software and costs much less than competing products. Offering such a high value for customers, it is easy to understand why Intuit has a 60 percent share of the personal finance software market.

Inc. magazine (April 1991) described Intuit's success this way:

> Suppose you could provide a product or service that was better than [they] expected, for less money than anyone else charged. Suppose that anytime you brought out anything new it was just what buyers wanted. Suppose your after-sales service was so good that customers went away feeling better than before. What would happen? You'd own your marketplace.

Common Misconceptions about Value

The value balance sheet and the accompanying examples provide a framework for addressing some common misconceptions about value and the often related concepts of price, quality, cost, and value-added.

Value vs. Price

As Peter Drucker notes in his book *Management,* "Economists think they know [what value is]—value is price. This is misleading, if not actually the wrong answer."

The value balance sheet shows that price is only one of many factors that influence the value provided to the customer. Price does not take into account all of the costs of acquiring the product or service. Furthermore, price and value are inversely related: If all other factors hold constant, the lower the price, the higher the value that the product or service provides to the customer. As the high-value case studies show, high customer value can come from providing more benefits for lower prices.

Companies such as Hewlett-Packard could charge more than competitors, if their products significantly outperformed competitors' on the benefit side of the value balance sheet, and/or in reducing other, nonprice costs.

There are the rare products, notably luxury goods, where high prices signal value, especially where the psychology of prestige is involved. Even the definition of prestige is being rewritten, however, in the less frivolous 1990s for luxury cars, upscale stores, and premium products.

Value vs. Quality

In further comments on the definition of value, Drucker said, "[M]anagers are quite sure that they know the answer. Value is what they, in their business, define as quality. But this is almost always the wrong definition."

Value is a much broader concept than quality. As the value balance sheet shows, quality is related to only some of the items, such as the reliability of the product and the ease of doing business. Understanding quality in the context of the value balance sheet can help managements avoid the "quality-cures-all" delusion. Too many companies have pursued single-minded quality programs as a way to address major problems such as high cost structures. Some work under the false assumption that higher quality will enable them to charge higher prices and so cover their excessive unit costs. Quality programs like this usually last about a year. Then the company's underlying cost problems start to shift management's attention to maintaining profitability and market share.

Managements need to recognize that, given increasing competitive pressures, the winning companies will be those that deliver the highest value to the customer. Many times, the winner will be the company with the highest quality and lowest prices. Instead of pursuing a quality strategy, the company should focus on a value strategy in which quality plays an integral role but is not the sole objective. Under such a strategy, the company maximizes the perceived benefits of its products while it seeks to minimize all perceived costs, including (but not restricted to) prices. Note that quality can play a role on both sides of the value balance sheet, for example, by improving the product's longevity (a benefit) and by reducing product maintenance and failure rates (costs).

Value vs. Cost

Costs are irrelevant to the value provided to the customer. No item listed in the value balance sheet relates to the company's costs. The company that believes that the value of its products or services is high because the products or services cost a lot to make is seriously deluding itself. In instances where management does not understand what customers value, cost and value can be inversely related. Such a company might, for example, provide a product with a lot of features and options that are costly to produce and that the customer does not value. The extra options might even be a nuisance to the customer.

Multiple car keys are a classic example. A study done by the Saturn Division of GM showed that most customers want a single key, that having to carry several keys is a bother. (Most of us already know that from firsthand experience.) As you might expect, Saturn also discovered that it costs more to make two keys than one. Yet the single car key was introduced by Toyota only in 1970. Surprisingly (or maybe not), Ford and GM are the only major car manufacturers in the world who continue to insist on providing multiple car keys. *The Wall Street Journal* (December 29, 1992) noted, "Most automotive engineers today agree that the single, multipurpose car key is a blindingly obvious, inexpensive, and low-tech innovation that in retrospect should probably have come earlier."

Value vs. Value-Added

Usually the term *value-added* refers to features added to a product to increase its value to the client. It is a "more-for-the-same-price" scheme. This can be a good strategy, but it is not without its pitfalls.

The so-called upstart of international airlines, Virgin Atlantic, is a good example of the value-added concept. Virgin Atlantic offers first-class service at business-class fares and calls it "Upper

Class." As it describes the service in its literature, "You get a first-class-style service with more amenities, more comfort, and entertainment, all for the price of a business-class fare." Virgin Atlantic offers door-to-door limousine service at both ends of the flight, sleeper seats with ample space, and individual video screens with a choice of movies. With such an increase in value, it is no wonder that Virgin Atlantic has British Air concerned.

Virgin Atlantic's strategy, however, hinges on one thing: the price of a business-class ticket. Many companies permit their employees to fly business class on transatlantic flights; thus, it is an obvious choice for employees to choose Virgin Atlantic's accommodations rather than another carrier's business class. Virgin Atlantic's strategy works well as long as competitors do not reduce their prices for business-class service below the level where it is still feasible for Virgin Atlantic to provide first-class services.

The pitfall in a value-added strategy is the assumption that the customers want more for the same (or a higher) price, when in fact they may prefer a little bit less for a much reduced price. From a production cost perspective, it is often possible to cut costs by curtailing some of the product or service's features. Often, 50 percent of production costs are driven by 20 percent of what, from a customer's point of view, are the most expendable features. HP used this strategy to dominate the laser printer market. By stripping frills from low-end printers, it was able to lower its operating costs and yet offer the market a high-quality laser printer for affordable prices.

AutoDesk used this "less-for-much-less" strategy to dominate the market for the computer-aided design software that it sells to mechanical designers, engineers, architects, and other design professionals. This market had been serviced by software companies whose products used expensive mini- and mainframe computers. Then AutoDesk came out with the first PC version, called AutoCAD, which provided 80 percent of the functionality of existing systems at 20 percent of their prices. So much for the notion of value-added. AutoDesk must have figured out the customer's value balance sheet just right, since it has 72 percent of the market. Its next largest competitor has a mere 8 percent of the market. A study conducted by the London School of Economics claims that AutoDesk was the most profitable company in the 1980s.

The Dynamics of Value

The definition of customer value is always dynamic; over time many factors can alter customers' preferences and tradeoffs. The definition of value changes with each consumer generation as a result of economic conditions, political events such as wars, and the advent of new technologies that create new ways of doing things. Not least of all, it changes when innovative competitors offer a quantum leap in the value of their products and services.

Consumer values changed dramatically between the 1980s and 1990s. As *Management Review* noted:

> Now the '90s are upon us and there seems to have been a 180-degree shift in consumer attitudes. Perhaps it can be blamed on the recession, or the guilt over the excesses of the '80s, but whatever the cause, one thing is for sure—this is the decade of value. [Reprinted by permission of publisher, from *Management Review*, May 1992. American Management Association, New York. All rights reserved.]

Value in the 1990s appears to be defined by a product's or service's true economic value, that is, it favors the economic benefits and costs in the value balance sheet. In fact, prestige is now gained by making smart economic decisions; high price is no longer a signal of value. Prestige means shopping at Wal-Mart, not sacrificing product quality but getting it at a discounted price. This shows that the individual is a "smart buyer," not a wasteful one.

This trend favors companies like the Gap, which has fashionable clothing at modest prices, and A&P, which has developed a line of premium products under the America's Choice brand. All of these products are lower priced than comparable national brands. A&P does most of its product advertising in-store, thus avoiding the expense of media advertising incurred by national brands. A&P passes the savings on to its customers, giving them a premium product at reasonable prices.

The 1990s trend will hurt those companies whose products are seen as excessively expensive in relation to their intrinsic benefits and costs. In response to this trend, BMW includes in its new models bigger engines and passenger air bags for nearly the same price it charged for earlier models without those features. In an article entitled "BMW Roars Back from Yuppie Hell" (*Fortune*, May 3, 1993), BMW's CEO, Karl Gerlinger, stated, "We've changed the image from trendy, high-price yuppie automobiles to products that are worth the money and generate a certain excitement."

Industrial customers have also changed. They are being driven by the intense competitive pressures introduced in part by foreign companies, notably the Japanese. Businesses can no longer bear high-cost overhead and far-flung ventures in unrelated businesses. Either they have squeezed costs already or they soon will, by eliminating middle-management positions or tightening up supplier relationships and insisting that suppliers deliver goods using JIT methods. To sell to the corporate customer, the supplier must justify how the product will provide substantial value to the customer. This trend is not likely to reverse itself.

Technology also changes the definition of customer value. For instance, the widespread use of electronic mail, portable phones, faxes, and other devices have raised our expectations. Consumers place a higher value on easy access to people at all times, in all locations, and with quick turnaround time. The traditional value of central control that accompanied the mainframe era no longer exists. The PC, using client server technology, has changed corporate customers' values by allowing access and sharing data across the enterprise.

Finally, nothing changes value expectations like a nimble, intelligent new competitor. Unencumbered by past business practices, assertions about customer value, and bloated cost structures, this "new kid on the block" introduces a product that delivers far more value than established competitors, transforming customer expectations and setting a substantially higher level in delivering value. Lexus and many of the other case studies I have discussed have done just this. In commenting on Lexus, for example, *Automotive News* (September 28, 1992) observed: "By presenting a challenge that few thought attainable—a superior-quality, volume-produced luxury car priced below $40,000—Lexus almost overnight moved the price/value bar in the luxury segment to stunning new highs."

Maximizing Customer Value

Maximizing customer value is actually quite simple, once you know the concept. All you really need to do is perform the proper research to determine what customers value, then realign your company's strengths/weaknesses, product designs, and strategies to reflect what customers value the most.

The techniques and approaches for maximizing customer value, however, differ in their scope of effort whether they represent strategic changes or simply fine-tuning. The best way to consider the issue of scope is by considering these steps: Make sure your company optimizes the value provided to the customer in major product or service features, such as price and key elements of the product's functionality, and continue to improve value offered to the customer by fine-tuning existing features, adding valuable new ones, reducing prices, and attending to any other small details that contribute value to the customer. Especially make sure that your company is doing the right things regarding major elements of the company's product, such as price, key service levels such as turnaround time, major product options, and other important functions. The list of major considerations should include five to ten items; although price should always be one of these, the other elements will vary according to product.

There are three broad approaches for defining what these major right things are—firsthand experience, qualitative market research, and quantitative market research. These should be used together.

Firsthand experience is appropriate for managements that are so close to customers and the marketplace that they intuitively know what customers value and what their tradeoffs are. Most companies rely on some form of periodic market research to define the right things, or to at least test their existing assumptions. Whether this is done internally or with the help of a market research firm, there are two alternative approaches: conducting extensive qualitative research (e.g., personal interviews and focus groups), or conducting more limited, qualitative research to ensure you are evaluating the right things and then using quantitative research to assess the relative importance of these factors to the client. Either way, management participation throughout the whole process is critical, particularly listening firsthand to what customers are talking about.

Toyota used the qualitative research method in developing the Lexus, and key staff participated significantly in the process. Toyota's multiyear market research effort involved thirty executives and designers, each of whom performed direct observations such as visiting dealerships, interviewing customers, and sitting in on focus groups. Their close involvement enabled them to develop deep insights into, and a successful strategy for, the image-intensive luxury car market.

While qualitative research permits you to probe more deeply into customers' values and perceptions, quantitative research enables you to make a statistically valid assessment across a larger sample collected by telephone, mail, or some combination of the two. Furthermore, if you use quantitative research, you can take advantage of the statistical methods called "choice models." These simulate real-world purchase decisions by asking survey respondents to make choices among a hypothetical group of products with different prices, features, and options. If respondents make enough choices, it is possible to put a dollar value on each component of the product.

A good example of this process is that of a bank that wanted to extend its retail financial services business by offering auto and homeowners insurance. Being new to the business, the bank faced the challenge of designing every aspect of the business, from sales and service functions to pricing, and was not sure about customers' priorities for product/service features.

The bank approached this design challenge by using a type of choice model to determine what customers valued most. The bank created a number of hypothetical products that consisted of different combinations of features and prices and then asked panels of customers to pick which products they preferred. This forced them to make tradeoffs among product features just as they would in making real-life purchase decisions.

By analyzing a large collection of hypothetical choices, the bank was able to quantify customer value across all major components of the product. (See Exhibit 5-2. Note that for simplicity, some features have been omitted.) The numbers in the exhibit indicate how much each product option contributed to, or detracted from, overall customer value. For example, customers valued a local sales office 50 percent more than a telephone-based sales office; sales done only through the mail decreased total value. Since the numbers are additive, it's easy to determine that the most highly valued product offering is the one with a local sales capability, a 10 percent discount, and servicing handled by a product specialist in auto and homeowners insurance. Not surprisingly, this is roughly the same product configuration offered by the industry leader, State Farm Insurance.

Armed with facts about customer values, your next step is to compare the importance of product/service features with how satisfied customers are with them. You can determine customer satisfaction by including satisfaction questions in the same research study used to determine what customers value. Once you

Exhibit 5-2. Customer value analysis for consumer banking services.

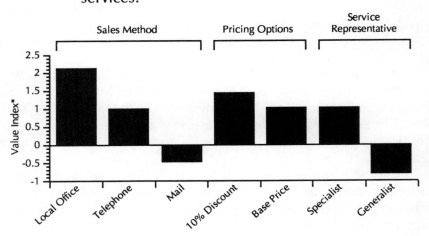

have collected the data, it is useful to graph importance and customer satisfaction for each key product/service feature. I call this the value scorecard because it tells you precisely how well you perform on those things that matter most to clients. (An example of the value scorecard is provided in the case study later in this chapter.)

The value scorecard graph clearly highlights your company's key priorities for maximizing customer value. For example, your highest priority should clearly be to excel on those product/service features that customers value most. Conversely, the value scorecard may indicate that you are overinvesting in some features that matter little to clients. The value scorecard is an important way to conserve your company's scarce resources and to invest them in those features to matter most to clients.

In analyzing many of these value scorecards, I've found that they clearly reveal how well companies (1) know who their clients are and what they value and (2) focus their resources on doing the right things to maximize customer value. Invariably the informed/focused companies have scores much higher in customer satisfaction than those of their competitors for the product/service features that customers value most. In contrast, the value scorecard for uninformed/unfocused companies looks like scattershot: The companies score very high on some features that are relatively unimportant to customers, and poorly on some that customers value most. The unfocused company may work hard to improve its products and services; it just doesn't know what the right things to do are. Thus, it overinvests in things that are of little value and overlooks some of the things that matter a great deal to the customer.

Armed with a solid understanding of customer value and an importance-versus-performance chart, your company is well prepared to take three important steps towards significant improvement:

1. Revise the company's strategy to incorporate the new understanding about customer value. Include such things as a mission statement, pricing strategies, and competitive positioning.

2. Redeploy the company's development efforts to improve radically the high-priority elements on which the company has scored poorly. Cut back on investments in product elements that are less critical to the customer. (Often the increased investments in the high-priority items can be completely funded by disinvesting in the low-priority ones.)

3. Revise the company's marketing programs to focus on what customers value most and on how the company can best deliver them. The revisions should include reorienting the sales organization, revising advertising messages, and making any other needed changes to the company's communications programs. This step should not be launched until steps 1 and 2 are fully implemented.

Diversified Investment Advisors—Part Two

As you may recall from Chapter 4, Diversified decided to develop a strategy to focus on the two "keep it simple" segments with the "Diversified Makes It Easy" theme. By definition these segments valued simplicity, and Diversified knew that it would have to develop a "hassle-free" service that was easy for both the corporate staff that handled the pension plan and the employees who were members of the plan.

The next step was to determine what specifically the "keep it simple" customers valued in terms of product and service features and options. Using the same market research data, Diversified was able to rank the following product/service features in terms of the percentage of customers that cited each feature as being "critically important" (numbers indicate percentage of respondents):

- *Accuracy* in information provided to employees and to the corporate customer regarding the status of the 401(k) plan (90%)
- *Timeliness* in producing reports and statements to the corporate customer and its employees (83%)
- *Quality of statements* in terms of form, readability, and quality of paper (75%)
- *Problem resolution*, the ability to respond quickly and professionally to problems identified by customers (70%)

- *Investment Performance,* the rate of return on invested money from the 401(k) plan (70%)
- *Employee enrollment,* the ability to provide on-site assistance to help employees sign up for the 401(k) plan (53%)
- *Investment options,* the number and variety of investments available to employees (32%)

Diversified then used these rankings in combination with customer satisfaction data to determine how important each product/service feature was and how well Diversified performed in providing it. Exhibit 5-3 indicates how much customers value each feature and how well Diversified performs in delivering it. The horizontal axis indicates the value of each feature to customers, as indicated by the percentage ranking; the vertical axis indicates how satisfied customers were with Diversified's various service features compared to the industry average (a score of zero means that Diversified's customer satisfaction was equal to the industry average).

Exhibit 5-3 highlights Diversified's strengths and weaknesses. It also indicates Diversified's key investment priorities for maximizing the value of its product offering to customers in the targeted market. Chris Cumming, vice president of marketing, called it "our scorecard."

The value scorecard indicated that Diversified's success in winning "keep it simple" customers depended on improving its service quality. Specifically, Diversified had to provide quicker turnaround in delivering reports and statements, eliminate errors and defects in statements, and retrain employees to handle customers' problems

Exhibit 5-3. Diversified's value scorecard.

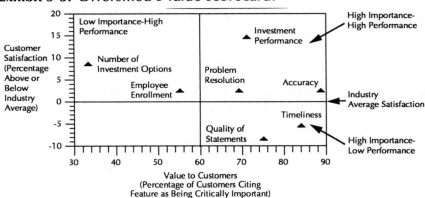

better. It also had to enhance its statements, a simple matter of editing computer-generated reports and using higher-quality paper.

The value scorecard also indicated that Diversified's highly rated investment performance would be a significant asset in winning "keep it simple" customers and that it had sufficient investment options to satisfy them.

To address its weaknesses, Diversified embarked on a total quality program. The company revamped work flows, developed an installation team to ensure that new customers were set up properly from the outset, and created a comprehensive measurement system that linked quality performance to the company's bonus system. Diversified also instituted programs to obtain feedback from clients several times each year. Finally, it set a goal to improve customer satisfaction by 20 percent each year and surveyed clients twice a year to track its progress.

As a result of these initiatives, Diversified saw a dramatic improvement in its quality results and in customer satisfaction. Turnaround in producing reports improved from twenty to ten days on average; the number of errors per one hundred reports dropped from fifteen to one; and Diversified achieved its goal of having all of its top one hundred clients as willing references for acquiring new customers.

As a case study, Diversified illustrates the point that is difficult to know how to maximize customer value unless you seek the answer directly from your customers. Diversified, like most of its competitors, believed that success in the 401(k) business was driven strictly by investment performance, when in fact customers valued service quality as much as or more than performance. Once Diversified did its research, it knew precisely what its priorities should be and how to position itself in the market. Its competitors, meanwhile, continued to act on their mistaken beliefs.

Second, this example shows that maximizing customer value does not necessarily require additional costs or investments. Diversified's cost to fix its reports was minimal; its total quality program paid for itself by reducing rework (i.e., the inefficiencies associated with fixing mistakes, which is like performing the task twice).

Finally, the case illustrates the proper role of quality improvement in the broader context of customer value. Diversified did not automatically embark on a quality program but instead logically proceeded by (1) envisioning its targeted customer (the "keep it simple" group), then (2) defining what this targeted customer valued most and (3) determining its key priorities for maximizing the value of its products and services to the targeted customer.

In this instance, improving service quality turned out to be Diversified's highest priority. Conversely, the key priority for one of Diversified's competitors could well have been to improve its investment performance instead of its service quality.

Improving Details

I have talked about maximizing customer value in the major elements of the product or service. However, success requires continuous fine-tuning of the details of the product or service. This fine-tuning often involves making the product easier to use, maybe adding new features and services, perhaps finding ways to lower prices. The company can't do this in a vacuum; to know what improvement means to its customers, it must determine customers' values and preferences.

Quantitative market research is useless for this type of research. To obtain this information, the company must expose its product options directly to customers via focus or user groups. In product design today, manufacturers use customer input throughout the process of creating prototypes. As author Michael Shrage commented in *The Wall Street Journal* (February 7, 1989), "Industrial designers are now taking customers back to the old drawing board with them." And as Professor Dan Droz of Carnegie Mellon noted in *The Wall Street Journal* (September 9, 1991), "Companies should get physical fast—that is, construct tangible, palpable prototypes as soon as possible. The prototype becomes a cheap way to manage risk. If the group doesn't like one, throw it away."

Intuit, the software company I talked about earlier in this chapter, uses prototyping to improve customer value. In addition to conducting extensive formal market research, Intuit develops early versions of new screens and software options and shows them to customers to see if the new features really are easy to use and to understand. Intuit also has what it calls its "Follow me Home" program: Staff members go to computer dealers and ask customers there if they can go home with them to observe firsthand how the user learns how to use the product. By doing this, Intuit learns what important improvements to make.

Diversified Investment Advisors brings in clients three times a year for two-day working sessions in which they discuss ways to improve service, get feedback on proposed changes, and determine if recently introduced improvements are working as planned. As Marketing Vice President Chris Cumming commented, "We describe the changes that we have made and then ask the customers to describe how the changes affected their use of our product. These meetings also provide tremendous feedback on what our competitors are doing."

The concept of continuous product improvement is critical to the success of any company. It's safe to assume that one or more competitors is diligently working to gain a competitive advantage, so a company should take advantage of every opportunity to enhance its products and periodically to introduce major breakthroughs that substantially improve customer value.

Whether you're making major improvements or fine-tuning a product or service, understanding what your customers value is a critical step in making sure that your company is doing the right things. Knowing who your targeted customer is and what that customer values provides your company with an enormous competitive advantage. It is the foundation for developing a market ownership strategy.

Chapter 6
Improving Customer Retention

Of all the hallmarks of market ownership listed in Exhibit 1-1, customer retention is the most revealing. Almost any organization with superior retention compared to industry norms has some special affinity with its customers and prospects and is likely to have some degree of market ownership. In fact, market ownership is impossible unless the company retains its customers far longer than its competitors do.

In this chapter I clarify the benefits of customer retention, explain why customers leave, and develop a framework for a comprehensive customer retention strategy. Retention is a building block in the middle of market ownership development.

I also demonstrate that customer retention is closely interwoven with the company's strategy. Top management should not undertake customer retention as a stand-alone program; there must first be a clear idea of who the target customer is. Retention is driven by the company's strategy, and it in turn drives many marketing, organizational, and operational requirements.

The Benefits of Customer Retention

It is very costly to acquire new customers and put them on the books. In almost any industry, these one-time costs (both upfront and back-end if the client is lost) generally range from two to four times the annual cost of serving clients on an ongoing basis. These one-time costs include such expenses as:

- All selling and prospecting costs (the company's total sales and prospecting costs per year divided by the number of sales per year)
- All one-time costs to set up the new client with the company's systems, such as accounting
- All costs associated with learning the new client's business and how to service it
- All costs in dealing with a departing client, including taking the client off the books, transitioning the client to a competitor, and fulfilling any residual obligations (none of which generates revenues for the company)

With these and other up-front costs, it is easy to believe the claim in the *Harvard Business Review* that it costs five times as much to generate a new client as it does to retain an existing one.

Quite simply, the longer a company keeps its clients, the more years over which it can spread its up-front costs and reduce its unit cost. High customer defection creates a very real, but often hidden, element of the cost structure, as illustrated in the following example.

Assume Company X has a 5 percent profit margin and 85 percent customer retention rate. (The latter statistic indicates that the company retains clients, on average, for 6.6 years.) Now, further assume that the company's up-front costs are three times its yearly cost to serve a customer. Therefore, its up-front costs equal 26 percent of its revenues, and ongoing costs are 69 percent of revenues (see Exhibit 6-1).

The high up-front costs are caused mostly by the fact that the company retains its clients for an average of only 6.6 years, the relatively short time over which the costs are spread. The exhibit also demonstrates the impact of improving customer retention from 85 percent to 90 or even 95 percent. As retention improves, the up-front portion of the company's cost structure declines 62 percent (i.e., from 26 to 10 percent), while profits increase more than four times. At 95 percent retention, the company's cost structure is substantially reduced because the up-front costs are spread, on average, over 20 years.

Improved customer retention creates many other economic advantages. Longtime clients are:

Exhibit 6-1. Impact of customer retention rates on costs and profit margins (percent of revenue).

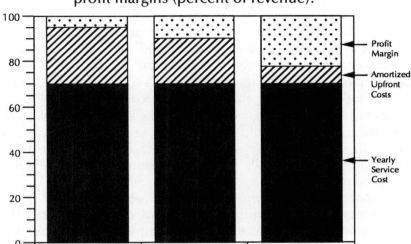

Customer Retention Rates (Percentage of Customers Retained per Year)

- Generally less price-sensitive, enabling the company to maintain its price levels when threatened by competitors
- Likely to provide free word-of-mouth advertising and referrals
- More likely to purchase additional products with less marketing effort than would be required to sell the same product to a new client

Customer retention is a critical driver of net growth. In many industries, the fastest-growing companies are those with superior retention rates, rather than those with the highest rates of new sales.

The fact that improving retention can be the easiest and cheapest way to grow is so simple as to be overlooked. To illustrate, let's assume that our Company X has a sales organization that can increase the number of new clients at the rate of 20 percent per year. If Company X has a customer retention rate of 85 percent per year, then it grows at a net rate of only 5 percent per year (20 minus 15). Many companies have similar growth statistics.

However, if Company X is able to improve customer retention to 95 percent, then it will have a net growth rate of 15 percent. While this math is obvious, the implications are more subtle. In this case, Company X will have tripled its net growth rate without spending so much as one additional dollar on sales and marketing. It would require a tripling of the company's sales organization to achieve the same results—a massive investment for the company, and one that it probably could ill afford.

But what would it cost to improve the company's retention rate? It most certainly would cost less than investing in a threefold increase in the company's sales organization. Quite possibly it would cost nothing at all, given the economic benefits of improved retention.

Another benefit of improving customer retention is that it provides sustainable advantages in comparison to other strategies that are more easily replicated by the competition, such as sales or advertising. For example, sales promotions, ad campaigns, and new product introductions are all highly visible. Competitors can quickly copy the new sales efforts and, in some cases, even derail them via their own marketing tactics.

In contrast, efforts to improve retention are low-visibility efforts between the company and its clients. Competitors usually have no idea about their rivals' retention rates or what those companies have done to improve retention. (In any case, there's not much they can do about retention rates.) All the competitor knows is that it is hard to win clients away from a company with high customer retention. It's as if the company's clients have disappeared from the market and are no longer viable prospects.

The automotive market in the United States is a clear case. In this market, customer retention is the easiest and least costly way to grow sales. Growth in real incomes is limited in comparison to auto prices, and customers are keeping their cars. These facts contribute to the stagnation of the auto market, where the growth of new car sales is about .5 percent per year. In addition, repeat-purchase loyalty is increasing and is now about 50 percent, which means that the market for new customers is shrinking.

The picture is especially bleak for U.S. manufacturers, whose repeat-purchase loyalty has stayed flat at around 43 percent, while Japanese car makers have increased their repeat-purchase loyalty to an average of 57 percent. This dramatic rise in repeat purchases is a major reason why the Japanese manufacturers were able to increase their share of the U.S. market from 17 percent in the 1970s to 34 percent in 1990.

With a stagnant market and a declining population of new customers (i.e., non-repeat purchasers), many car manufacturers spend a lot of money trying to attract potential market prospects through advertising and price rebates. Not surprisingly, the amount that the manufacturers spend on such sales tactics is generally inversely related to the rate of repurchases by existing clients. Logically, the more repeat purchasers the company has, the less it needs to rely on winning new customers away from competitors. For example, car manufacturers with the highest repeat purchase rates (about 70 percent) provided no rebates and spent only $150 per car on advertising. Companies with the lowest repurchase rates (about 20 percent) gave away $1,200 on rebates and spent $400 per car on advertising. These are staggering differences, given that auto manufacturers make only several hundred dollars' profit per car.

Honda Motor Company provides an excellent example of the benefits of customer retention. In 1990 Honda ranked number one in repurchase loyalty, with a 68 percent repurchase rate for existing customers. Not surprisingly. Honda is also the largest foreign supplier of cars in the United States, even though it spends far less on advertising than do other Japanese car makers. This is because it gets a significant majority of its customers "free" through repurchase. In fact, as shown in Exhibit 6-2, there

Exhibit 6-2. The financial advantages of high customer retention.

	Customer Loyalty (Repeat Purchase Rate)	Amount Spent on Advertising per Car
Honda	68%	$150
Toyota	53%	$300
Nissan	40%	$400

Source: Presentation by John Schnapp, "Coping with the 90s: The Significance of Repurchase Loyalty."

is a strong relationship between customer loyalty and the amount of money that Honda and the other two leading Japanese car makers spend on advertising.

With its high repeat-purchase rate, Honda also has enormous competitive advantages over the typical U.S. car maker, which, on average, has only a 43 percent rate of repurchase. If you assume for illustration that Honda and a typical U.S. company each start out with the same market share, the U.S. company will have to attract 78 percent more new customers per year (57 versus 32 percent) just to stay even with Honda. While this is not impossible, it would be prohibitively expensive for the U.S. company to achieve this higher rate of new customer acquisition.

Given the clear benefits of retaining clients, it is easy to understand the current popularity of customer retention programs. These benefits, however, accrue only if the company is focused on profitable customers. Too often, companies embark on customer retention programs without knowing enough about their clients, especially the profitability of different client segments. These stand-alone retention programs can hurt, rather than help, the company's profitability.

You have seen the benefits Company X has received from improving its customer retention rate from 85 to 95 percent. But what happens if the company's customer base consists of half A-level customers and half B-levels; unbeknownst to management, the As have a profit margin of 20 percent while the Bs have a negative 10 percent margin (which, taken together, produce the company's average margin of 5 percent). Assume further that As and Bs have retention rates of 90 and 80 percent respectively, which average out to the company's 85 percent rate. Furthermore, for simplicity, let's say that the company brings in A and B customers at a rate proportional to their respective retention rates. In other words, the company sells more Bs and the Bs turn over more quickly, thus keeping the As and Bs in even proportion.

If Company X is able to improve the retention rates for both As and Bs to 95 percent, a number of things happen. First, as you saw before, Company X's net growth rate triples from 5 to 15 percent per year, causing sales to double in five years. At the same time, however, the company has retained so many more Bs that after five years, Bs account for 64 percent of the company's customer base, and because Bs are less profitable, Company X's overall profitability declines; Company X's profit margins decline from 5 percent to near zero after two years (see Exhibit 6-3). After five years, the company loses as much money as it was making before it embarked on its retention strategy.

Why Customers Defect

To understand why customers defect, you have to begin with the assumption that competitors are constantly striving to steal your clients, especially your best ones. Most customers, if they are reasonably satisfied, stay with their existing suppliers—if for no other reason than convenience. They are, after all, in the business of selling their own goods and services. They're not interested in continually switching suppliers. In fact, there are many advantages to customers and suppliers in developing strong ties.

There are those clients who are chronic "shoppers," the ones who are always seeking to cut a better deal. However, these clients are not the type on which you seek to build market ownership. In fact, among the many retention programs dis-

Exhibit 6-3. The potential adverse effect of customer retention.

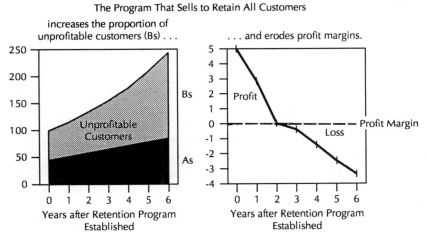

The Program That Sells to Retain All Customers

increases the proportion of unprofitable customers (Bs) . . .

. . . and erodes profit margins.

cussed in this chapter, the mere act of focusing on the relationship-oriented segments and shunning the shoppers is the most
potent way to improve overall customer retention.

The subject of customer retention often provokes a standard
response: "Isn't that just quality management?" It is true that
customers defect when they experience poor-quality products
and services. However, they leave for many other reasons, as
well. While quality is indeed essential to customer retention, the
most effective programs should involve much more than quality.

There are seven major reasons why customers defect. The
importance of each varies according to the industry:

1. Poor quality of service, product defects, and the supplier's
   inability to meet the client's time frame for repurchase
2. A significant change in price or in the value of the product
   or service compared to competing offerings
3. Unrealistic initial expectations and subsequent disappoint-
   ment
4. The absence of a relationship
5. The loss of a relationship
6. Other changes in the client organization
7. Poor reputation and negative word-of-mouth advertising

The importance of quality is self-evident; in many industries,
quality is strongly correlated with retention. In other industries,
however, lack of quality may drive customer defections less than
fluctuations in price (up or down) or product value.

Two good examples are health insurance and personal computers. Health insurance rate increases run in double digits
almost every year; sometimes they reach more than 30 percent.
The value added in competing personal computers changes dramatically each year as prices drop and performance escalates. In
both of these volatile markets, customer defection rates are
strongly correlated with the rate of price increases and are unrelated to quality ratings in the industry.

In such industries, when the expected gains from finding a
better price begin to outweigh the goodwill generated from quality products and service, changes in price and product value
encourage customers to consider competing products. In this

situation, good service is largely a defensive measure: It discourages competitive shopping, but it doesn't prevent it. This can be very puzzling for managements that believe they run high-quality operations, but still experience high rates of customer defection. Often, in these cases, management sees customer defection in their industry as a fact of life, beyond their control. But, as I explain later in this chapter, there are a number of strategies that enable management to improve retention even in volatile industries.

Customers rarely make repeat purchases when they believe they were oversold—or poorly sold—in the first place. This problem is usually attributable to an overzealous sales organization that, in striving to meet ill-conceived sales goals, makes promises on product benefits and features that cannot be kept and sells products and services that the customer does not need. (This is the common perception of auto dealers, life insurance salesmen, and stockbrokers, which some companies are striving to change.)

Worse still, an angered client may cancel an order, give the company negative word-of-mouth publicity, or take other adverse steps. How a company plans to keep clients should, to a very large extent, influence how it plans to sell to them in the first place.

When a company has a minimal relationship with its customers, customers are clearly more susceptible to competitive solicitation. Take, for example, HMOs, which often have defection rates of more than 25 percent per year. Part of their problem is attributable to members who have not yet used the HMO's services and thus have not established relationships with either the company or its physicians. To these people the HMO is little more than an unused card in the wallet. When a competing HMO comes along offering the slightest advantage, they switch. The story can be quite different once members actually use the HMO's services. At this point, retention becomes more a matter of satisfaction and relationship.

Worse than a minimal or absent relationship is the loss of an established one. Most often, customers' relationships are with individuals serving in sales and/or service roles instead of with the company, and when these personal ties are severed, the company stands a good chance of losing the client. This most often occurs as a result of employee turnover or a reassignment of staff to new clients or duties, or when the company's key contact with a corporate client leaves or is reassigned and is replaced by a new individual. The new contact may wish to take a fresh approach to purchasing services, including reevaluating suppliers. In the worst case, the new person may bring in his or her own favorite suppliers, with whom there is already a relationship. Such changes occur continually throughout corporations.

Other changes within corporations influence customer defection. For example, reorganizations, acquisitions, and new strategies may all change not only the players in the customer relationship, but the nature of what the company requires or values. Thus, the odds of customer defection are increased.

To a lesser extent, changes that occur within individuals' lives influence defection. For instance, changes such as divorce influence future purchase decisions. So also when people move, change jobs, buy a house, or have children. All these changes affect needs and/or purchase decision making and may contribute to defection.

Finally, a company's poor image and reputation can cause customers to defect—or at least make them more likely to do so. Negative press and word-of-mouth create concern about whether the company will meet future promises. Poor corporate image influences cognitive dissonance—conflict caused by the discrepancy between the customer's self-image and his or her actions. Few people, for example, would like to reveal that BCCI was their bank.

Improving Customer Retention

There are many cures for customer defection and several ways to improve retention. Programs for improving customer retention are mutually reinforcing and can be grouped into three categories:

1. Quality management for building a base of goodwill in the face of competitive solicitation, and for minimizing problems that can cause customers to leave
2. Strategic programs for moderating the price volatility that

often induces competitive shopping and for reducing the company's sensitivity to price competition
3. Tactical responses for intervening in or influencing the customer decision process and for building customer relationships

The degree to which each of these three management levers can be used effectively depends on the service intensity and price volatility of a particular product market. Strategic programs are the most critical for those markets with a high degree of volatility. Quality management and tactical programs help, but alone they are not sufficient. Quality management is more important for low-volatility markets and can be greatly augmented by strategic tactial responses.

Customer Retention in High-Volatility Markets

The link between customer retention and quality is self-evident. In this section I examine the various strategic programs that management can use to improve retention, particularly in volatile markets.

It is not surprising that companies that operate in markets with high customer turnover believe there is little they can do about customer retention. Market research tells them that price is everything and that their markets are driven by external forces such as price wars, raw materials costs, litigation, and interest rates. These factors seem to be beyond the companies' control, unalterable facts of doing business.

There are, however, a number of ways for management to gain control over customer retention in even the most volatile of markets. Sophisticated market research reveals that customers have a strong preference for stability in prices and product values. There are two groups of strategies that can offer a greater measure of control over a company's fate by reducing actual or perceived volatility and by reducing the company's sensitivity to rate volatility.

The first group includes strategies that can be used to reduce price volatility:

- Smoothing prices over the customer's life cycle
- Pricing for relationship profitability as opposed to the profitability of a single product
- Changing from fixed to variable pricing schemes
- Exiting/outsourcing volatile products or product components

Smoothing prices means charging the customer a stable price for a product over time, regardless of fluctuations in cost. This may involve, for example, charging a relatively high up-front price and using the extra margin to subsidize the sharp rises in costs that can be expected to occur in subsequent years. From the client's point of view the company's rates seem stable and reasonably competitive over time.

A related strategy is to smooth out prices by charging a rate that reflects the overall cost and profitability of a client relationship. Thus, the company can periodically subsidize volatile products to even out the price. This concept is related to the notion of a loss leader, a key anchor product that periodically may lose money but that creates a profitable customer relationship.

For both of these strategies to work, however, the company must have a distribution system that does not always focus on selling at the lowest price or that makes the best deal without regard for loyalty to the company or that unbundles products priced to sell as a package. The company also needs reliable profit data to ensure that it can manage overall profitability of the client relationship across products and over time.

For example, an automobile insurer with exceptionally high customer retention employs both of these strategies. In years when earnings exceed expectations, the insurer creates a reserve to offset unexpected surges in costs. Thus, it moderates its prices and does not drive customers away with sticker shock when they renew their policies.

This particular company also considers the total profitability of the customer relationship on a household, rather than an individual, basis, including all the products sold and involving all the people connected with the household. Unlike many other insurers, then, this company rides out the volatile and potentially unprofitable years associated with new drivers in the expectation that it will earn a desired profit from the whole-household relationship. It may achieve a high payback if it can retain the youthful drivers until they hit their more predictable years as experienced drivers.

Software companies are also employing strategies of this kind. These companies give deep discounts on the core software programs, such as spreadsheets, for example, that are bundled with hardware purchases. The company may not make any money on the initial sale, but it can expect to achieve profits over the life of the new relationship as the customer purchases upgrades and related software products.

The emergence of adjustable rate mortgages (ARMs) is a good example of a way to deal with volatility by changing from a fixed to a variable pricing scheme. In the past, mortgage bankers had been at the mercy of interest rate volatility. As interest rates dropped, clients left, refinancing with another bank to take advantage of its lower rates. No matter how loyal the customer was inclined to be, it was too costly to retain a mortgage product when a newer one would save the customer 3 percent or more each year in interest payments.

The last strategy to use in moderating volatility is to either exit or outsource a product or a piece of a product—even a component of the business—that is the main source of volatility, while retaining those elements that are more predictable.

Again, the personal computer industry provides a good example of how to deal with volatility. When the previously stable cost of hardware components began to decline rapidly, the decline was especially apparent in IBM-compatible machines, with numerous clone manufacturers all selling comparable products and competing on price. Some companies chose to exit hardware manufacture altogether and to focus instead on software development. Apple's strategy was to get out of hardware manufacture, at least temporarily, by outsourcing the manufacture of its Macintosh PowerBook to Toshiba. The company thus shortened its time to market and focused on its key strengths in overall design and software. IBM's fate in the personal computer business might have been quite different had it focused on the software component and outsourced the hardware component, as opposed to the other way around.

The second group of strategies deals with volatility by reducing the company's sensitivity to it. While good service and reputation, satisfied clients, and deep customer relationships insulate the company to some degree from the impact of volatility, there are six additional strategies that the company can employ to improve customer retention:

1. Targeting less price-sensitive customers and avoiding those who shop frequently
2. Relying on sales channels that attract customers less sensitive to volatility
3. Selecting distribution channels that are less likely to shop frequently for their clients
4. Exerting control over distribution channels to make sure they target the right customers in the right way and do everything necessary to retain clients
5. Promoting cross-selling to deepen client relationships
6. Creating pricing incentives/disincentives to customer defection

Perhaps the biggest impact that a company can have on improving its customer retention comes from targeting the right customers in the first place. Market ownership should be built on attractive target customers, i.e., those who are oriented to long-term relationships rather than to frequent shopping around. Any customer who shops regularly on price is going to be part of a high rate of turnover, and turnover generates losses.

Careful choice of sales channels is critical to attracting the right clients. It is not surprising that clients who come from referrals are generally the most loyal. Relationship-oriented prospects tend to be more cautious about the choices they make because they are seeking quality and more than just low price. At the other extreme, the shopper relies heavily on such sales channels as the Yellow Pages, especially as a vehicle to check prices—lots of them. Not surprisingly, prospects that come in via this route are likely to be the least loyal.

There is a strong parallel between customers' and distributors' loyalty and shopping behavior. Some distributors shop their accounts annually to protect themselves from price competition.

These distributors don't look for a relationship with their product providers beyond the latest deal. More often than not, these distributors have shoppers as clients. They are probably (rightfully) concerned about losing their clients if they don't provide the latest, best price. Other distributors seek long-term relationships with both clients and product providers, and they usually attract like-minded clients who themselves are less prone to shop.

The company should also strive to exert a high degree of control over its distribution system. This ensures that it is focused on the desired customer segments and that it promotes post-sale satisfaction by avoiding overselling or selling products and services that the client does not need. The company must also make sure that its sales organization keeps close track of the continual changes that take place inside customer organizations (and individuals' lives) so that the company does not lose a client relationship unnecessarily. Monitoring systems that track the sales organization's behavior, incentive programs that reward retention, and training on customer orientation are examples of important control mechanisms.

Too often, companies abdicate responsibility for the repeat purchase process, leaving it entirely to their distributors. Perhaps these companies presume that the channel will in its own best interest do whatever it can to retain clients. But this leaves too much to chance. Too often, companies hear about problems only when the client leaves. Indeed, while some enlightened distributors will do the right things, most will not. The company needs to intervene in the repeat purchase process, exert control over its channels, and make sure it is doing everything possible to keep clients.

For businesses with predictable repeat purchase or renewal cycles, the company may consider interviewing customers at an appropriate time prior to the repurchase decision. Interviews can be conducted either from the home office or by the distribution channel, even by using low-cost part-time or temporary employees. Interviews can be used to discuss new developments in products and pricing, to determine if the client's situation has changed, and to listen to the customer's responses to any new developments. Interviews enable the company to deal proactively with the customer's concerns and to propose measures to address them, rather than passively learning about problems after the customer leaves. Also, the company can learn about new product needs and can upgrade products and cross-sell new ones in response. Added revenue and savings from improving retention usually more than offset the cost of the customer interview. Not least of all, clients are pleasantly surprised with post-sale attention and efforts to better understand their needs.

The automotive industry needs to exert control over distributors to influence repeat purchase buying. Distributors often tend to oversell, which leads to customer dissatisfaction with the dealer and perhaps with the manufacturer. For some people, this can create a barrier to purchasing a car at all. Customers will avoid the oversell dealer in the future and may switch brands altogether.

The Saturn Division of GM addressed the distributor control problem by stipulating a single price at all dealers. Saturn then capitalized on this strategy via advertising promoting hassle-free shopping. Several Japanese manufacturers have taken a similar route. Other car makers have instituted dealer quality programs that include interviews and surveys of new customers and shoppers to determine their satisfaction with the salespeople and the sales process.

The second problem for auto manufacturers is that they are minimally involved in the initial sale and virtually absent from any repeat purchase process. So are most of their dealers. Yet the manufacturer has virtually no contact with the customer except through the dealers. Since most repeat purchase decisions occur after product warranties expire, a few manufacturers try to bond existing customers to the dealers through servicing and maintenance contracts. Manufacturers could do even more if they anticipated the timing of a repurchase decision—by the age of the car, for example, or by having dealers ask about repurchase plans during servicing calls. If the manufacturers had this information, they could intervene directly in the repurchase process—with or without the dealer—by contacting the customer via mail, telephone, or promotions.

Another valuable strategy is to sell additional products and services to existing clients. Cross-selling deepens client relationships and makes it harder for the client to defect. Customer retention generally improves with the addition of each new product sold to the customer.

As the company sells more products to the customer, it causes the customer to be more dependent on the company, thereby strengthening the relationship with the customer. Logically, selling more products to the client reduces the number of relationships the customer has with the company's competitors, thus narrowing competitors' opportunities to penetrate the client's business.

Cross-selling creates its own burden, of course, in that the customer may expect better service (and certainly deserves it). The company must reasonably meet these expectations or risk losing the whole account.

Another tool that reduces a company's exposure to volatility and competitive solicitation is image management. A strong image provides insulation from competitive threats. A weak image encourages clients to consider alternatives and can hasten their departure. At the very least a company should build a strong image through the quality of its products and services, by avoiding visible mistakes and by fixing the unavoidable ones in an honorable way. Overall image is a critical ingredient in market ownership.

The final strategy is to structure product pricing so that the customer pays an additional fee if he or she leaves too soon before the up-front costs have been recouped. An intelligent pricing scheme such as this can be beneficial to both buyer and seller of products with high up-front costs. It enables the company to spread the up-front cost over a longer period of time and to charge the client a lower price. At the same time, the company does not have to risk having the client leave before the company recoups its up-front investment. (However, some clients may find this pricing approach to be too restrictive.)

Customer Retention in Low-Volatility Markets

In low-volatility markets, the primary focus of retention strategies is on value and product/service quality.

There is almost no justifiable reason for losing clients in this type of market. Management can completely control the quality assurance function, and companies should achieve and maintain retention rates of 95 to 99 percent. This range may be the practical limit, given the truly external causes of defection I discussed earlier in this chapter. Even given these unavoidable events, however, a company may be able to retain the client (or its successor) through diligent sales and service efforts during the transition. For example, it is not a foregone conclusion that a company always loses a business client once the customer is acquired by another company. An attentive sales organization can often retain the client and get the acquiring company as a customer as well.

While customer satisfaction is the key driver of customer retention in low-volatility markets, this does not mean that quality is the sole driver of customer retention. At the same time that management is emphasizing quality management, it should also be employing strategic programs and tactical responses, especially those that tighten customer relationships and insulate the company from competitive solicitation.

Under its tactical umbrella the company should include the critical topic of personal relationships, which covers anything that builds bridges with clients. I have already discussed some of these bridges; other opportunities include stabilizing relationships with employees, institutionalizing relationships, maintaining contact with the customer, and establishing electronic linkages.

As I mentioned earlier, loss of personal relationships and the reassignment or turnover of staff are key causes of customer defection. Reassigning employees is unavoidable if the company is growing and the staff is taking on new duties. However, the company must be careful to develop transition plans and discuss them with clients.

A company cannot excel at retaining clients if it has high employee turnover. This is obviously true in industries where personal relationships are important, and to a large degree it is true in other businesses as well. At worst, high turnover leads to the immediate loss of clients as staff with critical client relationships moves customers to their new company. Even in industries where personal relationships are a minor factor, high employee turnover can be a problem because it creates a chaotic situation where too many employees are too new to the job, leading to customer frustration caused by poor service and incompetent employees. Customers immediately detect an undercurrent of negative attitudes and can be persuaded to leave. In fact, customer and employee turnover can be closely correlated.

The company should also strive proactively to maintain a presence with clients even when the situation does not demand such contact. This prevents the inevitable withering of relationships that can happen over time and it enables the company to stay on top of changes in the client organization and keep up with other factors that may prompt customers to leave. For very large, lucrative client relationships, it may be desirable to set up an office at the client's site to house the account executive. IBM is famous for doing this with major corporations. For smaller clients, the company should maintain visit schedules to make sure that the client is covered. Finally, mailings, newsletters, and seminars are low-cost vehicles for maintaining relationships with all types of clients and enhancing customer relationships.

In industries where personal relationships are critical, the company should strive to institutionalize its value and connections with clients. The company must insulate itself from employee defections and competitors' ploys to hire (at premium prices) key employees (with their books of business).

In a business such as a law firm, the organization should strive to be more than a collection of practitioners. It should try to provide value as a company by offering a differentiated product that creates bonds stronger than individual relationships.

This strategy may have been the motivation behind Merrill Lynch's creation of its innovative Cash Management Account (CMA), which provides a consolidated statement and an integrated investment account that is proprietary to Merrill Lynch and creates bonds with clients that exceed their relationship with individual stockbrokers.

Another important tactic is to build multiple personal relationships with each client that involve people from sales, service, R&D, and other departments. It is important for the company to create a culture that proclaims that it, not specific individuals, owns relationships with clients. This obviously works best when the overall value of the company to the client transcends the client's relationship with one or more of the company's employees.

Electronic linkages between the company and its clients for such applications as electronic reordering are now coming into their own and are becoming more important by the day. They are essential to such companies as Wal-Mart, J. C. Penney, and AT&T. These vehicles build yet another bridge to clients, providing for ongoing service and ease of reorder and making it harder for the client to defect. Bank of America, for example, has developed a number of products that link it electronically with its corporate clients; the bank's CFO, Lewis Coleman, described the benefits of these links as follows: "When you get wired into a customer's information system and they get wired into you, it becomes mechanically difficult to lose that business" (*The Wall Street Journal*, January 31, 1994). Companies that can't offer this technology will be left behind, both in selling new clients and in retaining existing ones.

Clubs, membership cards, and frequent-user programs are other relationship-building tactics that are being used by many industries. Started in the airline industry, they have spread rapidly to other industries—to credit card companies and to many varieties of retail businesses from Wal-Mart to Staples (the business supply company) to the local grocery store. These programs influence the consumer's shopping behavior at least a little, and they may bond satisfied customers with the company.

Tactical responses include any way that management can augment strategic and quality programs, such as modified billing methods and defection intervention programs. Installing automatic billing systems, for example, requires the customer to take action in order to leave (i.e., to stop the process), in contrast to conventional mailed invoices, which allow customers to leave through inaction (i.e., by not paying the bill). Another tactic is to switch from annual billing to quarterly or monthly billing in order to reduce the perception of high rates. Still other tactics include providing consolidated statements and offering private-label credit cards, as many retailers do. There are dozens of these tactical programs that can be employed, and all of them help support a retention program.

If your company has sufficient lead time before the customer actually signs up with the competition, you can intervene in the customer's process of defecting. It makes good sense for any business that receives requests for cancellation by phone, mail, or in person to install a customer "preservation/reacquisition" function and staff it with the most skilled customer service employees. These company representatives listen to the client's reasons for defecting and offer remedies for the problem; they may also offer incentives, such as a period of free service or other rewards for staying with the company. This tactic can also bring back customers who have recently left. If the retention desk can save 10 percent of defecting clients, the financial rewards more than pay for the program.

Developing an Integrated Approach

Contrary to common belief, management can exercise a lot of control over customer retention and can employ many tools and methods (see Exhibit 6-4).

For full impact, these tools must be integrated into a comprehensive strategy for improving customer retention. The need for a coordinated approach is especially important given the close interrelationships among the various elements that drive customer retention. For example, a reputation for quality service and stable channels may be required to attract less price-sensitive customers; stable customers and distributors may not tolerate voltality or poor quality products or service. Small incremental efforts will improve retention by only a few percentage points at best; at worst, a narrow approach will backfire, making no impact and leaving the company with a credibility problem.

Analyzing customer defection and employing the tools I have outlined can take place within an eight-step staged approach for improving customer retention:

1. Define the customer.
2. Analyze the economics of retention.
3. Analyze retention/defection trends.
4. Conduct interview research.

Exhibit 6-4. Summary of options for improving customer
retention.

- Improve the quality of products and services.
- Target relationship-oriented clients.
- Control distribution systems:
  —Restrict sales to targeted clients.
  —Select non-shopping-oriented distributors.
  —Ensure proper sales tactics to avoid over- or improper selling.
  —Train sales staff to be customer-oriented.
  —Make sure that the sales organization stays on top of clients' changes.
  —Cross-sell additional products and services.
  —Provide incentives to retain customers.
  —Interview customers prior to their repeat purchase decision.
- Maintain a stellar image:
  —Manage the company's image on an ongoing basis.
  —Avoid problems that suggest the company has low integrity.
  —Recover from those problems that do arise.
- Price to address volatility:
  —Smooth out prices over time.
  —Charge on a multiproduct relationship basis.
  —Change from fixed to variable pricing.
  —Charge fees for early departure.
- Exit/outsource volatile components of products or aspects of the business.
- Make service and production employees attentive to customers:
  —Train on customer relationships.
  —Give incentives, where appropriate, for good retention.
- Employ relationship-building tactics:
  —Retain employees as long as possible and improve job satisfaction.
  —Manage the continuity of employee-customer relationships.
  —Institutionalize relationships to involve more than a single employee.
  —Maintain contact via visits, mailings, and telephone calls.
  —Build electronic linkages to clients.
  —Offer private-label credit cards, frequent-user programs, and clubs.
- Other tactical approaches:
  —Create a retention desk to intervene in the defection process.
  —Offer consolidated statements.
  —Change to automatic and/or more frequent billing methods.

5. Analyze competitors' practices.
6. Employ retention tools.
7. Develop an integrated retention process.
8. Design information systems.

The first two steps are to precisely define the target customer and to understand the economics and profitability associasted with acquiring, servicing, and retaining the targeted customers. As I noted earlier in this chapter, efforts to improve retention pay off only when the targeted customer is profitable to start with.

In the third step, full understanding of the causes of customer defection requires synthesizing the results of several analyses that provide different pieces of the puzzle. One of the first tasks should be the collection and analysis of internal records to assess patterns in customer defection. These analyses help identify key issues to research further, including:

- Do customers defect at different rates during the year?
- Do customers defect at different rates over the customer's life cycle
- Does retention vary by office, region, sales representative, or distributor?
- What is the relationship between retention rates and changes in prices?
- What happens to lost customers, and where do they usually go?
- What are the retention norms for the industry, and are they increasing or decreasing? Which companies retain customers the longest?

Step 4 helps determine the root causes of customer defection by interviewing a cross-section of existing and lost customers, as well as various employees who have direct contact with customers. This research is not always easy, and the company should proceed cautiously, synthesizing the inputs from all of the various parties. For example, asking existing customers what would cause them to leave usually produces bland results that tell very little, since it calls for pure speculation on the customer's part.

Even probing lost customers can be misleading, especially in more volatile industries. For example, one executive was confounded by a survey of lost customers. The survey indicated that even though these customers had recently defected to competitors, they claimed they had been satisfied with his company's service, would in fact recommend his company to others, and would even consider using his company again in the future. Market research in this case provided no indication of how the executive could improve customer retention.

Nevertheless, it is important to interview people, both inside and outside the company, who have different perspectives on why customers defect. In particular, interviewing lost customers is critical—but it must be done in a way that will reveal the often subtle reasons why customers choose to defect. Qualitative research such as open-ended interviews, either in person or by telephone, and focus groups provide far more insight than surveys conducted by mail or telephone. Interviewing sales representatives and outside distributors is also important for gaining a different perspective. Salespeople usually have unique, incisive, insights on retaining customers. However, it is a good idea to consider their potential biases. For example, sales staffs are quick to say that prices were too high or that there was something wrong with the product; they are less quick to confess to having been outsold by a competitor. Other interviews should include any service staff that has close contact with customers, deals with their problems and complaints, and hears firsthand why some clients leave.

Step 5 is helpful in understanding how to retain customers longer. Direct competitive analysis is more important than broad-scale benchmarking, because retention practices employed in other industries may not be applicable to the subtleties in your company's industry. The company should start by identifying the competitors with the highest retention rates in the business. These statistics are sometimes compiled and published by industry associations and other such sources. Information on specific retention practices, however, must come directly from the competitor or those who know the competitor well. Some of the needed information can be obtained via a survey conducted with the competitor's cooperation, as is often done in benchmarking studies. More likely, the process will require extensive interviews with the company's distribution system, customers, and other parties.

To properly utilize step 6, the company should develop an integrated retention strategy by definining all root causes of customer defection and designing retention programs to address them. This provides a useful tool for linking causes of customer defection and remedies to minimize it. It facilities the identification of a large number of retention programs and indicates their interrelationship; multiple programs can be used to address the various causes of defection.

Customer retention should be treated as a management process, not a series of improvement programs. Thus, in step 7, the company should develop a comprehensive process that integrates all the retention programs defined in the step 5 retention matrix. The company should start by creating a timeline that indicates all key events and interactions with the customer, starting with the initial contact via the selling process and extending over the life of the client, including when and if the client leaves. In fact, it is helpful to start the process before the client makes contact with the company. For example, it is important to consider how word-of-mouth advertising shapes the company's image with prospective customers and influences their propensity to be loyal.

The next step is to place the various retention programs on the timeline, indicating when they occur during the customer's life cycle, and so design a comprehensive process. Since this comprehensive retention process inevitably cuts across various functional operating units, such as sales and customer service, the company should consider designating a special staff person to track customer retention results.

Too often the company's only information concerning customer retention is the rate of defection; after defection, however, it is too late for management to intervene. Accordingly, the last step addresses the need for the company to create a management information system that tracks all the key events identified on the timeline and the process developed in step 7, the company's performance, and indicators of customer behavior. In particular, the company should identify ten or more early warning signals that indicate the likelihood of customer defection. These signals can include such items as uncharacteristic late payment of bills, complaints, and changes in the client company or in the individual's life (e.g., having children).

Chapter 7
Acquiring Customers

"If you build a better mousetrap, people will beat a path to your door"—a quaint notion reminiscent of the village store. In fact, strong sales and marketing capabilities are essential for the survival of all but the handful of businesses with few buyers and sellers. While word-of-mouth advertising is highly advantageous, it is seldom enough to sustain a thriving business. Companies that own markets excel at sales and marketing; business surveys frequently rank their sales organizations and advertising campaigns among the highest.

During the creation of the commercial computer industry nearly fifty years ago, the critical need for sales skills was clearly evident. Although most people credit IBM with founding the industry, UNIVAC actually built and sold the first computer at a time when IBM was still selling relatively low-tech devices such as punchcard readers and adding machines. IBM followed UNIVAC into the market with a less powerful machine (i.e., a worse mousetrap), yet it quickly surpassed UNIVAC because of its powerful and very professional sales organization. While IBM went on to own the computer market for nearly five decades, UNIVAC went bankrupt waiting for the world to beat a path to its door.

Similarly, a now-forgotten company called Visicorp created the first spreadsheet software program, Visicalc. But Visicorp was displaced by Lotus and its 1-2-3 product. Although Lotus was able to copy and improve its own product, much of its success is attributable to the substantial advertising program that established the Lotus name and led to its ownership of the market for several years.

Market ownership requires a unique approach to sales and

marketing. On the one hand, the company needs an aggressive sales and marketing effort to establish a large presence in the target market. On the other hand, the company must establish itself in a way that builds relationships and strengthens its image in the market. This is, in fact, how many of the top-ranked sales organizations operate.

In this chapter I outline a philosophy and an approach for building an aggressive, yet relationship-building, sales and marketing capability. In the first section I describe how to build a relationship-oriented sales force. Next comes a framework for successfully cross-selling new products to existing customers, thus deepening relationships and improving customer retention. In the last section I provide ideas for developing, maintaining, and managing the company's image in the marketplace.

Relationship Selling

The role and behavior of the sales organization is a major factor in retaining clients. It is a critical component of any market ownership strategy.

First, the sales organization is the predominant (if not the only) means by which the company actually acquires the clients it has targeted as part of its strategy. Once a company defines its target customer, it faces a huge challenge in developing the sales organization that will actually go out, get the right clients, and do so in a quality way. In other words, the sales force must function effectively and in a way that adds value to the product or service and fosters relationships.

The sales organization should be the company's bridge between strategy and implementation. In addition to reaching the right prospects in the right way, the sales organization is the company's primary link to the customer and the competitive marketplace and is its eyes and ears.

In terms of making the sale, customers often rate the quality of a company's sales organization as highly as the quality of its products. In fact, as we will see, highly competent salespeople can become an integral part of "the solution"—as opposed to merely "the product"—that the customer ultimately purchases.

The sales organization is (or should be) integral to many of the company's key processes beyond pure selling. These include strategy formulation, customer retention, order processing, billing, and product delivery. Depending on how it is managed, the sales force can be either a significant contributor or a barrier to the efficiency and the quality of these processes. Finally, sales organizations are usually one of the company's larger cost items, and the efficiency of the distribution system can dramatically affect the value of the company's products in the market.

Too often, companies fail to appreciate how critical their sales organizations are to success, and they tend to undermanage them. Such managements view salespeople as independent "entrepreneurs"; they develop their sales organizations by hiring "Lone Rangers," paying them pure commission, firing those who fail to make quota, and sending the top performers to a resort to listen to a motivational speaker. This formula can produce sales— but it also creates chaos. It is an approach that is inconsistent with building customer relationships and market ownership for these reasons:

- A few people in the sales organization usually generate a disproportionate share of the company's profits, while a majority posts losses.
- The organization develops a heterogeneous customer base that differs from the company's target markets, has varying needs, and is difficult to serve. As a result, the links to customers are weak. The company has almost no direct relationship with customers and therefore insufficient knowledge of their needs.
- The organization's customer retention average is low, with some salespeople deliberately "churning" accounts each year to earn higher commissions for new sales. The channel cannot maintain effective barriers against competitive inroads. This exposes the company to intense price and quality competition and the danger of a rapidly eroding base of customers.
- The organization provides uneven, and sometimes poor, service to customers, which directly reflects on the company's reputation and image.

In all of these ways, undermanaged sales organizations weaken a company's profitability, quality of service, and ability to implement its market ownership strategy. The solution to this dilemma isn't in weeding out the poor performers. It is in revamping the whole undermanaged approach to selling.

What Makes a Great Sales Force?

The concept of market ownership requires a wholly new philosophical and organizational approach to selling if the concept is to work. Although there may be many other qualities that are important for a sales organization, five characteristics are critical to a market ownership strategy. The sales force must:

1. Be tightly linked to the company's strategy in selling the right products to the right prospects in the right way, with the right offering in the right way
2. Employ a value-based sales approach that focuses on solving the client's broader problems instead of pushing a product
3. Be aggressive in pursuit of sales, yet do so with the highest degree of professionalism
4. Have a high degree of loyalty, with many salespeople staying with the company as a career
5. Have favorable economics in terms of the cost-per-sale

Many of the best sales organizations exhibit these five characteristics. One excellent example is Hewlett-Packard, which is the only company ever to displace IBM from the number one rank in *Sales and Marketing Management* magazine's Best Salesforce Award. HP's sales strategy is articulated in the magazine (September 1991) by Manuel Diaz, director of sales and marketing for North and South America: "Our goal is to deploy the best sales force in the industry. That means fielding the best quality people at the lowest cost and at the highest levels of customer satisfaction." HP's commitment to value selling is further described by Mr. Diaz: "The company that thrives . . . will be the one that offers the best solutions . . . and that can best articulate that strategy to the customer . . . in terms the customer can understand. [We]'ll have to deal with a number of partners . . . even competitors." (Reprinted with permission from *Sales and Marketing Management* magazine.)

It is vitally important to link the company's strategy to the actions of its sales organization so that it targets the right clients and sells the intended products and services in the right way.

The second characteristic, using value selling, is a powerful sales approach. In contrast to just selling a product, salespeople employing this strategy determine what the client's true, broader problems and needs are and then develop a creative solution to meet those needs. Value selling is nearly synonymous with "system selling," which implies the sale of a solution, not just a product. Value selling forces the sales organization to be highly client-oriented and to outflank "product-pushing" competitors. Employing value selling, the company changes the rules of the game by selling solutions to the client's underlying needs, while competitors sell only products. Further, solving the client's broader problems creates a satisfied customer who is likely to remain loyal to the company and provide it with referrals.

Hewlett-Packard is a strong advocate of value selling throughout its many operations. This is illustrated by its efforts to sell its Sales Force Automation service. First, an HP task force analyzes the prospect's sales organization. Then it recommends specific opportunities to improve the company's sales efficiency and bottom line by using a method that HP calls a "benefit analysis process," which quantifies the benefits of sales force automation. HP then proposes a tailored system solution and guarantees that benefits (i.e., value) will be produced or HP will refund the cost of the hardware and the software. This is a very strong value-oriented sales approach.

Value selling, however, requires considerable discipline and a much more sophisticated way of selling than does traditional product pushing. It has six key requirements:

1. *Focus on the client.* Value selling requires uncovering clients' problems, even ones that the client may have been unclear about at the outset of the sale. Instead of trying to persuade the client that he needs a particular product, the salesperson tries to

understand what is on the client's mind. Then the salesperson presents solutions that tie in with the client's thinking, rather than the other way around. This requires the salesperson to do more listening and to ask penetrating questions, rather than closing the sale and handling objections in the manner associated with product pushing.

2. *Problem-solving skills.* Value selling requires that the sales organization have the conceptual strengths, client knowledge, and technical skills to propose creative and valuable solutions.

3. *Team selling.* Effective problem-solving capability requires a team effort. Each salesperson should bring the company's best resources and people with appropriate skills to understand the client's needs and to propose solutions; the "Lone Ranger" approach is inappropriate. The salesperson must also bring the team together so that participants are equal partners presenting a "one-company" approach to the client.

4. *Adaptability.* Value selling requires the salesperson to hear clients' problems in terms that may go beyond the company's proprietary products. It requires the company to have the breadth to consider incorporating even competing products into the solution. This is as true in information technology and other high-tech businesses as it is in selling trucks or life insurance. Value selling also requires walking away from sales opportunities when the company cannot effectively solve the client's problems.

5. *Higher-level sale.* Value selling is oriented towards delivering bottom-line payoffs; the higher the stakes, the more important it is for the salesperson to call on the most senior level of decision makers. HP, for example, sells its Sales Force Automation to senior vice presidents of marketing at large companies; Paychex sells its products to owners of small businesses.

6. *High-caliber salespeople.* To accomplish these strategies, the sales organization must field highly competent, well-trained salespeople, support them with effective sales processes, and guide them via capable managers.

The third characteristic, being aggressive yet professional, is required to break through the noise of competing sales efforts. It employs calling activity and persistence, done in a way that is highly professional and consistent with how the customer expects to interact with salespeople. Surveys of buyers' perceptions of salespeople (see Exhibit 7-1) show that customers see professionalism in terms of honesty, integrity, a long-term view of client relationship building, responsiveness rather than manipulation, and an attitude that is friendly but not too personal.

The study also debunks many common myths about successful salespeople, in particular the idea that they are fast-talking, wining-and-dining schmoozers who do business mostly on the golf course. In the survey, these are all negatives. Furthermore, a June 1993 article about successful selling in *Inc.* magazine says, "Clients are too concerned about survival to worry about golf." The reality of truly successful sales professionals is that they excel

Exhibit 7-1. How customers evaluate salespeople.

Best Characteristics	Bad Characteristics	Worst Characteristics
• Is honest. • Loses a sale graciously. • Has problem-solving capabilities. • Is friendly but professional. • Is dependable. • Is adaptable. • Knows my business. • Is well prepared. • Is patient.	• There is no follow-up. • Walks in without an appointment. • Begins by talking sports. • Puts down competitors' products. • Has poor listening skills. • Makes too many phone calls. • Offers lousy presentation. • Fails to ask about my needs. • Lacks product knowledge. • Wastes my time.	• Has wise-guy attitude. • Calls me by inappropriate names. • Gets personal. • Condescends. • Is a complainer. • Is a bull-shooter. • Wines and dines me. • Plays one company against another. • Is pushy. • Smokes in my office.

Source: Sales and Marketing Management magazine, November 11, 1985.

at asking penetrating questions and listening to the answers. As the saying goes, "You can't learn anything while you're talking."

The fourth characteristic, retaining loyal salespeople, is important to retaining clients. Customer turnover is related to turnover among employees, especially salespeople. The longer the company retains salespeople, the more professional and skilled they become and the more they contribute to value selling. Loyal salespeople are also more productive and confident. Their belief that they are working for the best company in the industry comes across to clients; this, in turn, builds clients' confidence in the company. Finally, it often takes many thousand dollars to recruit and train a salesperson, and high turnover can adversely affect the company's cost structure.

The last characteristic is having favorable economics. Sales organizations are expensive and can significantly affect the value of the company's product in the market. Companies usually manage sales force economics in one of two ways. The company driven purely by sales may pay higher compensation than its competitors, hoping to attract seasoned salespeople away from competitors and to motivate them to sell a lot of business. The high compensation increases the cost of the products and makes it harder to sell, so the company increases compensation to drive the sale of the lower-value product.

The company that takes a customer value approach pays lower compensation rates than the competition, which, in addition to other factors, makes the product more valuable to the customer and thus easier to sell. In this model, salespeople are well compensated because they are highly productive and at the same time contribute to lowering the company's unit costs.

This correlation between product value and the cost of the sales organization is very evident in the life insurance business, where sales charges drive much of the product's cost and value and where almost the whole industry is sales-driven. A rare exception, Northwestern Mutual (NML), is value-driven, selling the highest valued life insurance product among all those companies selling through in-person sales organizations. Part of NML's formula is to minimize the cost per sale. It pays lower rates of commission and even makes salespeople pay their way to the annual sales conference, a traditional perquisite in the industry. The conference is nevertheless very well attended. Further, NML agents are loyal. They are also very well compensated, because the company's higher valued product makes their sales job easier and they are therefore more productive. The NML model is a winner for the customer, the salesperson, and the company. It is very difficult to compete against and even harder to replicate.

Management Tools

The five characteristics of a relationship-oriented sales force can be developed in the company's sales organization by applying six primary tools or levers (see Exhibit 7-2). The application of these tools may vary somewhat according to the type of distribution system. In this section I explain how to apply these tools to the common in-person sales force that sells directly to the end customer.

Sales Strategy

The first step is to develop a detailed sales strategy that translates the company's overall strategic plan into specific steps that can be implemented by the sales organization. The sales strategy is essentially a blueprint for managing the behavior of the sales organization and should include the following items:

- A carefully thought out profile of the targeted customer
- Definitions of the roles that the salespeople and other staff play in the sales process (e.g., the various roles in team selling)
- A description of the tasks involved in the sales process
- A detailed plan for managing the sales force
- A procedure for linking the sales organization to the company's strategic planning process

One of the most important keys to success in a market ownership strategy is the company's ability to focus its sales organization on selling to the company's targeted customer. Left

Exhibit 7-2. Management levers for achieving desired characteristics of sales organization.

Desired Characteristics	Sales Strategy	Hiring	Training	Reward System	Management	Information
				Management Levers		
Link to strategy	Develop a blueprint for sales.	Hire people with the right background.	Communicate the firm's strategy.	Support strategic objectives.	Manage the implementation of the strategy.	Monitor performance and obtain feedback.
Value selling	Define the sales process.	Hire the right personality.	Build the right skills.	Influence customer orientation and teamwork.	Control the sales process.	Equip sales force with valuable information.
Professionalism	Define the sales process.	Hire the right type of person.	Build skills.	Reward professionalism.	Manage the sales process.	Obtain feedback from prospects.
Loyalty	Employ a manageable process.	Hire team players.	Indoctrinate for company loyalty.	Reward teamwork and company perspective.	Use support management styles.	Track employee satisfaction.
Favorable economics	Develop target economics.	Hire skilled and loyal staff.	Build competence.	Manage major cost items.	Manage resources.	Track unit costs.

on their own, salespeople are inclined to believe that any sale is a good sale; they sell to any prospect they think they can close. It is important for the company to provide a clear definition of the targeted customer and to establish procedures and incentives to ensure that the stream of new prospects fits the definition. Of course, the sales organization must also develop the discipline to walk away from opportunities that do not fit the profile.

In defining the sales process, the company should describe all the players and their roles. This is especially important for a team selling approach. In particular, the description should include a definition of responsibilities and measurable goals for each player.

The sales process definition should indicate the tasks and procedures that should take place at each stage of the company's sales cycle. It should, for example, indicate which people in the target organization to contact, how to approach them, what the criteria are for qualifying a valid prospect, and how to prepare for presentations.

The more detailed the process description, the more focused and successful the junior salespeople will be in achieving the company's strategy. Seasoned salespeople need less direction, but they must still adhere to the basics, such as focusing on the target customer.

Finally, the sales process should be manageable over the long term. It must not be so demanding that it causes early burnout and high turnover.

Once the sales process is defined, it becomes important to outline the company's sales management process, which essentially defines the role of the sales manager. The definition should describe the specific tasks required during the sales management cycle, such as weekly meetings, performance reviews, participation in sales calls for coaching, and key points of intervention in the sales process.

The management process should include all the gatekeeping or sign-off roles of the sales manager, such as the review of prospects to determine whether and how to proceed. At Hewlett-Packard, for example, sales managers are responsible for orchestrating the meetings with prospects that may involve sales, technical, and product specialists. For large projects, sales managers may arrange for as many as 80 to 130 employees to visit the client over a two-year period.

The sales strategy should indicate how the company will incorporate the sales organization in its strategy development process. The linkage should work two ways. First, the sales organization should have the additional ongoing responsibility of reporting trends and events in the marketplace, and the company should provide a forum to obtain this valuable feedback. Second, the company should create formal mechanisms to communicate periodically the company's strategic direction to the sales organization and to obtain its feedback. Paychex, for example, brings its top ten salespeople together with the CEO to discuss the direction of the company and to make high-level policy recommendations.

Hiring

The second tool, recruiting, requires that the highest quality sales staff be attracted, people who demonstrate professionalism and the ability to succeed at value selling. Most of the attributes listed in Exhibit 7-1 can be learned, but only to a point; innate talent is critical. Companies with strong professional sales organizations leave little to chance in hiring; they are very savvy, disciplined recruiters with a specific profile for their ideal sales candidates. Most important, they stick to it. Their hiring processes are at least somewhat centralized at the regional or corporate levels to ensure consistency. They recruit college graduates or people with only a few years' experience so that they can mold the new hires in their own culture. They are very selective. They develop deep relationships with a small group of colleges, and they ask professors to find the best students. They are very selective, interviewing thirty to one hundred candidates for each person they hire.

Many companies employ an ad hoc approach to hiring their salespeople, letting local sales managers apply their own sense of who they think would make a good salesperson. If such a company has thirty sales offices, it will hire thirty different types of salespeople. Many companies rely strictly on business contacts, friends, newspaper ads, and letters from people looking for a job. Predictably, these sources produce a mixed assortment of salespeople who may not fit the ideal profile. The inevitable result is a very mediocre sales organization.

While companies all have different criteria for selecting new salespeople, common attributes used to identify those candidates who are most likely to succeed in sales and in building customer relationships are described in Exhibit 7-3. The first four attributes relate specifically to the requirements of value selling and building relationships and also describe the type of person most likely to be loyal to the company.

Training

Training is important for enhancing the level of the sales organization's professionalism. The sales force's ability to provide value to clients and prospects depends on superior training in product knowledge; the background of the company, industry, and competitors; and the company's strategy and sales process. Companies with the most effective sales organizations manage training, like hiring, by maintaining a heavy corporate commitment and at least some degree of central control. They invest heavily in initial training; one to three months of off-site training is common, and there is usually substantial ongoing training thereafter.

For example, managers at Hewlett-Packard believe that their product and sales training is one of the keys to the company's success. HP provides three to four months of initial training in sales, products, and the computer industry. After that, every salesperson must complete twenty-two days of product and sales training (nearly 10 percent of the work year) every year.

Anheuser-Busch, which also has a highly rated sales organi-

Exhibit 7-3. Profile of an ideal candidate for relationship selling.

- Empathy with client needs
- Partnership with clients
- Ability to build rapport; people-oriented
- Collaboration with team members
- Ability to learn quickly and think conceptually about client problems
- Presentation skills
- Task and mission drive
- Resilience in dealing with rejection
- Initiative to make things happen
- Tolerance for ambiguity
- Ability to plan and organize
- Self-starter

zation, stresses continual development of its sales staff. It constantly monitors the skill levels of its existing salespeople, who are required to attend two seminars per year.

Training is also important for indoctrinating new salespeople into the company's culture, methods, and value system. This is especially true if the company employs a heavy off-site training program for groups of new salespeople and reinforces it with continual training each year. The programs help sales staff build bonds with the company and with each other and can be a major factor in retaining these valuable employees.

It is especially important for the company's training program to be consistent with value selling and relationship building. Many commercially available sales programs are a poor fit because they are oriented toward product pushing. They stress stating the benefits of the product at the outset, before learning about the client's needs, and suggest various tricks for handling objections raised by the prospect regarding the product and for closing the deal fast.

Reward System

A company's reward system is an especially potent tool. Salespeople tailor their actions and behaviors to how they are measured and rewarded, financially and otherwise. If the rewards are inconsistent with salespeoples' efforts, the salespeople leave the company. The company's reward system must be consistent with its sales strategy, philosophy, and process. In particular, a sales strategy must be oriented to value selling and retaining customers. When Sears, for example, changed the compensation of sales representatives in its tire stores from fixed salary to pure commission, the sales staff sought to maximize its income by recommending that unnecessary work be performed on customers' cars. This ultimately led to serious legal and public relations problems for Sears.

For market ownership to work, the company needs a compensation system that rewards customer orientation, team selling, and relationship building. Although there seems to be no definitive model for compensating salespeople, it is clear that pure commissions and variable compensation are incompatible with a market ownership strategy, especially in selling business-to-business. Although the pure commission approach is convenient for the company, it downplays teamwork and is too product-oriented. It also creates an independently minded sales organization that is hard to influence. Such people will leave the company when the next better offer comes along. The pure commission approach works best in situations where there is little need for a post-sale relationship, where the salesperson works alone; in companies that constantly hire and turn over their sales staff; and in companies that are unconcerned about repeat business or their reputation in the market.

A more appropriate approach is to provide monetary rewards for team performance, especially if it is hard to determine who in a team selling effort contributed what to the sale. This can include various forms of shared revenue credit.

Another tactic used by companies with superior sales organizations is to emphasize recognition, career tracks, and other nonfinancial rewards. The latest trend is to tie sales force compensation to customer satisfaction. General Electric, Chemical Bank, and other companies are attempting to do this by linking compensation with annual customer surveys.

Management

The quality of a company's sales management is perhaps its strongest tool. It takes a high-quality sales manager to recruit, develop, and retain a high-quality salesperson; the quality of a company's sale organization can be no better than the quality of its sales management. The sales manager is responsible for implementing the company's sales strategy and processes. The manager must employ an effective management style that builds skill through coaching and that fosters salesperson retention through support and leadership.

Hewlett-Packard carefully selects its sales managers in a process that includes its CEO. And, contrary to common practices, HP does not necessarily promote salespeople with the hightest sales records. Instead, the company considers a broad array of candidates. Once they are promoted, HP trains its sales managers in leadership, in employee coaching, and in business fundamentals. It also frequently measures the performance of sales managers by using upward feedback systems in which salespeople evaluate their managers.

Senior management plays a visible role in leading sales organizations. It is critical to reinforcing the company's strategy, its values concerning customer orientation and integrity, and the company's commitment to its sales organization. The participation of senior management on sales calls and other such involvement with the sales organization is vitally important and is standard operating procedure in companies with customer-oriented sales organizations. HP reinforces its commitment to its sales organization, for example, by routinely staffing management positions with people from its sales organization.

Information

Information is a major tool for supporting the sales effort and controlling the behavior and results of the sales organization. An absence of information is a significant barrier to managing the sales process.

A relationship approach to selling also requires performance measures that go beyond closing ratios and other traditional metrics to track customer retention, penetration, and satisfaction. At a minimum, management should have information that enables it to assess sales productivity; whether the sales process is being followed; the development and satisfaction of the sales organization; and, most important, customer satisfaction with the company's sales organization. Lexus and some other car dealers, for example, routinely survey customers to assess how satisfied they were with their experience.

Companies now equip their sales staffs with information tools that facilitate value selling by enhancing the salesperson's analytical and problem-solving capabilities. These tools include expert systems to help analyze customers' needs and to develop solutions, such as laptop PCs that provide product information and generate documentation in real time at the client's site. Laptops with modems can be used to report milestone information back to the home office and to connect the client with the company for access to account status data and automatic reordering. Although these information applications can enhance a good sales organization, they cannot improve an ineffective one.

Deepening Relationships via Cross-Selling

Selling additional products to existing customers can deepen customer relationships and improve customer retention, important elements in a market ownership strategy. Although the concept is sound, many companies have developed cross-selling strategies that fail to produce sales results and in the worse cases may actually sour relationships with existing customers.

The financial services industry illustrates the mixed success of companies that attempt to cross-sell multiple financial products to the same customer.

The 1980s may be remembered as the decade of the rise and fall of the financial supermarket. At the beginning of the decade many leading financial services companies believed that their industry would consolidate around a few leading companies that were "supermarkets" for financial products. This led to a spate of ill-conceived product ventures. Worse, many companies, including American Express (Shearson), Prudential (Bache), Sears (Dean Witter), Primerica, Xerox, Travelers Insurance, and Mutual of New York, made big-stake acquisitions. Since then, the industry has been trying to unload financially disastrous ventures and is abandoning many cross-selling ventures.

Despite these failures, cross-selling remains a viable and important concept—even for financial services companies. The survival of many banks, for example, depends on their ability to spread their costs, sustain their profitability, and protect their clients from competitive inroads. Thus, banks are now cross-selling mutual funds, insurance, and other nontraditional products.

When cross-selling works well for both the company and the client, the company may have a closing rate (i.e., sales success per attempt) that is many times higher than that achieved by competitors attempting to sell to the customer on a stand-alone basis. More important, successful cross-selling can eliminate up to 80 percent of the expenses associated with a new sale, including advertising, prospecting, and proposal development—even developing the information about a customer necessary to determine pricing. If it is pursuing a successful cross-selling strategy, often the company already has all or most of the information it needs.

Developing Sound Cross-Selling Concepts

In this section I first assess the soundness of cross-selling strategies and then describe the criteria that indicate the strategic fit of those strategies with the company's core business. (The stronger the fit, the more successful the cross-selling strategy is likely to be and the easier it will be to implement.) I close with guidelines for maximizing the success of the cross-selling strategies.

Six factors determine the strategic fit of a company's cross-selling strategy:

1. *Customer match.* The new product has the same customer as the existing one.
2. *Point of need.* The company is present when the customer's need for a new product emerges.
3. *Preference for comparative shopping.* The customer desires to evaluate carefully product alternatives.
4. *Value added.* The cross-selling provides some value added to the customer.
5. *Sales and service match.* The requirements for selling and servicing the new product are similar to those that the company already provides.
6. *Credibility.* The company's credibility with the customer indicates that the new product would be a safe purchase.

1. *Customer match.* To succeed at cross-selling, the right product must be matched with the right customer. Although this may sound simplistic, many cross-selling ventures fail because management does not fully understand who are its current customers, who are the most likely customers for a new product, whether different decision makers are involved in the purchase of the new product, and to what extent other intermediaries or advisers are involved in the purchase.

2. *Point of need.* Cross-selling is greatly enhanced when the sales organization is in direct contact with the client as soon as the need for the new product emerges. This is called "the point of need." For instance, the purchase of major consumer goods creates an immediate need for ancillary products. In particular, the purchase of a home creates an immediate need for inspection, improvement, insurance, financing, and the many other products that can be cross-sold to the home buyer if the company is present at the point of need. Among the various service providers involved in buying a house, the real estate broker is the closest to the point of need. Some brokers—Century 21, for instance—have been very effective at cross-selling a full array of products and services, such as mortgage financing, homeowners insurance, title insurance, mortgage life insurance, home warranties covering appliances and systems, engineering and survey services, and extermination and various maintenance services.

Few companies, however, can count on being present at the piont of need. To succeed at cross-selling they must closely track the client for indications of newly emerging needs. This is referred to as "life event marketing," and it applies equally well in selling to individuals, such as home buyers, and to companies. As mentioned earlier, USAA has a sophisticated tracking system that monitors the life events of its members.

3. *Preference for comparative shopping.* Even if the distribution channel is present when the need arises, it may gain no advantage if the customer has a strong preference for comparative shopping. A preference for comparative shopping varies by product and consumer segment. It tends to be high for products that are expensive or where the performance of the product has a significant impact on the buyer (e.g., the choice of a doctor) and easily compared in terms of price and performance (i.e., commodity-like items) or that vary widely in price and performance from one company to another. For example, it would be much easier for a bank to cross-sell its discount brokerage service, which is simple and low-cost, than its investment advisory services, which are expensive and could significantly affect the net worth of the customer.

The preference for comparative shopping also increases with the sophistication of the customer, especially those individuals or corporations who are aided by lawyers, accountants, and other advisers, and especially for important purchases. Sophistication—and the resources to be sophisticated—generally increases with company size. Essentially, the more sophisticated the target customer, the more the cross-sold product will have to stand on its own competitive merits.

4. *Value added.* Cross-selling obviously works best for buyer and seller when the customer receives some added benefit from purchasing the cross-sold product (e.g., lower prices or added convenience) compared to buying the competitors' product; cross-selling should add value. The company should be especially cautious about venturing too far afield and should avoid cross-selling in areas where doing so might actually diminish the value of the company's offering to the client.

5. *Sales and service match.* Generally, the more the sales and service aspects of a new product resemble those of the channel's core products, the easier the cross-selling becomes. A close match is especially important in the servicing process, where a mismatch can lead to the sale of products without having adequate servicing available, resulting in frustrated customers and a distribution channel fearful of selling the new product in the future.

6. *Credibility.* Of course, the best guarantee of success in cross-selling is a base of satisfied customers who trust your company more than any of the others selling the same product. This explains the success of *Sports Illustrated for Kids,* Gap Kids, and Disney's many movies, stores, and other products and services it cross-sells to its customers. This is a hallmark of market ownership. Companies that hold such positions are significantly advantaged in offering products that customers trust.

Paychex's strategy is to provide an array of products to small businesses. As the recession trimmed Paychex's revenue from its traditional payroll processing business, it introduced three new services for existing clients: preparation of tax statements, employee benefit administration, and life/health/disability insurance. An assessment of these three product strategies according to the cross-selling criteria I have discussed is presented in Exhibit 7-4.

Exhibit 7-4. Illustration of cross-selling criteria applied to selling additional services to payroll customers.

Criteria	Tax Preparation	Employee Benefit Administration	Employee Benefit Insurance
Customer match	1	1	1
Point of need	1	2	3
Preference for shopping	1	2	5
Value added	1	2	5
Sales and service match	1	2	3
Credibility	1	2	3

All three products in row 1 have a good customer match because they have have the same buyer as the core payroll product. Paychex's customers are small businesses in which the business owner makes most of the purchasing decisions. This is not true for larger businesses in which the purchase decisions for the four products might involve different, and often multiple, buyers.

The other cross-selling criteria, however, favor tax preparation over the other two products, especially insurance:

• *Point of need.* Since Paychex already prepares payroll tax information for the client, it is clearly present when the need for the product arises. This is less true for the other two products, especially the purchase of insurance, which is independent of payroll activities.

• *Preference for shopping.* The tax product is inexpensive, especially in contrast to products like health insurance. This is one of a company's major business expenses, and small businesses aggressively shop for the lowest price each year.

• *Value added.* The tax preparation product saves the business owner precious time and thus provides value. It is unclear whether Paychex provides any extra value in selling insurance compared to insurance agents, and the Paychex salesperson must have product knowledge comparable to an insurance agent's to provide comparable value to the customer.

▪ *Sales and service match.* The tax product is relatively simple to sell and takes little extra effort to service. By contrast, insurance products represent a very complex sales service process that includes knowledge of the technicalities of insurance coverages, rating, and resolving disputed claims.

▪ *Credibility.* Paychex's popularity with customers easily extends to tax preparation, as it is seen as a logical extension of its core payroll business. Its popularity no doubt helps with selling insurance products, but that is a much larger stretch for Paychex.

Not surprisingly, Paychex is able to cross-sell is tax preparation product to an additional 15 percent of its payroll clients each year. After only four years, the new product accounts for 35 to 40 percent of Paychex's total revenue. If its strategies are properly executed, Paycheck may well succeed in cross-selling additional products to small business owners.

Following through with Sound Execution

The next consideration is the execution of cross-selling strategies. No matter how close the strategic fit, a lack of organizational and process design and other execution details can doom a cross-selling effort to failure.

The six areas that require special attention when implementing a cross-selling strategy are:

1. Supportive organizational structures
2. Product focus
3. Reward systems
4. Marketing support
5. Information systems
6. Organizational harmony

1. *Supportive organizational structures.* There are four organizational approaches to cross-selling. The appropriateness of each depends on the degree of strategic fit.

a. *Product bundling.* When a group of products has a strong strategic fit, they can be bundled together, creating a seamless package that is easy to implement. The cross-sold product becomes an almost integral feature of the company's core product.
b. *Generalist distributor.* When the cross-sold product has a good strategic fit, yet needs to be sold separately with some effort and against competition, then the generalist distributor is an effective model. The salesperson takes full responsibility for the client relationship and for cross-selling all products to clients.
c. *Team selling.* When new products are unlike existing ones and the strategic fit is weaker, team selling becomes important. The generalist may still control the client relationship but is assisted by product specialists who aid in closing the sale and who may assume full responsibility for after-sale service.
d. *Referral systems.* When a new product differs radically from existing ones, referral systems are often the best method of cross-selling. The existing channel takes the role of referring leads generated from its customer base to an entirely different unit.

These four organizational approaches form a spectrum of strategic fits for cross-selling strategies. With product bundling, the strategic fit is so strong that the customer may significantly benefit from the cross-selling strategy and readily purchase it, thus deepening relationships. Referral systems are at the other end of the spectrum; the strategy may be so weak that cross-selling may be disadvantageous to building customer affinity. Whenever products are sold to a client without necessarily increasing the value to the customer, the sale exposes the company to potential servicing problems that could hurt the core business.

Paychex has followed this organizational approach in its cross-selling efforts. Tax preparation has a very strong strategic fit. It is relatively easy for the existing sales organization to sell tax preparation at the same time that it sells Paychex's payroll processing service. The other two new products have a weaker strategic fit, and Paychex has created a separate sales organization to cross-sell them to existing payroll customers.

2. *Product focus.* Product focus, which deals with the problem of channel overload, gets lost when a company overwhelms the sales organization's ability to understand and professionally handle the broad product portfolio. When this occurs, few of the new products get sold. Worse, clients get confused about the direction of the company and its expertise in these new lines. To avoid this problem, the company can create a strategic product calendar that coordinates the introduction of new products with a set schedule. The calendar alerts management to similarities and differences in products, and assesses the channel's ability to absorb new products.

3. *Rewards system.* Many cross-selling ventures fail because existing rewards systems do not encourage the sale of the new product. This is true whether the system uses monetary or nonmonetary rewards. Sales personnel are quick to reject new products if the effort required to learn about and sell them outweighs the rewards available. Thus, a compensation scheme that does not directly reward cross-selling will merely maintain the organization's focus on its core products.

4. *Marketing support.* Cross-selling must also be supported by marketing programs such as training, market and competitive research, and promotional material. Training is particularly important, because if the sales staff feels uncertain about a new product, then it will stick with old habits and avoid the new product. At a minimum, training should include information on product details, the need the product meets, the sales process required to sell it, and the after-sale servicing required.

5. *Information systems.* The information systems category is critical; it is hard to see how cross-selling can happen without excellent information. For example, the company must know everything there is to know about existing product relationships, the potential needs of customers, and what they value. Without such information, the distribution channel wastes a lot of time prospecting for cross-selling opportunties in a large customer base that at any time contains only a small percentage of likely

prospects. Advanced cross-selling strategies, such as life event marketing, must be driven by effective information systems.

6. *Organizational harmony.* Organizational harmony, the final item on the implementation list, requires effective coordination among all parties involved, including product managers, sales support, product divisions, and the sales organization.

Two organizational harmony problems that often emerge to stifle cross-selling efforts are turf wars and home office seclusion. Turf wars should be minimized at the outset by setting clear roles, responsibilities, and reward systems that support the company's cross-selling objectives. Home office seclusion can cause many problems as the company attempts to support its cross-selling effort with people who are out of touch with day-to-day culture of the frontline distributor. This results in late response to inquiries, ineffective and uninformed advice, and literature that is unusable for marketing purposes.

These problems can be remedied by requiring that product development staff receive greater exposure to field operations. A number of excellent consumer goods marketers, for example, require new product managers and support personnel to spend several weeks each year making calls with local sales representatives. This practice brings them in tune with the end customer and the dynamics of the distribution system.

Managing Image and Reputation

For a company to own a market, the company must be widely known in its target market and must have the distinct image of being the logical, safe purchase. It must have high integrity and high-quality products and services. It must be a well-managed, stable company that is committed to the business for the long term.

Like other corporate assets, the company's image can have enormous value, especially in terms of reduced marketing costs. The strength of Disney's brand image, for example, helps it to sell its movies, stores, TV channels, hotels, toys, and so forth; Disney anything sells well.

Image is a manageable phenomenon. The authors of *Image*

By Design, Clive Chajet and Tom Schachtman, comment: "Corporate images have the power to conjure up impressions in the minds of employees, competitors, consumers, special interest groups, the financial community, and the public at large. And it's in your power to make sure those impressions are positive." Too often, managements view image as something to be fixed occasionally by calling in the advertising agency to paper over a recent spate of problems. However, as the authors point out, "Many executives use the word 'image' casually, as though an image can be manipulated easily with puffery, deceit, or tricks played on a gullible public. Nothing could be further from the truth."

A company's image and reputation is shaped by virtually everything that touches the customer (see Exhibit 7-5). Direct response companies such as Fidelity and L. L. Bean touch the customer only through their telephone service, merchandise, and mailings; companies in the hospitality and leisure business have intense customer contact. This is why Dell puts so much emphasis on the quality of its telephone operations, while Disney treats its theme parks as living theaters where all but the backroom employees are considered to be actors and actresses.

Of the items listed in Figure 7-5, advertising reaches the broadest audience, yet viewers see it as less credible than other forms of communication. Its impact per encounter is usually low and can even be negative if the advertising conflicts with the viewer's image of the company. Among the most credible forms of communication are the things that customers see as hard

Exhibit 7-5. Examples of image-shaping factors.

• Company name	• Products and services
• Logos	• Quality of interaction
• Signage	• Community relations
• Word-of-mouth	• Mention in the media
• Labels	• Major actions (e.g., acquisitions)
• Advertising	• Disaster recovery (e.g., recalls)
• Promotional material	• Company staff
• Physical presence	• Senior management
• Location and address	• Financial performance
• Telephone number	• Joint ventures and affiliations

evidence of its character: the quality of its people, the way it responds to critical problems such as product recalls, how well it honors its promises, and the way it handles actions such as alliances and acquisitions. For instance, Avon's acquisition of Tiffany and the subsequent efforts to meld the two companies' marketing sent a conflicting and unhelpful message to the typical upscale Tiffany customer.

Actions speak loudly, as well illustrated by The Moorings' policy of honoring the prepaid contracts of competing (yes, competing) yacht charters facing bankruptcy. Charlie Cary, chairman and cofounder, established this policy in an effort to maintain the integrity of the industry. Cary believes that customers of bankrupt charter companies lose not only their $6,000 prepaid fee but also the long-term commitment and planning they've invested in their vacation, usually to some remote part of the world. He believes that such substantial losses damage the overall demand for yacht chartering and that these losses would ultimately hurt The Moorings.

Although The Moorings is out $6,000 for every contract it honors, it gains a client for life—and much more. Jean Larroux, head of investor relations for The Moorings, believes that no equivalent amount of paid advertising would be as beneficial to the company's image and word-of-mouth advertising, both of which are very important in the yacht chartering business.

The quality of a company's people is among the strongest influences on the company's image. No amount of advertising will compensate for a low-quality sales organization. Customers are loath to buy from salespeople they do not trust or respect. This is the reason that, years ago, IBM adopted its legendary blue-suit-and-white-shirt dress code: IBM salespeople conveyed an image of trust and professionalism. So also with people who serve customers in the health care and airline industries. How comfortable would you feel about using a doctor who wore dirty clothes or an airline whose pilots wore cut-off blue jeans?

Many small details can be important; taken altogether, they can significantly influence the company's image. In his book *Customers for Life*, author and Cadillac dealer Carl Sewell has a whole chapter entitled "If that's how they take care of the restrooms, how'll they take care of me?" In it he comments, "It may be a little thing, but when customers are forming an opinion of you the little things add up." A detail such as The Gap's practice of stitching its labels onto its merchandise has helped make Gap products one of the strongest clothing brands.

Since so many things influence image, the company needs to develop a coordinated image strategy and the internal mechanisms to monitor and manage it. In developing the image strategy, it is important that the company first define its current image with clients, prospects, employees, suppliers, and any other relevant party who could, through word-of-mouth, influence the company's image.

Developing an Image Strategy

Image consists of perceptions in the mind of the customer; these perceptions cannot be known to the company without some customer research. Yet, the subject of company image is as sensitive to management as personal image (indeed, the two are linked).

In assessing the company's image in the market, management should have few preconceptions. Too often, management's perception of its company is shaped by no information, by misinformation, or by the interpretation of information that fits its preconceptions.

In developing the Lexus brand, for example, Toyota assumed it knew nothing about the U.S. luxury car market or the Toyota image in it. Although initially it planned to introduce its luxury car line under the Toyota name, research indicated that Toyota's image was inconsistent with luxury cars, despite the fact that Toyota's cars are consistently ranked among the highest in quality. Armed with this research, Toyota went beyond just creating a separate brand called Lexus; it created a completely new business with the image desired by the target market and with its own separate dealer network.

Image research should include a cross section of customers, prospects, distributors, sales staff and other employees, and other parties, since they all influence the company's image. The research should also use qualitative methods (such as in-person interviews and focus groups), which provide deeper insights into the customers' thought processes. Quantitative research, such as mail and telephone surveys, washes out the important, subtle nuances. It is also important for management and technical staff to be closely involved in the research, whether doing the interviews or observing focus groups, so that they can develop first-hand interpretations. Finally, the research should provide specific examples of how the company's people, actions, and other operational aspects influence its image; for example, are there specific behaviors of the sales organization that especially shape perceptions?

Disney values its powerful brand image. Always concerned about how its broadening product line affects customer opinion, Disney does intensive research to track its image. Disney has what it calls the "Brand Image Group," which regularly conducts telephone surveys, focus groups, and personal interviews.

After evaluating market research on the company's existing image, management should address how the company needs to be seen to own its market. In addition to having the general characteristics previously discussed, the image must be consistent with what the targeted market expects and values.

For example, if the company's customers expect the company to deliver the latest technology, it cannot project an image of being a laggard in introducing new products. Toyota understood this well when it positioned Lexus as a car with superior performance and styling, modeled after Mercedes, yet with a significantly lower price. Toyota thus met the expectations of its younger, value-oriented, affluent, target market.

The final step is to develop a strategy to achieve and maintain the desired image for the company, following these steps in order:

1. Change the company's operations, organization, management style, culture, etc., to make the company's behavior and quality of people, products, and services consistent with the company's desired image.
2. Review the company's corporate identity.
3. Develop a well-managed public relations program.
4. Use advertising and promotional media.

Why not just get on with it and spend several million dollars on advertising? The fact is that the money might be wasted if items 1 through 3 are not first addressed. It is particularly important to make sure that the company's actions are congruent with how it wants to be seen. Customers and even the press will inevitably spot discrepancies between the company's claims and its actions. In reviewing how it would like to be perceived in the market, the company should think hard about what message it communicates via its actions, culture, and product and service quality and via the quality of its employees. It should question how congruent these real-world attributes are with the company's desired image.

To quote again the authors of *Image by Design:* "To have the most positive impact on corporate audiences, the company's image must reflect, not distort, reality. In particular, companies that use advertising to proclaim themselves to be something they are not at best waste their money; at worst they breed cynicism and mistrust in the market." To have a strong, lasting, positive image, the company should first be sure that it can deliver on its promised values. The elements that touch customers and prospects must project the right image, because they are more convincing than advertising. Conagra, for example, ran initially successful advertisements promoting the health advantages of its product line, Healthy Choice frozen foods. Later, the company ran into significant image problems when its health claims were challenged.

On the surface, the Gap's success derives from its creative and extensive advertising. Yet its advertising program would have been a waste if it had been begun before the Gap had crystallized its retail concept, getting its house in order by changing its merchandise and even the appearance of its stores. In repositioning The Gap, and before embarking on the ad program, management wanted its stores and everything in them to appear as if they had been designed "all in one mind."

Selecting corporate identification is the logical next step. This includes all of the outward identifiers of the company—its name, logos, trademarks, and so forth. Before spending money on media advertising, it is important that the company make sure these elements are the chosen identifiers and that they portray the desired image for the company. It is also important to maintain the integrity of these identifiers. For example, Disney entered the adult film business using separate identities (Touchstone

Films and Hollywood Pictures), thus preserving the Disney name's association with entertainment for children.

Public relations is a deliberate effort to shape a company's image through mentions in the media, endorsement/sponsorship of various causes, and similar activities. It is a major management tool because it is more believable than media advertising. The author of *Relationship Marketing*, Regis McKenna, believes that the primary focus of a company's marketing program should be to establish favorable relationships with journalists, product analysts, investment analysts, retailers, suppliers, and customers, all of whom play a significant role in building the image of the company.

A good example of the efficacy of public relations is Mobil Oil Corporation. If you first ask people about their image of the oil industry in general and then ask them about Mobil, you will probably find that Mobil is perceived very differently from and in a more positive way than the rest of the industry. Much of Mobil's positive image is a result of its public relations campaign, in large part its sponsorship of *Masterpiece Theatre* for the Public Broadcasting System (PBS). After all, who could have been more credible than PBS and Alistair Cooke (and his so-carefully-chosen successor, Russell Baker)?

Of all the many strategies for good public relations, involvement in community relations and popular causes is especially important for building trust and an image of integrity. Anheuser-Busch started out by making a significant donation in 1906 to help the victims of the San Francisco earthquake; it has since maintained as one of its primary values that of being a good corporate citizen. Today it contributes $25 million to charity and requires its distributors to make a similar commitment (*Sales and Marketing*, September 1992): "It's part of the charter agreement they sign with us that they'll be involved in charity projects in their community." Virgin Atlantic takes a similar tactic in expressing concern about the children of Romania; it requests that passengers join in the charitable cause by donating spare foreign currency left over from their trips abroad.

As concern about the environment grows, so-called green marketing is becoming a powerful public relations tool. A 1992 study by market researchers Yankelovich Clancy Schulman found that 63 percent of adults they polled said they were more likely to purchase environmentally sound products than they were three years earlier.

McDonald's is a prime example of a company that was not only *not* part of the pollution solution but clearly a major culprit. McDonald's has responded to criticism of its environmental policies by creating the position of vice president of environment affairs. The company has committed to using recycled materials where possible and has a stated goal of using 100 million pounds of recycled material to build and remodel its restaurants. RubberMaid offers a recycling system to customers that includes a guide on recycling and a container system to store recyclable materials.

Finally, media advertising can be a very important tool for building the company's image—so long as the company has in fact achieved a level of credibility and can demonstrate that it can deliver on promises. The world listens when a company spends lavishly in the media to advertise that it can provide something of value to customers far better than its competitors can, especially if the company can support its claim with independent sources. For example, its claim about reducing cavities, supported by recommendations from dentists, is what put Crest toothpaste in the lead. Saturn's advertising of its haggle-free dealership sales is another good example. Before it advertised, it had to establish that its new style of customer treatment in its dealerships was something that competing brands could not deliver.

Northwestern Mutual promised—and was able to deliver—the highest-value product among its peer companies. It created a huge stir in the market when it advertised on TV during a Super Bowl game to spell out the product differences. Similarly, Hewlett-Packard stirred up the computer industry when it advertised its significant price and performance advantages, which were well documented by highly credible independent industry consultants.

Market ownership is based on relationship building and the firm's reputation for trust and integrity. Yet without an aggressive sales and marketing effort, customers may never learn about your better mouse trap. Both relationship building and aggressive marketing are needed to own a market; the key challenge addressed in this chapter is how to achieve both at the same time.

Chapter 8
Improving Operations

How can you make operations faster, cheaper, and better within the context of the market ownership model? A key theme to creating lean operations is that operational excellence is essential to maximizing customer value. That is, you must consistently produce the highest quality products and services at the lowest prices. Take as examples Harley-Davidson and Smith Corona, both of which owned and nearly lost their markets due to fat, wasteful, noncompetitive operations.

For decades, Harley-Davidson owned the heavyweight motorcycle market, with a market share in the early 1970s estimated by *Forbes* to be about 90 percent. By 1983, however, its share had dropped to 12.5 percent, largely due to poor quality manufacturing practices that produced motorcycles with significant defects—to the point where dealers had to repair brand-new motorcycles before they could sell them. According to *Sales & Marketing Management* (April 1991), "Stories abounded about customers who bought two bikes—one to ride and one to cannibalize for spare parts." By borrowing operational concepts from its Japanese competitors, Harley-Davidson was able to regain its market ownership, boosting it to a 63 percent market share in 1993.

Smith Corona traditionally held over 50 pecent of the typewriter market. (Its home base in Cortland, New Hampshire, was once known as the typewriter capital of the world.) But its share, given a combination of its own inefficient operations and the impact of low-cost Japanese manufacturers, dropped to about 30 percent in the late 1970s. Smith Corona made its typewriters at seven old-line plants, which, by its own admission, wasted space, material, inventories, transportation cost, and manufacturing time. By redesigning the product for ease of production and by improving its manufacturing processes, Smith Corona was able to fit all its operations into a single plant, gain substantial efficiencies, and rebuild its market share to 54 percent.

Before I get too deep into the subject, I want to note briefly the role of this chapter in the context of the book as a whole. Literature on operational improvement often captures management's attention because it promises quick cost savings. However, managements are too quick to embrace operational improvements before first thinking through other, more fundamental issues (such as those I explored earlier in this book). For example, it makes no sense to streamline operations that support unprofitable customers, products, or business units that should not exist in the first place. It is only logical to attend to the more strategic issues first. Accordingly, operational improvement comes at the end of a long sequence of more strategic considerations, as illustrated in Exhibit 8-1. Furthermore, as you know, the major theme of this book is building a focused business through streamlining the corporation. Operational improvement represents the last element in this theme.

The vast literature on operational improvement offers numerous concepts and ideas, but here I'm going to focus on seven

Exhibit 8-1. Operational improvement in the context of this book.

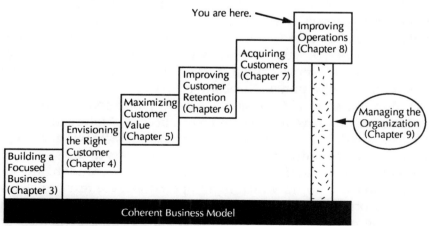

fundamental themes that are compatible with the concept of market ownership, especially those that take a long-term, employee-oriented perspective. The current concept of "lean manufacturing" is particularly compatible with the market ownership concept, especially relative to the dehumanizing and grossly out-of-date mass production school of thought. These seven themes are:

1. Continuous improvement and quantum-leap improvement goals
2. Training
3. Self-managed work teams
4. Reduced complexity and waste
5. Information
6. Improved support functions
7. Easy access to the firm

Implementing Continuous And Quantum-Leap Improvement

Your ability to achieve substantial improvement in operations starts with senior management's committing to continuous improvement and to setting quantum-leap performance goals. Continuous improvement requires that the "forever" search for better ways to do work becomes part of everyone's job. Quantum-leap goals are necessary to drive the company's improvement to new heights that, once attained, become the basis for new, even higher, goals. The goal should involve some multiple improvement; a tenfold improvement in ten years seems to be popular among those who pursue this course.

A number of U.S. businesses have pioneered this type of operational improvement with great success. Motorola, for instance, developed the now famous goal of achieving a "six-sigma" rate of product defects. (The sigma refers to the statistical measure *standard deviation*; six sigma means six standard deviations above the norm, which in an operational context translates to 3.4 errors per million transactions or process steps. Six sigma above the norm is analogous to having a having a genius IQ of

160.) Motorola has found that a four-sigma producer has a repair rate equal to 10 percent of revenues, while a six-sigma company spends only 1 percent of revenues on repair, giving it a significant cost advantage.

Federal Express has a goal of zero defects and has achieved a tenfold improvement in its Service Quality Index, which is a composite of items such as complaints and missed pickups. Xerox, having achieved its goal of a tenfold improvement in product quality, now uses a process it calls "A-delta-T," where delta stands for change. The process begins by defining performance levels that are theoretically the highest achievable and then setting quantum-leap goals to close the gap between existing performance and this theoretical high level. Hewlett-Packard achieved similar goals by measuring failure rates to improve the quality of some its hardware products tenfold over the 1980s and is now setting quantum-leap goals for the 1990s.

Although these companies have given their improvement efforts different umbrellas and banners with names like TQM, process improvement, and reengineering, the successful programs have several common ingredients. First, whatever the programs are called, they focus on making improvements that translate into enhanced customer value. This requires simultaneous improvement in both quality and productivity—and anything else that contributes to maximizing value provided to the customer.

The concepts of continuous process improvement and reengineering are usually used interchangeably, despite purists' attempts to distinguish them. Although both concepts promise major gains in performance, the speed with which improvement can be achieved is different: continuous improvement implies steady incremental change that adds up over time, while reengineering calls for revamping or "obliterating" whole processes within a short time.

There will always be opportunities to improve your operations incrementally. Reengineering opportunities, however, arise only when the company has neglected continuous improvement, thus becoming grossly inefficient, or when new technologies emerge that all of a sudden make existing processes obsolete.

Reengineering purists also downplay incremental improvement gains of 5 to 10 percent, touting the more dramatic 50 percent-plus gain that reengineering promises to achieve in a short time. These 5 and 10 percent gains add up, however, to substantial improvement over a multiyear period. After a few decades of tinkering with its operations, Toyota's culture of continous improvement enabled it to build cars in half the labor hours required by many of its American and European competitors.

Another distinction between continuous improvement and reengineering is their impact on the company's workforce. The incremental gains from continuous improvement make it easier to avoid layoffs by enabling the company to redeploy employees and by shrinking staff through attrition. Achieving the quick and massive gains promised by reengineering, on the other hand, inevitably requires significant layoffs. While such layoffs may be necessary to get the chronically inefficient company back on track, quick gains accompanied by layoffs are no way to build the trusting and motivated workforce that is central to market ownership.

If You Think Training Is Expensive, Try Incompetence

The title of this section, a variation on one of The Body Shop's mottoes, says it all. Training frontline employees contributes to the company's operational efficiency in productivity, reduction of reworking and waste, better customer servicing, and reduced job injuries. Training reduces absenteeism and turnover and improves employee morale. Workers feel the satisfaction that comes with succeeding in the job and appreciate the company's investment in their skills. The alternative to adequate training is extreme waste.

Quantitative evidence reveals that employee training produces a high return on investment. The Brookings Institute found that training in job skills has increased productivity in the United States more than twice as much as technology over the past few decades. Other research noted in *Training & Development Journal* (November 1990) found that trained employees were 30 percent more productive after one year than were untrained employees. The American Society for Training and Development (ASTD) found that $1 spent on training saved $10 that would otherwise have been spent on employee turnover alone.

Motorola has conducted three studies using outside auditors and has concluded that each dollar of training produces between $29 and $33 in benefits to the company each year. By training employees to simplify processes and reduce waste, it has cut its costs by $3.3 billion since 1987. As William Wiggenhorn, president of Motorola University, noted in *Industry Week* (February 19, 1990), "We have seen a great increase in the quality of our products and services since we formally began our training and education programs."

Honeywell found that its employee training improved productivity by 40 percent and reduced work-in-process inventories by 60 percent, customer delivery time by 50 percent, and rework and waste by 50 percent.

These findings make it clear that training frontline employees is one of the most attractive investments that a business could make—a $1 investment in training that produces a $30 payoff per year is a 3,000 percent return on investment. Furthermore, training is essential if you are going to reap any benefits from other high payoff initiatives such as teams, continuous improvement, total quality management, or other programs that require frontline employees to assume greater responsibility and to perform broader job roles. Management should never initiate any of these programs without adequately training frontline employees.

Given the logic of investing in training, it is shocking to find that the majority of U.S. employees are largely untrained and increasingly ill-equipped for beginning their jobs. American businesses have virtually ignored worker training. This contributes to the inefficiency of the typical U.S. company and threatens both U.S. competitiveness in global markets and Americans' standard of living.

To start with, compared to workers in other developed countries, the average U.S. worker receives inferior basic education. *The Economist* (September 22, 1992) noted that "[a] third of America's frontline workers are high school dropouts, often illiterate and innumerate. There are, unlike in Germany, Sweden, and

Denmark, few schemes to help students make the transition from school to work." Ray Marshall and Marc Tucker, authors of *Thinking for a Living*, note:

> Twenty-five percent of Canadian high school seniors know as much chemistry as the top 1 percent of American seniors; 78 percent of South Korean thirteen-year-olds have acquired intermediate math skills versus only 40 percent in the U.S.; and only 25 percent of young adults in the U.S. know how to use a bus schedule.

A 1989 study by the Department of Labor found that "[t]wenty to 40 million adults have literacy problems, making it difficult for them to be trained or retrained. One-half of all eighteen-year-olds have failed to master basic language, mathematics, and analytic skills." Finally, the National Commission on Excellence in Education in 1983 concluded poignantly, "If an unfriendly foreign power had attempted to impose on America the mediocre educational performance that exists today, we might well have viewed it as an act of war."

Furthermore, the United States spends relatively little on vocational training to help those students who will not be attending college to prepare for frontline jobs. As a percentage of gross national product, Sweden spends 1.7 percent, Germany 1.0 percent, Britain .7 percent, and Spain .7 percent on vocational training, while the United States spends .3 percent. The Commission on the Skills of the American Workforce concluded that "[t]he transition from school to work in the U.S. is the worst of any industrialized country."

Most U.S. companies spend little or nothing on company-sponsored training. Although the ASTD estimates that U.S. businesses spent about $47 billion on training, the actual amount spent on frontline employees might as well be zero, because (1) 75 to 90 percent of the training money is spent on training college-educated employees in managerial and professional jobs, and (2) one-half of one percent of all corporations account for 90 percent of the money spent on training.

The bottom line is that only 10 percent of U.S. frontline employees receive any form of company-provided training, compared to 70 percent of the frontline workforce in Japan and in Germany. In the United States, *OJT* might as well mean "only job training."

Worse still, the concept of on-the-job training (OJT) is weak in the United States compared to other developed countries. In the United States, OJT usually means being thrown into the workplace fray and using initiative to pick up job skills. In Japan, workers from across all levels of seniority are expected to teach one another job skills and to share knowledge and information. As *Training and Development Journal* (March 1990) noted, "On-the-job training is the heart of training in Japanese companies."

Finally, the United States lacks rewards for self-study. Self-study is usually done outside work on the individual's initiative for purposes of self-development, not necessarily for advancement in one's current job. Conversely, Japanese employers expect employees to pursue self-study to help them advance in their current jobs.

U.S. management is primarily accountable for the failure to invest in training. The success of foreign companies operating under foreign management philosophy in the United States and using U.S. workers clearly attests to how strong U.S. employees are when adequately trained. *Fortune* magazine (Spring-Summer 1991) noted, "One thing the one thousand Japanese factories in the U.S. teach is that the oft-maligned American worker can be a powerful competitive asset." Marvin Runyon, president of Nissan USA, commented in *Training and Development Journal* (March 1990), "Japanese companies are much better than American ones at training employees, a key to the enhancement of productivity."

Worst, American managements apparently do not believe they have a training problem. This fact emerged in a 1990 survey conducted by the National Center on Education and the Economy, which found that only 5 percent of American management believes that U.S. workers have a low-skills problem. In 1989 MIT's Commission on Industrial Productivity reported, "There seems to be a systematic undervaluation in this country of how much difference it can make when people are well educated and when their skills are continually developed and challenged. This underestimation of human resources becomes a self-fulfilling prophecy."

Economists widely concur that this low-skills problem is a serious national issue. The book *Thinking for a Living* (Ray Marshall and Marc Tucker, 1992) lays out a dire scenario in which U.S. workers retain only the least skilled jobs. Lester Thurow notes in his book *Head to Head* that "[t]he United States, an educational laggard, is in trouble. If the bottom 50 percent of the work force isn't educated enough to learn new high-tech processes, those processes can't be employed. If German and Japanese workers can learn them easily, they'll get the best jobs." And *Business Week* (June 25, 1990) wrote, "The U.S. is on a de-skilling binge for the sake of short-term productivity growth that could prove disastrous for business and the economy in the long run."

If training is so obviously beneficial, why has it escaped American management? No doubt the answer derives in part from the short-term orientation of U.S. management, which favors today's earnings over investing in tomorrow's success, whether in training, R&D, or other investments. This is especially true where the current outlay in hard dollars for training provides an unproven (to management) future benefit. It is an American cliché that "[w]hen budgets get tight, training is the first thing to go."

And where would American management learn that training frontline workers is critical? Do business schools stress training as a top management tenet? I doubt it. Since our business culture is oblivious to the need for training, there are no leadership models within companies to pass the message down to future generations of managers. Only the intuitively bright managements know the wisdom of training their workers.

Furthermore, our model for jobs and productivity dates back to mass production and Henry Ford early in the century. It calls for splitting jobs into small functions that require little thinking on the part of the worker, paying low wages, treating employees as cogs that are easily replaceable, and applying automation to replace people whenever possible. In November 1990 *Training & Development* described our system as a "high-turnover, low-wage model that assumes a large uneducated, undeveloped people, using automation to create simple work tasks and jobs that are idiot-proof."

This model contrasts with that prevalent in other developed countries, especially Japan, where employment with the same company is viewed as a lifetime obligation. In fact, Japanese workers stay with one company for an average of twenty-two years, compared to thirteen years for workers in the United States. Also, Japanese workers enter the workforce from high school with superior general backgrounds. The employer is responsible for training employees in job-related skills and rotating them through different jobs every three to five years.

The first solution to your company's particular training needs is to assume that the government will not bail you out. If it does provide assistance, by the time it does, you may be out of business. And although it is not your company's responsibility to provide basic education, you have no choice but to try to hire the best people you can and to train them very well. By *train* I mean that you must fill in the gaps in basic knowledge that you expect (and pay for) their schooling to provide.

This is what Motorola has set out to achieve. The company created Motorola University with the objective of training and retraining more than 100,000 employees around the world and requires every employee from the chairman on down to complete at least forty hours of training each year. The program has twenty-eight different courses covering everything from general skills such as math and reading to how to work in teams to solve problems. It costs $60 million per year to run and represents an investment of about $6,000 per employee per year. Motorola's goals are to have all production workers able to read, write, and comprehend at seventh-grade levels at a minimum.

Your first important step is to become completely convinced that training is a high-yielding investment that is critical to your company's success. For those who need further convincing, visit companies that are committed to training. Any of you who are still on the fence should just start in and observe the benefits in your own organization. As James Houghton, chairman of Corning Glass, observed in *Training and Development Journal* (November 1990), "We talked about the importance of training for years, but until we instituted comprehensive and mandatory programs, our efforts never matched our intentions."

Another step is to work with local educational institutions to offer training in basic skills such as math and reading on the company's premises, during convenient hours, with costs subsidized by the company. Honeywell, for example, used local community colleges to conduct courses on-site from 4 to 7 P.M. and achieved a 60 percent participation rate among employees.

Finally, make a sufficient investment in training the entire workforce in job-related skills. Continue to train them every year, not just at the outset. Using as models companies like Motorola, IBM, Corning, Xerox, and others who are committed to training, you will probably determine that a good benchmark for your training budget means spending about 5 percent of payroll each year on employee training in job-related skills. Remember, training is one of the highest-yielding investments you can make.

Self-Directed Teams

Another major opportunity in streamlining operations is to organize work around teams that are largely self-managed. Although this is a radical departure from the traditional reliance on heavy supervision in mass-production environments, the team concept has proven effective for many decades; Toyota has effectively used self-managed work teams since 1950.

Successful self-managed teams typically do the following activities: schedule their own work and give assignments to team members; change the configuration of work processes; solve operating problems; participate in the hiring and firing of team members; prepare labor and materials budgets; make quality inspections; appraise team and individual performance; participate in pay raises; and assume many other supervisory jobs that managers and administrative support staff perform in most operations.

Fred George, vice president of manufacturing at Campbell Soup, described his company's approach to using teams this way for *Business Week* (March 1, 1993): "We turned the business over to them. Self-managed teams take the place of most supervisors, meet with vendors, and set their own schedules. They even propose capital expenditures, complete with calculations of internal rates of return."

Employees know firsthand the details of day-to-day operations. They are well equipped to make decisions, solve operating problems, and improve the processes they live with every day. The benefits of having them work in teams are improved quality and productivity, which foster better decision making in production scheduling and goal setting and give employees a chance to resolve quickly operational problems as they arise. Teams share workloads so that everyone is about equally busy, unlike the traditional system in which one worker might be overloaded while another is idle. Teams can also resolve disputes that arise within the team organization without resorting to management intervention.

Self-directed teams assume greater responsibility for traditional management tasks, thus reducing the need for supervisory and managerial positions. *Business Week* (March 1, 1993) noted that "General Electric Company has made self-managing work teams a centerpiece of its organizational approach to the point of running some plants without supervisors."

Teams provide much greater motivation for productivity and quality work than do traditional supervisors. And teams do a better job with performance appraisal, feedback, and on-the-job training. Furthermore, teams improve employee morale because team members are challenged and motivated by greater job flexibility, increased involvement, and a sense of ownership and control over what they do day to day. Reduced absenteeism and employee turnover are other benefits of work teams—and when an employee is absent, other team members fill in.

The American Society for Training and Development conducted a survey of companies that use work teams and found that 77 percent of respondents indicated that productivity improved, 72 percent indicated that quality improved, 65 percent reported improvements in job satisfaction, and 57 percent cited improvements in customer satisfaction. Further evidence of the benefits of work teams comes from General Mills, which estimates that the introduction of teams improved productivity by 40 percent, and from Kodak, which found that a single shift with teams does about the same work as three shifts without teams.

Two Case Studies

The following case studies should give you a sense for the use of work teams. There are examples for both a manufacturing and a service operation. Donnelly manufactures mirrors and related products for the auto industry and has employed work teams for many decades. Sun Life is a Canadian life insurance company that adopted self-directed teams with great success as recently as 1989.

Donnelly Corporation

Donnelly instituted work teams in the 1950s as part of a broader effort to improve overall productivity. Currently, every worker is a member of one of two hundred teams, each consisting of ten to twelve members. The mission of each team is to satisfy customers.

Each team member is assigned to a specific job and is often cross-trained in other team members' jobs. Employees are also trained in how to work collaboratively in teams; the teams meet regularly to discuss their performance and possible improvements to the manufacturing process.

Teams are responsible for setting their own goals in the context of larger organizational goals and have a great deal of influence on their work. As Maryam Komejan, corporate vice president, commented, "Team members have a great deal of influence on their work, often including the design of the process and how best to do the work. When a problem arises, they solve it right on the floor as it comes up; they can stop everything to fix it right there and are encouraged to call in other resources they need."

Donnelly has no time clocks. Employees are accountable to their teams for their performance. Supervisors function more like facilitators than like traditional production-line bosses. While team members willingly fill in for those who may be absent, they are cautious about excessive and unexplained absenteeism on the part of other team members. As Maryam Komejan observed, "Employees exert considerable peer pressure upon one another to achieve team goals."

In exchange for creating this stimulating work environment, Donnelly expects its employees to perform at very high levels in terms of productivity, quality, self-sufficiency in problem solving, and the continual improvement of Donnelly's operations. Robert Levering and Milton Moskowitz, authors of *The 100 Best Companies to Work for in America*, note that "[the teams] are expected to be part of finding solutions . . . to involve themselves fully in the work with others on their team . . . to make a difference. A premium is placed on personal responsibility, not only for product quality but production effectiveness and efficiency as well."

While Donnelly cannot precisely calculate the payoff from its team approach, Maryam Komejan says that "[w]e have low absentee-ism and have less than a 2 percent turnover rate; teams are continu-ally improving yields to meet customer demands. Teams have a goal of zero defects. You can go into any facility and see our goals and where we are on a month-to-month basis presented on the walls, and you can see the improvements achieved. People will work extra hours to get the job done. We don't miss customer deadlines, and we win the highest quality awards from our customers. For example, we are in the elite category of suppliers at GM, Ford, Chrysler, and Honda of America, to name a few. It's all because of the extra effort people put forth."

Sun Life Assurance Company of Canada

Sun Life substantially improved productivity, quality, and employee satisfaction in one of its U.S. divisions by installing self-directed teams. The division, called the Sun Life Annuity Service Center, handled investment products sold by the firm's large agent network. Like most life insurers, the division was run by a hierarchy of managers; in some areas it had eight levels of management from top to bottom, and management in one form or another accounted for about one fourth of total employment in the division. The division also had excessively high costs that required it to be subsidized by other parts of the business.

When Ian Kennedy took over the division in August 1990, he was given a mandate to make the Center financially self-sufficient, which would require a substantial improvement in operating effi-ciency beyond traditional budget-tightening. Ian had learned about self-managed teams from consultants, books, and articles, and he decided to install the team structure. He did so in January 1991, giving the frontline workers many of the responsibilities and tasks that had previously been performed by their bosses. The company also instituted higher performance standards and an incentive com-pensation plan that rewarded employees for meeting divisional, team, and individual productivity goals.

At an employee meeting to announce the team approach, Kennedy mentioned that while everyone "has a home," the performance standards for the division were going to be greatly increased. Those who did not meet the new standards would have to go. Otherwise, the planned workforce reduction would come from attrition, rather than layoffs.

Team members picked up most of their bosses' duties, such as scheduling their daily work and making assignments to individuals; enforcing disciplinary actions for tardiness and other poor work habits; changing processes to improve productivity; and directing the hiring and performance appraisals for the team.

Several employees described their day-to-day work as follows:

> We watch over our own time, set our own schedules, and agree as a team on the hours within Sun Life's flexible work-hour system that each of us will work. We are constantly talking to one another to see who needs help. We used to perform small and narrow jobs; now we have bigger jobs where everyone on the team is involved in all aspects of the work, which provides a good variety.

The teams determine staffing requirements. They are not eager to add staff, even to fill open positions, because the team is rewarded on its productivity. They interview all job candidates and have the final say as to who eventually gets hired to join the team.

Teams are also responsible for performance appraisals for all of their members. All team members except the person being reviewed meet to discuss the individual's performance. The group must reach consensus and then present the results as a group to the individual. Teams are also charged with distributing the team bonus pool.

As Ian Kennedy noted, "Most of us who have been around for a while and were used to more traditional performance appraisals would find this process thoroughly intimidating." He was absolutely right; there is just about no way to blame someone else or to come up with personal excuses in this process.

Team members commented on their peer review process:

> We believe that this is a more accurate and immediate way to assess people that is not subject to misinterpretation. We always suspected that supervisors had favorites, which can't happen in a work team. The process is better because you have multiple inputs from people who work closely together. Teams really know how someone is performing, and

reviews are much more honest and reflective of the person's true performance.

The team members are trained as specialists in some particular type of product or technical process but are cross-trained to function as generalists capable of performing any job within the team. This enables them to trade jobs, filling in for employees who are absent or assigned to other projects. They also mix day-to-day servicing work with problem-solving and process improvement initiatives.

Sun Life did not experience immediate success in implementing the work team approach. Kennedy recalled, "We struggled for a year with cross-training employees and weeding out nonperformers and the disbelievers." He confronted managers who were mentally entrenched in the old ways of managing people, telling them, "We will work with you to change your mind, or you can go to work in a more traditional place where you can exercise your need for power and authority." Looking back, employees observed that the transition was hard at first because, as one of them commented, "We needed to build trust and teamwork."

By weeding out the disbelievers and transferring other managers to teams as workers and in support positions, Kennedy reduced the number of line managers from fifty-three to two, while adding eight "coaches" who facilitated the work teams but did not manage individual employees. He told the eight coaches, "As coaches, you are part of the team for as long as the team needs you; your job is to make yourself unnecessary from a day-to-day perspective."

After the first six months, the division's performance started to improve dramatically. By the end of 1993, three years after installing the teams, the division's head count had shrunk from 189 to 136 employees while sales had almost doubled and the average unit cost of serving new and existing customers was cut in half. At the same time, the division's quality improved. For example, Sun Life reduced the time it took to license and appoint agents to sell its annuity products from five to two days.

When they were asked how the team structure specifically contributed to such impressive improvements in productivity gains, team members responded with these observations:

> [*Higher skills through better on-the-job training*] "New people get right into their jobs. We have team lunches, introduce them around, and it is our responsibility to train new people to work within the team. We know immediately

what a person can and can't do, and so they are put to work earlier in areas where they are strong and we know where to focus training on their weaknesses."

[*Making workloads even*] "In a traditional job you are told to just do this particular job, and when you are done you just kill time. Meanwhile, someone working next to you is unbelievably busy, but it's not your job to help out. It's the supervisor's job to make this decision. In teams we even out the workload among team members. A critical element is trust. You can trust that work you are responsible for will get done well when handed off to another team member. We are not afraid to go outside the bounds of our jobs to get the work done."

[*Plain old teamwork*] "We ask for help and volunteer to help each other out. We have our own specialties, and we can help each other out when problems come up. Getting answers from team members [i.e., multiple people] is a lot more effective than getting an answer from individual supervisors who only know what they know."

[*Greater responsibility*] "We take more responsibility for decisions and our work. Before, we had multiple layers of management and no one was willing to take any risks. We had too many people covering for themselves."

[*Continuous improvement*] "We do a lot of streamlining that traditional managers couldn't do because they are not in the front line and don't see improvement opportunities like we do. We get together and decide to streamline a particular process and just do it. Previously we would have to go through five levels of management to get the work done. So many existing procedures are useless. The business has changed, but the rules remain the same. We get rid of them. First we ask why we did it in the first place, and then we hash out the pros and cons, who will benefit and who will be affected."

[*Improved communication*] "Communication is so much better. People in the past were afraid of their supervisors and would not raise problems. We own these problems and fix them instead of passing them off to other departments like the traditional way of doing things."

[*Cross-team coordination*] "Coordination through the

division is much better than it was previously. Before, cutting across functional lines made everyone defensive, like passing the blame. Also you had ten layers of management to get things done. You'd go up several levels in your area, wait for top management to have a coordinating meeting, and then wait for it to pass down several layers on the other side. It might take months, or it might never happen. With the team structure, we can go to another team and raise an issue, and they will address it because they have been empowered to solve problems."

[*Quality of work*] "We ultimately have an attitude of 'get it right or get out'; poor-quality work increases the team's workload and reflects poorly on the team. We also have more feedback from team observation on how well everyone is performing and whether someone is continually screwing up. We are also fully responsible for handling every aspect of clients' problems as opposed to handing the client off to some other department to solve it for them."

When asked to compare how they feel about their current team structure with their previous, traditional work setting, team members commented:

"It makes you feel like an adult on the job. You have more freedom, and there is more trust. You feel more important because no one is second-guessing you from management. Your job makes you feel good because you are empowered with decision-making ability and work isn't dictated to you. Your work is more interesting and varied. It's good to get away from the day-to-day to mix things up a bit. It's these little things that make you want to come back to work. It's the flexibility, the ability to pick the work you want to do for variety and team members that help you. Work doesn't pile up when you're absent because someone else on the team will handle it. When you come back from vacation, your desk looks the same as when you left because the team handled the work. Also, with the absence of layers of management, we have easy access to top management, and we are more visible. Today we would think nothing about walking into a senior manager's office to discuss a problem. In the old system we'd never do that."

"You can hide from your supervisor, but not from your team" was the response to the question of what motivates a team member to be effective. Other comments included,

> "It is definitely more motivating. In the old system you knew how to play the manager, but you can't fool your team because you work too closely together. Besides, the team reviews our performance. Also, you need to retain your self-respect within the team. If I was doing someone else's job day after day there would be a big problem, though this hasn't happened. We are close enough to say 'need some work; need something to do' in a friendly way of course.
>
> "We try to get people to fit into the team and we do everything in our power to help them. When that doesn't work, we suggest that the person moves on. If we have a problem, the team needs to solve it on its own. We don't want the team to look bad. If we had to go to management to solve our problems, it would be like running to Mom."

There are several key lessons to note from the Sun Life example. First, the combination of installing teams, creating incentive compensation, and getting rid of the disbelievers was critical to Sun Life's success. As Ian Kennedy noted, "We had to get management people to focus on coaching, advising, and working on facilitywide strategic areas in which they could add more value than simply supervising people. The people who do the day-to-day work are capable of supervising themselves, managing their work, and getting the job done." Sun Life demonstrated that quantum leaps in improvement can come from employee-friendly programs such as teams and continuous process improvement, not just from productivity programs that require massive layoffs.

Shrinking Complexity, Waste, Time, And Everything Else

Operational efficiency can be significantly improved by shrinking elements of the company's production process. This is analogous to the old, old notion of "minimizing the number of moving parts" as a way to keep things simple. A more modern analogy is the ever-shrinking integrated circuit; the smaller and denser it is, the faster and cheaper it runs. The items listed in Exhibit 8-2 are good candidates for the kind of shrinking that will improve operational efficiency.

There are three logical steps for shrinking inefficiency. I explain these using manufacturing terms and concepts, which apply equally to service operations and can serve as metaphors for improvement.

Design for Manufacturability

Logically, the first thing to do is to design the product/service to make it easy to produce in the first place; in manufacturing terminology this is called "design for manufacturability." The next logical step is to design highly efficient processes that produce the goods or service; in manufacturing lingo this is called "lean manufacturing." The last step is to apply technology to automate the plant, which too often is seen as the quintessential quick fix and as the first step in the process.

Support for this logical sequence is presented in the book by James Womack et al., *The Machine That Changed the World* (1990), which found that 41 percent of the difference in manufacturing cost between a high- and a low-cost car was attributable to design for manufacturability. For example, the bumper in the lower-cost car had only ten parts, compared with one hundred parts for the high-cost car. Another finding was that the most efficient auto manufacturing plant in the world is only moderately automated,

Exhibit 8-2. Things that can shrink.

• Product/service complexity	• Packaging of any type
• Number of parts per product	• Setup and changeover times for
• Job classes and specialization	machines
• Number of suppliers	• Downtime with scheduled
• Cycle time in every process	maintenance and rebuilds
• Rework	• Number of warehouses
• Transportation costs	• Paperwork
• Surplus plants	• Legal contractual work
• Inventory of all types	• Space between machines

while some of the most automated plants in the world rank among the least productive.

Although this sequence of priorities is logical, American manufacturers too often reverse the process, seeking quick-fix solutions from technology and automation rather than first simplifying what they are planning to produce and then streamlining the processes to make it.

The first step, design for manufacturability, is achieved by creating cross-functional design teams that represent marketing, engineering, manufacturing, and other relevant functions. In addition to creating a superior product in record time, these teams design a product that is easy to make.

One example of a logical design concept is to minimize the number of parts in the product. Roy L. Harmon, in *Reinventing the Factory II*, notes, "The importance of limiting the number of components can't be overstated. A product that uses fewer parts automatically requires less labor and fewer purchases, tools, fixtures, and machines." He estimates that superior design for ease of manufacturing can reduce manufacturing costs by 30 to 50 percent.

Here are some examples of companies that have successfully designed products that are easy to make:

DIGITAL EQUIPMENT designed an easy-to-manufacture computer mouse that had no screws and that reduced overall assembly time by 53 percent, materials costs by 47 percent, and packaging materials by over 50 percent.

SMITH CORONA simplified its typewriters to make them easier to build by radically reducing the original three thousand parts in earlier models, many of which were moving parts.

BELL AND HOWELL redesigned its projector using plastic molding to reduce the number of metal parts from one hundred to six.

IBM's head disk assembly plant substantially reduced the number of parts per product, which enabled it to reduce (1) production hours by one half, (2) manufacturing floor space by 50 percent, and (3) cycle time by a factor of three.

Design for manufacturability depends on cross-functional design teams in processes variously called "concurrent" or "simultaneous" design. Teams of people from all relevant functions work together, contributing their perspectives along the way. This maximizes the chances that the product will be something that manufacturing can easily make, that customers will want to buy, and that the company can sell at a profit.

In the traditional development approach, engineering finishes its design, then hands it off to manufacturing to make; manufacturing then sends it to marketing to sell. If problems arise with the design's makeability or salability, engineering has to go back to the drawing board for another cycle of design and rework.

Concurrent design eliminates this rework cycle and enables tasks with long lead times to be undertaken in parallel, greatly shrinking cycle time. For example, if manufacturing and engineering can agree on a preliminary design concept, manufacturing can line up suppliers early in the design process (as opposed to the end of it). Concurrent design can reduce product development time by 50 to 75 percent; for example, HP used concurrent design to reduce the time it took to develop its highly competitive computer printer products from four and one half years to less than two years.

Lean Manufacturing

The second step, lean manufacturing, is a concept well documented in *The Machine That Changed the World*, which was researched by an MIT team investigating the global auto manufacturing process. As the author noted, "Lean production is lean because it uses less of everything compared with mass production—half the human effort in the factory, half the manufacturing space, half the investment in tools, half the engineering hours to develop a new product in half the time."

Lean manufacturing is achieved by a management geared toward reducing waste of any type within the context of continuous improvement. Reducing waste includes anything from stopping rework at its source to sharply reducing inventories with better planning and coordination. Two important ideas that underlie lean manufacturing are cross-functional coordination and collaborating with external partners.

In cross-functional coordination, employee teams from different functional areas work together in close cooperation to solve problems, develop products, prepare strategic plans, and perform the day-to-day production of goods and services. This approach contrasts sharply with the traditional approach of narrowly defined jobs and frequent hand-offs to other functions or departments.

Cross-functional coordination has significant payoffs when it is applied to the actual production function, where work teams consist of multiple skills and all team members are cross-trained to do multiple jobs. The payoff comes in several ways. First, since they have knowledge of all the components of the process, cross-functional work teams can solve day-to-day problems on their own. Cross-functional teams are more flexible in adapting to changes in production cycles and manufacturing needs. For example, the United Motor Manufacturing joint venture between GM and Toyota created cross-functional teams and reduced the number of its job types from 180 to three. The three remaining were highly mobile jobs, able to adapt to changes in production cycles.

These cross-functional teams perform many of the tasks traditionally performed by specialists with narrowly defined jobs. Japanese auto makers rely on production teams to perform functions (e.g., machine maintenance) that their U.S. counterparts normally assign to a specialized maintenance crew. The efficiency comes from eliminating these extra support positions; the production staff performs these functions in and around peaks and valleys in the production process.

Collaborating with external partners means working closely with suppliers, joint venture partners, and partners in strategic alliances for operational improvements that neither party could achieve alone. To benefit from this collaboration requires ending the "not invented here" thinking and substituting a close working relationship for mutual gain, based on a lot of mutual trust.

Collaborating with suppliers requires a wholly new philosophy towards the purchasing function. Traditionally, the purchasing function has involved the buyer's solicitation of proposals from a large number of potential "vendors." The vendors respond to tightly defined specifications, and the one with the lowest price wins. The process is marked by mistrust, suspicion, a lack of cooperation, and—usually—low integrity. Suppliers and buyers play games at each other's expense; the buyer uses every opportunity to ratchet down bid prices; the suppliers seek to recover profitability by delivering less than they promised, increasing their prices with every change to the original specifications. In this environment, neither party is to be trusted, and for good reason.

In the collaborative model, the buyer chooses a few select suppliers. They establish collaborative relationships based on a commitment to continually improving both companies' operations. The buyer exempts the chosen suppliers from bid processes so long as the relationship lasts. The buyer also integrates the two companies' operations in coordinating, product planning and design, sharing improvement ideas, and R&D and may also train the supplier in process improvement.

In exchange, the supplier commits to strict quality and delivery standards, especially agreements to deliver supplies according to "just-in-time" (JIT) standards. (JIT requires the supplier to deliver parts or services right when the buyer needs them, which nearly eliminates inventories and the associated factory space and materials handling costs.)

It is important to understand that collaboration with suppliers is more than just the highly popular JIT. To require that suppliers deliver their goods according to JIT standards misses the point. Lean manufacturing means that each party helps the partnership by eliminating waste: The supplier is also expected to show improvements in its own operation that will be shared with the buying firm. JIT is but one element of a broader relationship dynamic.

The payoff for collaborating with suppliers is substantial. First, the buying company can delegate the preparation of much of the detailed design work and specifications, normally done-in-house, to the supplier. This practice is popular among Japanese auto makers, who do detailed engineering for only 30 percent of their parts (compared with 81 percent for American manufacturers). The closer working relationship also enables the supplier to understand better the buyer's requirements and the buyer to

understand better the supplier's capabilities. Ideas for improving
processes flow both ways.

The collaboration also simplifies the buyer's purchasing process by reducing the number of suppliers. A long-term contractual
relationship cuts the hassle of dealing with a lot of different
suppliers. *The Machine That Changed the World* credits this form of
collaboration to Toyota, which had only 337 people in parts
purchasing compared with GM's 6,000—despite the fact that
Toyota relied more on its suppliers than GM.

Trust and integrity, themes that run throughout this book,
are critical to buyer-supplier relationships. Once the deal is
struck, each party is expected to go to great lengths to meet
commitments and to help each other out when problems occur.
Patricia Moody's book *Breakthrough Partnering* lists trust as one of
the key elements in establishing truly efficient partnership relationships with suppliers. As she notes, "Trust lies at the heart of
all partnering activities."

Kingston Technology, which makes electronic components
that enhance PCs, attributes much of its success to trusting
relationships with its suppliers. An executive from Hitachi, an
important Kingston supplier, commented in *Inc.* magazine (October 1992), "Integrity, that is how I'd sum up Kingston in a
word. We have a strong partnership with Kingston. We don't
share that with a lot of its competitors."

Collaborative relationships can also include a range of external parties who share costs and/or profits and who perform
functions for the company better than the company could do by
itself. This includes all forms of outsourcing, as well as strategic
alliances and joint ventures. Taken to an extreme, a company
might conceivably exist as a minimal shell, outsourcing all functions to external parties. This concept is called "the virtual corporation."

Collaboration with external parties is especially beneficial
when the company needs to enter a market quickly and without
developing costly infrastructure. This is the case when the external parties have a significant functional advantage or when the
company does not have the resources to pursue an opportunity
on its own, as in the case of joint ventures to develop a new
technology.

Automation

The third step is to apply automation technology to replace labor-intensive tasks, better control operations, and collect valuable information that helps optimize work flow. The available technology for automating operations is vast and growing, including such popular technologies as computer integrated manufacturing, robotics, bar code scanning, expert systems, and electronic data interchange. Nevertheless, you should first employ the prior two steps—design for manufacturability and lean operations—before applying technology; otherwise you may automate functions and elements of the business that should not exist to start with. This thinking is similar to the reengineering notion of "don't automate; obliterate." As authors Michael Hammer and James Champy noted in their book *Reengineering the Corporation*, "Automating existing processes with information technology is analogous to paving cow paths. Automation simply provides more efficient ways of doing the wrong kinds of things."

Information as a Strategic Asset

Information is a vital strategic asset. Lacking information, management operates in the dark. Ill-informed decisions and myths fill the information voids, creating entrenched cultural barriers to operational improvement. Each new idea is met with "That will never work. We already tried that and it failed miserably." Facts about the business can quickly dispel myths, enabling the company to proceed with continuous improvement. What I am going to talk about here is the value of information in coordinating operations, assessing performance, improving operations, and capitalizing on institutional knowledge.

Coordinating Operations

Information is a major component of lean manufacturing. It is used to predict customer demand and to coordinate operations within the plant and with suppliers.

The ability to predict customer demand is critical if you want to know what and how much to make of a particular product. If you are able to predict demand precisely, you can schedule production processes efficiently. You might even be able to eliminate nearly all types of inventories. As far from reality as this ideal may be today, it is nonetheless important to get as clear a reading as you can on customer demand.

The sales staffs at Toyota dealerships in Japan, for instance, conduct door-to-door interviews with existing and prospective customers to determine the number and the age of customers' cars and when the family plans to replace them. Toyota uses this information to forecast customer purchases of cars and particular trends in the type of car that customers are likely to purchase. U.S. car makers, on the other hand, take a "wait-and-see" approach and design and ultimately produce cars in a multiyear process. When the cars finally hit the market, management desperately hopes it can sell what it has geared up to produce. Mistakes cost billions of dollars.

At a minimum, you should obtain the most recent sales data possible. If you can get instantaneous information, so much the better. This is where point-of-sale terminals and bar-coding play a key role, capturing purchase decisions the instant they are made and enabling managers to coordinate operations better. A sophisticated in-store computer system that coordinates consumer purchase data via a cash register that records product and brand type, as well as manually keyed-in data on the profile of the customer, helps managers of units of 7-Eleven Japan to know what is being sold, to whom, at what time of the day, and so forth. This enables the managers to stock their stores with precisely the right items in right amounts at the right time.

Sharing information within an operations center or plant is essential for running a lean operation. In the book *The Machine That Changed the World*, the authors observe:

> In a lean plant, . . . all information—daily production targets, cars produced so far that day, equipment breakdowns, personnel shortages, overtime requirements, and so forth—are displayed on . . . [lighted electronic displays] that are visible from every workstation. Every

time anything goes wrong anywhere in the plant, any employee who knows how to help runs to lend a hand.

With electronic sensors and other detection devices, production operations are flush with information that can be captured, interpreted, and shared to gain efficiencies through coordination.

Information is essential for coordinating with suppliers. The more closely coordinated your operations are with your suppliers', the more critical it is to have timely information on customer demand, production schedules, and required delivery times. JIT is unworkable without critical information linkages. Bar-coding technology is useful for collecting real-time sales data at the checkout counter; it enables the retailer to pass current purchase data along to key suppliers instantly for their own planning purposes. Such linkages are commonly used by Wal-Mart, 7-Eleven Japan, and Home Depot.

Assessing Performance

"You cannot manage what you cannot measure." So said W. Edwards Deming in his 1956 book *Quality, Productivity and Competitive Position,* and his advice remains ever true. It is impossible to pursue continuous improvement and to hold people and teams accountable for performance without factual scorecards and reasonable benchmarks to gauge results.

Most companies have few performance measures beyond overall profitability. What they need is a whole array of measures to indicate performance across critical areas such as market share, sales productivity, unit costs and productivity, error rates, and customer and employee satisfaction. Tracking customer and employee satisfaction is something that a well-run company should always do; this is a critical bottom-line measure for the company.

Furthermore, while most companies know their overall cost and profitability, very few have information broken down by customers, market segments, products and services, and geographic locations. In the absence of these cost and profit data, management is destined to make less-than-optimal pricing decisions, misallocate resources, and continue unprofitable operations while underinvesting in those that do contribute.

Improving Operations

Efforts to improve operations depend on collecting and analyzing information that reveals problems, their root causes, and improvement opportunities. Four important sources of improvement information are clients, employees, competitors, and other companies with functions similar to your own.

Customers flood corporations with valuable information on improvement ideas. These come in the form of complaints, inquiries, and suggestions voiced to salespeople, customer service workers, and other employees who have customer contact. The company needs an organized process for mining this information; otherwise, all of it gets lost.

Hewlett-Packard has a standard process for collecting and analyzing customer comments. As HP's Alan Bickell describes it: "Every large firm has enormous amounts of data on trends and actions, and most of it gets lost. We have a process to get information into a form that we can do something with by sharing it throughout the organization." HP's system involves about a hundred customer feedback analysts, located throughout the world. These analysts are responsible for obtaining information on problems that occur throughout the company, coding information on the specific nature of problems and their causes, and entering the information into a database. HP's business units can then tap into the database to collect information on related problems, and they can share it in a summarized form with the staff responsible for the particular process or products

Employees are a rich source of improvement information, and finding ways to tap their knowledge can provide a big payoff. Donnelly has a very effective suggestion system that yields three to five suggestions per employee (most companies with suggestion systems receive far fewer than one per employee). Donnelly notes that a high percentage of employee ideas are concerned with cutting costs and improving operations; the dollar range of payoffs in savings ranges from very small to hundreds of thousands of dollars. Donnelly attributes the success of its suggestion system to its policy of responding within two days to all employees who submit suggestions and recognizing employees' contributions with small tokens of appreciation—tickets for a movie, for example.

GE has a formal process, called "workout," that brings front-line workers together to discuss improvement ideas of all types and requires management to respond immediately to the assembled group with the company's plans. In a *USA Today* (July 26, 1993) interview, GE CEO Jack Welch described the payoff from this process: "We don't get just 10 percent or 15 percent of our ideas from hourly workers. We get 100 percent of the ideas from them."

Another source of improvement information is your competitors and companies outside your industry who perform similar functions especially well. The Japanese in particular are big users of benchmarking, or systematically comparing aspects of your operation to comparable functions in other companies with superior performance; it is a normal part of their continual improvement efforts. Donnelly Corp. is a strong believer in benchmarking and has formed an active network of companies outside its industry that exchange information. Maryam Komejan commented, "It is essential that we don't work in a vacuum. We have a way of learning from other firms."

Institutional Knowledge

The knowledge accumulated by your workers is a valuable asset that resides in the heads of individuals and is thus likely to stay buried deep in the organization. As someone once observed, "If we knew what we knew, we would be brilliant."

Information technology is making it much easier to mine the company's institutional knowledge. Three such technologies are:

1. *Groupware,* which allows many people to communicate with each other via electronic bulletin boards. Groupware enables "knowledge workers" to transform disparate data from around the company into valuable information and to make it available to all employees.
2. *Expert systems,* which enable companies to store facts, judgments, and relationships about a particular process

or activity that normally reside within the heads of experienced workers.

3. *Human resource information systems,* which store information on the skills and knowledge of every worker in the company, thus enabling the company to tap the right resources for a particular task. This information is normally unavailable in large organizations.

Although much of the literature on operational improvement focuses on the production function, the same concepts we have looked at so far are equally applicable to support functions, such as human resources and finance. In fact, most companies that are serious about significant operational improvement eventually get around to focusing attention on the quality and efficiency of support functions, regardless of whether the head of a support function volunteers for such a renovation process.

Typically, people in overhead and administrative positions are maligned as being too costly and as providing too little value to customers or the company. This is only partly true. Many companies are indeed burdened with hidebound administrative support functions. Roy L. Harmon and Leroy D. Peterson, authors of *Reinventing the Factory,* note that American and European companies typically have ten times more employees in administrative jobs than do comparable Japanese operations.

But support functions can be restructured to provide high-quality, low-cost services of significant value to the company's line operations and thus (indirectly) to customers. Human resources workers can make sure the company attracts, retains, and develops the highest-quality people possible; financial functions can help line management to make better business decisions by generating timely and cogent analyses of the business.

Managements of support functions must, however, adopt the same commitment to continuous quantum-leap improvement goals as their production counterparts. Like business units, support functions must start by defining who their internal customers are and what they value. Management should then set quantum-leap goals to improve cycle times, responsiveness, service quality, and productivity in performing the function. Motorola, Federal Express, Corning, and other businesses committed to continuous improvement have applied this approach to their support functions with much success.

Easy Access Is the Price of Admission

This discussion of operational excellence would be incomplete without the simple concluding note that however good—even technologically advanced—your products and services may be, customers will always view your company as a hopeless bureaucracy if they have any difficulty in getting through to the right person and having their matter quickly and courteously resolved.

Two decades ago, this practice of easy access was leading-edge and provided a competitive advantage, differentiating companies such as L. L. Bean and Fidelity from the pack. Today, it is a basic requirement for any company that hopes to be a major player in its market.

Management needs to audit all the many ways the company touches and communicates with the outside world. The audit should begin with the receptionist and go on to internal phone handling, external phone communication (facilitating access to the company through 800 numbers is standard practice today), written correspondence, and catalogs. Once it begins to use good communications practices, your company has got to adhere to the highest response standards, for example, picking up inbound calls quickly, answering more than 90 percent of the customer's questions without routing the call to someone else or promising to call back, completing transactions while on the line with the customer, and delivering the product the next day.

Chapter 9

Managing The Organization

As a topic, managing the organization is extensive and complex. In this chapter I discuss the five management qualities that are essential for market ownership to work. They are:

1. Integrity
2. Long-term commitment
3. Customer orientation
4. Employee orientation
5. Organizational connectivity

Together, these five management themes form a foundation for building a superior organization that can own its market. I provide a brief note on the importance of each and describe the key actions a company can take to incorporate these qualities into its culture and organization. I also address the importance of managing the key drivers of organizational behavior, such as the company's reward systems.

Because the five characteristics are closely interrelated, it is difficult to utilize any one of them successfully without also adopting the others. Many of them must be approached in similar ways. For example, all five qualities require that significant top management commitment be demonstrated in both words and actions.

The Integral Role of Integrity

Integrity is central to the concept of market ownership. I have mentioned integrity earlier in this book as critical to acquiring and retaining—and perhaps even selecting—customers and to dealing with suppliers.

Integrity means fairness, a soundness and an honesty that are integral parts of the company's functioning. Integrity means meeting commitments to the company's many stakeholders—all those parties that have vested interests in the company, such as customers, employees, providers of capital, suppliers, and the communities in which the company operates.

Integrity is essential to building a business that can succeed over the long term. When a company is consistently fair to its multiple stakeholders, it receives many benefits that have significant economic payoffs:

- With *clients*, integrity builds trust that enhances brand loyalty, deeper product relationships, free word-of-mouth advertising, and protection from price competition.
- With *employees*, integrity repays itself with stronger commitment to the company and its goals, and in higher productivity.
- With *capital markets*, integrity provides the company with a lower cost of capital, since investors trust the company's projections and do not need extra margins for uncertainty. It also means that the stock price will hold up when there are down-ticks in quarterly earnings.
- With *suppliers*, integrity is essential for building the strong partnerships that provide mutual competitive advantages.
- With *local communities*, integrity in dealings means that there will be better support when plans call for regulatory approval.
- With the *media*, integrity means that the company's spokespersons are more believable, which can have a significant impact on the company's image.

Like the market ownership concept in general, integrity is not the only way to create a profitable business. For sure, there are those executives who see integrity as a naive concept, something that impedes success. (This depends on how you define success. As Norman Vincent Peale and Kenneth Blanchard note in *The Power of Ethical Management*, "Nice guys may appear to finish last, but usually they're running in a different race.")

The ultimate benefit of integrity is long-term sustainability of the company's profitability. In the short term, it may well be easier to create a highly profitable business by cutting corners and doing what is expedient, rather than assiduously fulfilling agreements and ensuring fairness. However, over the long haul, small indiscretions mount up. When a company encounters tough times, as most companies do periodically, its various stakeholders will be reluctant to bail them out. Thus, if you seek to develop a company that sustains high margins long-term, integrity must become an essential building block in the strategy. It is perhaps for this reason that, in a 1989 study by Korn Ferry entitled "Reinventing the CEO," the majority of the CEOs polled believed that integrity was the most important quality for corporate leaders of the future.

Management Levers

Integrity is a cultural value that must be built and sustained through a long-term commitment. Management has three main ways to instill it in the organization:

1. Demonstrating leadership
2. Developing employees in a homegrown environment
3. Managing the company's behavioral drivers

1. *Demonstrating leadership.* Top management's commitment to, and strong belief in, integrity is essential for building it into the company's corporate culture. Moreover, top management must lead the organization by actions as well as words and must insist that the rest of the organization adhere to high standards.

Management must take every opportunity to state and restate the importance of integrity as part of the company's value and ethic, even at the risk of seeming redundant. It should also incorporate integrity into its mission statement and any other corporate announcements that outline values. Donnelly's statement of corporate values (Exhibit 9-1) includes integrity as one of the many characteristics central to the market ownership concept.

Actions speak even more loudly. They can run the gamut from setting a good example in day-to-day business decisions to charitable deeds. How top management deals with various stakeholders to honor its agreements, meet contracts, honor deadlines, and deliver on its promises sends a strong message to employees. Integrity in action means not cutting corners on honoring commitments with customers, not doing the expedient at the expense of some stakeholder, not wringing extra profit from suppliers beyond original agreements. During an interview with *Inc.* magazine (October 1992), Kingston Technology's co-founder David Sun commented on delaying the payment of suppliers' bills: "For a fraction of a percent you suddenly become an unethical person."

Maryam Komejan, corporate vice president for Donnelly,

Exhibit 9-1. Donnelly's "corporate values statements."

We believe these elements of be essential in operating our business:

1. We serve our customers with excellence; our existence depends on them.
2. We respect people. They are important and we empower them.
3. We are highly productive through participation, teamwork, and accountability.
4. We demonstrate integrity, high ethical standards, and respect for the community and environment in all of our actions.
5. We are a manufacturing organization thriving on change, committed to continuous improvement, and achieving zero defects in all areas.
6. We have strong leadership at all levels, which is critical to our success.
7. We expand and strengthen synergistic core competencies.
8. We select products based on strong competitive advantage, high profitability, and global potential.
9. We grow profitably to achieve security and above-average returns for employees and shareholders.
10. We support long-term cooperative relationships with excellent suppliers.

explained that her company manages integrity primarily by having top management present clear role models: "Top management models expected behavior. You never see senior managers
promise something they have no intention of delivering, or doing
something expedient to avoid uncomfortable situations."

Actions that demonstrate integrity include turning down
business from prospects who fail to meet the company's standards or who have requirements that management honestly believes its company cannot deliver. It also means refusing to do
business with suppliers who do not meet corporate standards,
even though they may offer a better financial deal. (Home Depot,
for example, has a policy of making sure that no foreign trading
partners use child or prison labor or engage in business practices
that are unacceptable to Home Depot. These practices underscore
its philosophy.) Integrity can also mean helping a valued supplier
who needs some assistance with financing. It means taking back
products from dissatisfied customers.

In December 1989, Lexus's management set new standards
in managing product defects by admitting to problems and undertaking an expedient recall. This helped build the Lexus reputation and stands in sharp contrast to various other auto makers
who tend to deny that problems exist. Such companies succeed
only in tarnishing their image and creating mistrust among all
stakeholders.

As I have noted, management's policies and procedures are
important tools for managing integrity. A good example is HP's
insistence that it will rely only on product and market share
rankings prepared by outside parties, such as the many consulting companies that follow the computer industry. This builds
HP's credibility in its marketing efforts, keeps employees from
making self-serving claims, and sends a strong message to the
organization.

Actions that support integrity extend even to corporate phi-
lanthropy. Home Depot, for example, invests money in its local
communities to develop or rehabilitate affordable housing for the
poor. It has an employee volunteer program called Team Depot,
which helps low-income families build housing projects. In the
aftermath of Hurricane Andrew, which ravaged south Florida in
1992, Home Depot sold plywood at a loss to those who needed

it, while other suppliers marked up their merchandise by as much as 40 percent.

Supporting integrity also means refusing to tolerate unacceptable behavior by the company's employees, especially by top managers and others who are seen as successful in the company. Management's toleration of undesirable behavior makes a mockery of corporate values and sends the clear message (in fact, the true message) that current profits mean more than shared values. On this point, Jack Welch, CEO of GE, commented in a *USA Today* (July 26, 1993) interview:

> Numbers [i.e., financial results] are no longer security. Values and numbers now mean job security. The hardest thing in the world is to move against somebody who is delivering the goods but acting 180 degrees [different] from your values. But if you don't act, you're not walking the talk and you're just an air bag. [Copyright 1993, *USA Today*. Reprinted with permission.]

2. *Developing employees in a homegrown environment.* The second management lever is the creation of a homegrown culture that stresses high integrity. This starts with taking care to hire entry-level staff who demonstrate strong innate personal integrity. This characteristic can be detected through interviews and tests. Although employee testing remains a controversial subject, research conducted by the University of Iowa in 1990 found that many personality tests can easily detect dishonest people, in part because, as one of the researchers quoted in *Personnel Journal* (May 1990) noted, "It is very difficult for dishonest people to fake honesty."

Training employees and managers in integrity and ethical business conduct is another important tactic for reinforcing desired behavior. Such training is especially important for the company's managers, who face numerous ethical issues that arise in daily business activity. Home Depot, for example, conducts management workshops on ethics and related workplace issues. And unlike some retail companies, it trains its salespeople to help customers not to overspend but to find low-cost solutions to their home improvement projects.

Developing a high-integrity organization is much easier to accomplish in a homegrown environment, promoting from within when at all possible. Hiring high-level entrants into the company not only sends a bad message about promotional opportunities to employees but also brings in people from different cultures with different attitudes regarding integrity. Hiring high-level entrants should be the exception, not the rule, for building the organization. When such hiring must be done, it should be done with great caution, ensuring that the new people fit the company's standards.

The company must also control its growth. Growth should not outstrip the company's ability to hire and develop employees. Too-fast growth creates extreme pressures to lower standards, hire people who do not fit the criteria, put people into jobs before they are fully trained, cut back on quality measures, fulfill an order any which way, and make any sale possible. It also makes it impossible to maintain a corporate value system and to manage integrity throughout the organization. Managed growth on the other hand, enables the company to acquire the needed resources in a planned way and to ensure that the integrity of the company's staff, management, and operations continues to meet high standards.

Similarly, seeking growth through mergers and acquisitions can pose a threat to managing integrity. In a merger, a company's value system goes up for grabs. The likely outcome is that one of the two corporate cultures will survive or that a third one will emerge. The same applies to major acquisitions, which can link the company with a different value system that does not place much importance on integrity. American Express's acquisition of Shearson dragged it into all sorts of controversial deals, such as a bid to buy RJR Nabisco. Prudential's acquisition of Bache Halsey Stuart Shields—now called Prudential Securities—has created enormous drains on its attempts to build an image of trust and integrity. While Prudential advertises that "the most important thing we earn is your trust," the government has ordered the company to pay about $300 million in restitution to the 400,000 customers who lost money on limited partnerships due to " 'false and misleading information' according to the SEC," noted *Business Week* (November 1, 1993).

3. *Managing the company's organizational drivers.* The third management lever is to control the drivers of organizational behavior to make sure they influence the company to act ethically. The company's reward system, which includes monetary compensation, promotions, and recognition, is a critical driver of organizational behavior. For example, it is important to avoid reward systems that drive employees to act out of desperation to cut corners, underserve clients, and otherwise demonstrate a lack of integrity. This is clearly a problem with salespeople who are compensated on pure commission.

Similarly, the company's performance measures drive employee behavior. If a company measures only throughput, for example, it will influence employees to do poor-quality work and to underserve customers. It is a good idea to ask customers to rate your company on integrity as part of your customer satisfaction surveys.

Taking the Long View

Market ownership requires that the company and its employees have a long-term commitment to stay focused on the company's core business, sticking with the company's strategy with sufficient commitment, and emphasizing long-term financial health over growth.

Staying focused on the core business is what Tom Peters and Bob Waterman, the authors of *In Search of Excellence,* called "sticking to your knitting"—staying close to the company's defined business scope and what it knows how to do best. This is critical to keep the company from straying into unrelated activities that can weaken it and waste its resources.

The second long-term commitment is to give the company's strategy sufficient time and resources to successfully implement it. Almost nothing worthwhile can be accomplished in the course of the annual budget cycle; three to five years is the minimum duration of a business plan. A long-term, dedicated commitment to a mediocre strategy will always beat out a brilliant, short-term plan that has little commitment behind it.

Donnelly's long-term commitment to its strategies has enabled it to further its lead in its industry. Unlike its competitors, Donnelly maintained its R&D spending during industry slumps and came out way ahead of its competitors. Donnelly's president noted in *IndustryWeek*, "If we had cut back on R&D spending for the short term we would have shown higher profits, but we would have hurt ourselves for the long term. Now we have the luxury of picking and choosing from so many opportunties while other companies in the automotive supply business are cutting back and trying to figure out how to survive or are downsizing." (Reprinted with permission from *IndustryWeek*, February 1, 1993. Copyright Penton Publishing, Inc., Cleveland, Ohio.)

The third long-range commitment is to the company's long-term financial health, which enables the company to weather industry slumps and to emerge much stronger than competitors that were financially stretched at the outset. As the weaker players cut back on staff and customer service, the stronger can pick up their disgruntled customers.

Goldman Sachs and Drexel Burnham Lambert provide an excellent contrasting illustration of financial objectives. Through its controversial and explosive growth in junk-bond dealing, Drexel rose to the top of the securities business within just a few short years, only to collapse and go out of business a few months later. In contrast, Goldman Sachs has grown steadily over decades in a managed way and with a strong capital base. As a result, it has emerged as a dominant company in the international securities industry.

Management Levers

U.S. companies' fixation with short-term and quarterly earnings reports has become so widespread that it has been singled out as a national crisis in global competitiveness. In fact, most companies operate quarter to quarter, and their annual budgets substitute for long-range planning.

Capital markets have been much to blame for top managements' short-term orientation. Indeed, it is much easier for privately held companies to commit to long-range plans. As Intuit's CEO, Scott Cook, noted in *Inc.* magazine (April 1991), "When you own the company, you take the long view so that management can attend to long-term interests." CEOs at publicly owned companies turn shortsighted when they fear that they will be ousted by a hostile takeover, or fired because the company's quarterly earnings and stock price have dropped.

Whether a company is privately or publicly held, there are five key elements that top management can use to build a long-term orientation within the company and to keep it from becoming a sitting duck for a takeover:

1. Developing long-term strategic plans
2. Investing in the company's future
3. Employing performance measures that influence long-term thinking
4. Treating shareholders like owners (which they are)
5. Sharing power

1. *Developing long-term plans.* Long-term perspective starts with a long-term vision of the business and investment in the future. Senior management must acquire skills in long-range strategic planning; it must see strategic planning as a critical aspect of its job and not something to farm out to support staff or outside consultants. If top management participates in the development of long-range plans and has confidence in its planning skills, then it will stick with its plans. Plans that fail to gain top management commitment get ditched at the slightest blip in earnings, causing the company to have a short-term orientation.

Long-range planning is not the same as long-range forecasting. No one can accurately predict the future of the economy or of an individual industry, customers, and competition. Planners should, however, be able to develop a set of plausible scenarios about the company's future environment that help set the context for developing long-range plans. Author Peter Schwartz, in his book *The Art of the Long View*, suggests that companies develop a range of future scenarios five to ten years out as a basis for long-range planning.

Donnelly has a ten-year planning cycle that it revises as needed and updates every three to five years. In the 1970s, it envisioned the increased global presence of Japanese auto makers, developed a long-range plan to secure them as customers, and stuck with it. Don Auch, vice president of marketing and sales, commented, "Looking five to ten years out, we knew that the Japanese market was very important to Donnelly when you look at it on a global basis. It took us five years of operating in Japan before we got our first job. Others would have walked away after six months. But our relationships in Japan made us the favored suppliers to the Japanese operations set up in the United States."

By using a clear definition of core competencies—the things that the company does especially well—to define the scope of the company and its future plans, the long-range plan becomes a tool to keep the company focused. Nothing attracts hostile takeovers like unfocused companies that have loaded up on unrelated business activities.

There are large numbers of once strong companies that were once dominant leaders in their businesses but that were weakened when they strayed outside their core businesses. The list includes Honeywell's venture out of its core instrument business into mainframe computers; Texas Instrument's venture outside its integrated circuit business into consumer electronics, such as watches, calculators, and personal computers; Southern Pacific's venture out of its railroad business into title insurance, real estate development, vineyards, telecommunications, and pipelines; United Airline's venture into the hospitality business; and Prudential's and American Express's ventures into the securities industry.

In contrast, there are a number of companies that have either stayed with their core businesses or have made sensible ventures into new areas that draw on their core competencies. Intel is a good example; the company has focused intensely on the integrated circuit business and is one of the few U.S. companies to lead the industry. Donnelly has carefully leveraged its core competencies in making mirrors for cars to producing special glass products used in computer displays.

To guide its scope of business, DPIC Companies uses what it calls its three core values, which include a belief that litigation can be avoided, a commitment to low-cost resolution to disputes when they arise, and specialization. DPIC's CEO, Peter Hawes, said this about diversification: "It starts with our core fundamentals. We wouldn't do anything that our approach wouldn't apply to." This is why DPIC has carefully chosen to branch into professional liability insurance for public accounting firms and, more recently, law firms. As Hawes noted, "The principles apply."

2. *Investing in the company's future.* The second aspect of long-term thinking is for management to invest in the future of the company by setting the right financial priorities. This means investing in the future by hiring and training people today who will serve the needs of the company five and ten years out. It includes sufficiently high and sustained investment in R&D and product development. Donnelly, for example, invests 5 percent of its revenues in R&D, which is five times the industry average. In contrast, the short-term-oriented company is quick to mortgage its future by scrapping hiring plans, R&D, and training, particularly whenever current earnings fall short.

The excessive use of corporate debt also causes companies to emphasize the present at the expense of the future. When a company loads up too much debt, as in the case of a mangement buyout, management's attention becomes completely short-term-oriented, focused on meeting the next loan payment. Excessive debt also causes management to make sacrifices, such as cutting the R&D investments that are the future of the company. In this environment, management gives little thought to strategic planning and to the long-term success of the company.

3. *Selecting a performance measuring system.* The third driver of long-term thinking is the company's performance measurement system. Profitability is a barrier to long-range thinking for those companies that rely on it as the only measure of success. Profitability is a very narrow, excessively short-term-oriented gauge of success. The truth is that current profitability measures past actions; it tells you nothing about the future. Peter Drucker noted in his book *Management,* "To emphasize only profit misdirects managers to the point where they may endanger the survival of the business. To obtain profit today, they tend to undermine the future."

What the company needs is a host of performance measures that track broader trends, such as market share, customer retention, and employee retention and development. The measures must also include leading indicators of performance. For example, customer satisfaction is a leading indicator of customer retention, which in turn is a major driver of profitability.

4. *Including shareholders in the business.* The fourth tactic for instilling long-term thinking is to include the company's shareholders in the business; communicate clearly, frequently, and

openly with them; and share with them the company's long-range strategic plan. In *Across the Board* (March 1992), Michael Jacobs, author of *Short-Term America*, noted, "Corporations have gone out of their way to make large owners unwelcome."

This lack of forthright disclosure to investors probably exists for good reason. How many companies have a long-term plan that is sound enough to give investors confidence in the company for the long term? How many companies obfuscate their quarterly and annual earnings, smooth over embarrassing details, and take short-term measures to manage earnings at the expense of future performance? Probably the vast majority of publicly traded companies do these things to give shareholders the serene, yet false, sense of ever-steady earnings growth.

The investment community employs hundreds of thousands of people whose job it is to break through the smokescreen and discern fact from fiction. As *Industry Week* (March 1, 1993) said: "Public relations blather won't do; the financial community is not easily taken in. What the Street wants is the straight goods—and no surprises." It is no wonder that this community looks to current earnings as the critical measure of veracity.

On the other hand, if management has a sound strategy that it believes in and that spells out the good with the bad, then it should share that strategy openly with the investment community. Those investors who buy into the long-term plan are likely to stick with the company regardless of fluctuations in quarterly earnings—so long as the company sticks with what its plan calls for it to do.

Assuming management is confident of its long-term plans, it should be forthright with the investment community. For example, Cooper Tire & Rubber has adopted an attitude of openness, and arranges for investors to tour its plants and interview its management. Cooper CFO Alec Reinhardt told *Industry Week* (March 1, 1993), "We gave the analysts a sense that we realized that what they were doing was important, that we wanted to help them."

5. *Sharing power.* A fifth related tactic is for to management to share power in running the company, starting by having a board of directors that is active in the business and not just a rubber stamp.

This means having a heavy board representation of large

investors, not a CEO-appointed board. The board should also be active in the business and have sufficient knowledge of the company's operations to make intelligent decisions regarding its future. The directors of Home Depot, for instance, are required to spend time as store employees in order to understand the business and to gauge its performance.

The author Michael Jacobs has a different model for the typical board member:

> [Directors] would spend significant time getting to know the company, talking to customers, talking to suppliers, looking at markets, understanding the strategy of the business, visiting plants, and so on. If the definition of a responsible director is not to disagree or argue with anything that the chief executive says, then I think we have totally dysfunctional boards. [*Across the Board*, March 1992].

Another tactic is for the CEO to share power by reporting directly to a chairman of the board. In the United States, the role of the CEO is something of an all-or-nothing proposition; the CEO, who usually holds the additional title of chairman, has all the power and thus is seen as totally to blame when the company gets in trouble. In other countries CEOs tend to hold the title of president. They report to a chairman, thus sharing power and making the CEO responsible to a powerful individual.

Jacobs has commented on this topic:

> The CEO is the number one employee of the corporation. And as an employee of the corporation, he should be accountable to somebody. . . . [CEOs] would prefer their labor do whatever they told them without ever asking questions or being allowed any input. That's what we all would prefer; we all would like to be potentates. [*Across the Board*, March 1992.]

A Customer-Oriented Culture

A major driver of customer satisfaction and loyalty is the employee's customer orientation. Employees must see customers as critically important and must understand that satisfying them is vital to the success of the business. They must always project a positive image and make the company seem easy to do business with. They must take responsibility for solving the customer's problems even when those problems go outside the normal scope of the employee's job.

To succeed in building customer affinity, employees must satisfy customers not just most of the time but all of the time. Since employees cannot be monitored 100 percent of the time, management must instill an attitude into the company's corporate culture that makes it standard to do business without much oversight. This can be accomplished by demonstrating importance through management actions; hiring and developing customer-oriented people; using behavioral drivers; and maximizing customer contact.

The company's customer orientation starts with top management's own beliefs, values, actions, and words. If management is more internally oriented, focused solely on profits or costs, for example, then there is little hope that the company will be customer-oriented.

Senior management's actions are critical signals of appropriate organizational behavior. At Intuit, for example, all top management, including the president, must spend a few hours each month serving customers in its telephone service department. An Intuit employee commented in an *Inc.* magazine (April 1991), interview, "What other company would have the president do the same thing I'm doing?"

The top two officers of Home Depot spend 25 to 40 percent of their time visiting stores, talking to employees, and asking customers whether they found what they were looking for. They also spend a day each month with all new store managers and assistant managers to instill the company's customer orientation. In an interview with *Fortune* (May 31, 1993), President Allan Blank said, "It's time consuming, but it's essential. When they hear it from us it means a lot more."

Another key tactic is to assign all top managers as senior advisers to clients, thus maintaining high-level contacts in the organization. This achieves three critical things: It keep top management plugged into the world of the client; it signals to every employee that customer orientation is critical; and—particularly important—it helps cement client relationships above and beyond anything that the company's sales organization could achieve on its own. Hewlett-Packard requires all its executives to maintain high-level relationships at client organizations. This ensures that the relationship is intact at the highest level in the client organization.

Another tactic is to hire the right people and to train them to be customer-oriented. As I have noted at several points in this book, management must be highly selective in recruiting employees who are empathic about customer problems and motivated always to solve them. Home Depot hires people who are extroverted and people-oriented and who have building-trade backgrounds.

However innately customer-oriented these select hires may be, they will inevitably lack a full knowledge of what they must do and what customers expect from them across a wide array of service interactions. They therefore need to be trained to satisfy clients in all the detailed encounters and different scenarios that they are likely to experience. For example, GM's Saturn Division identified all the major encounters its dealership staff had with customers and then trained the staff to handle each one.

The third tactic for instilling customer orientation is to use the company's key behavioral drivers to influence employee actions and attitudes. First, the company must make sure that its financial reward system supports a customer orientation and does not inhibit it. For example, compensation that is heavily commission-oriented can create a negative customer orientation by influencing employees to focus strictly on selling prospects and not on retaining customers. Conversely, cash rewards and other forms of recognition can be used to achieve positive results. For example, the company might pay a bonus to individuals or teams that achieve high levels of customer satisfaction.

Another behavioral driver is the company's performance measurement system. Management uses these systems to recognize top performers and uses peer pressure to address the laggards. But management must be sure to use the right measures to get the desired results. If, for instance, management stresses only profitability, it suppresses signals that employees should be customer-oriented. Management must use measures that reflect the things that drive customer satisfaction. Intuit's president, Scott Cook, commented, in an interview with *Inc.* magazine (April 1991), on his weekly employee meetings: "The first four numbers we go through have to do with customer service. Even before we get to revenues. It creates real peer pressure to improve service."

Finally, the company should create an annual customer survey to track customer satisfaction and changing values, to reward employees with high scores in customer satisfaction, and to address problem areas.

Organzational structure also influences customer orientation. Execessive management layers are a major barrier to promoting customer orientation. Every layer that separates the customer from top management filters out customer feedback, causing the organization to focus in on itself.

How the company aligns and defines its various functions and specific reporting relationships often has a significant influence on its customer orientation. For example, HP aligns most of its corporate laboratories with major product sectors to maintain the right balance between being close to the marketplace and maintaining enough distance to preserve some independence in developing new technologies. Alan Bickell, who is in charge of HP's geographic operations, commented:

> At HP, our corporate labs don't work in a vacuum. While they work on state of the art technology, they work very close to the business. The labs are lined up with our businesses, but not too tightly. Also, the person who heads our labs is a member to the president's staff and sits in on all discussions regarding our business operations.

The final tactic (and certainly one of the most important) is to maximize the organization's contact with the customer at every level possible. Richard Whitely advised in his 1991 book *The Customer-Driven Organization*, "Saturate your company with the voice of the customer."

Create formal mechanisms for a dialogue with the customer, including the highly accessible 800 number service discussed earlier. Put together a formal process for tracking complaints and for converting customer input into valuable management information. Encourage customers to call the company. This is the case at DPIC, where customers can call the company's president—who answers his own phone.

Involve the company's sales organization in the company's strategic planning process, as DPIC does twice each year, to learn from the employees who have day-to-day customer contact. Participate in customers' supplier councils and industry associations to play a key role and to establish relationships with industry leaders.

Send employee groups on visits to customers' plants to see how clients ultimately use the company's products. Donnelly sends groups of twenty employees to customer plants to watch how the final product is used in the manufacture of the automobile. Intuit has staff members go home with new customers to observe and help with any difficulties customers encounter in using its product for the first time.

One useful tactic employed by Donnelly is encouraging customers and prospects to visit the company, review its operations, and talk with its employees. Nearly every day, groups of customers visit Donnelly. They are encouraged to talk freely to employees, and vice versa. Customers walk up to employees on the plant floor and ask what they are doing. This tactic gives employees an unusually high level of contact with customers, thus furthering their customer orientation. With the right employees and the right culture, such tactics build customer confidence in the company.

The Employees Are the Company

Developing a highly motivated and qualified staff is much more than an idealistic notion. It is a powerful management tool that pays off economically. It is also the only course of action if the company is to reap the rewards of the self-directed teams and other highly efficient ways to organize work that I have discussed in this book. Although a number of managements are highly employee-oriented, there are those that hold cynical views about employees, and others still who are oblivious to the topic.

The employee-oriented model goes like this: Hire the best raw talent appropriate for the job; pay the staff fairly and somewhat more than competitors do; invest heavily in training and developing employees; provide a stable and livable work environment; and delegate substantial authority to workers to run day-to-day operations. This creates a loyal workforce with the initiative and the confidence to take actions independently. This workforce will do whatever is required to satisfy customers and to complete all necessary work on time and with high quality.

Although this model requires a greater investment in employees, the payback is quick, substantial, and sustaining. The benefits include higher productivity, lower turnover and absenteeism, less required management oversight; higher quality of service resulting from pride in the company and team pressure to maintain quality levels; and higher customer retention. The longer the company retains its employees, the less it spends to recruit and train new ones. The initial costs of hiring are spread over more years, employees' productivity is higher, and employees are more likely to provide free recruiting by word of mouth.

Donnelly has an employee turnover rate of only 2 percent per year. It also has fifty unsolicited applicants for every existing worker on staff. When the local community hears that Donnelly is hiring new employees, lines form at 2 A.M.

The cynical model assumes that employees are inherently lazy and untrustworthy and that they have limited job loyalty. Managements of companies that accept this premise pay minimal wages, invest little in training, and spend a lot on checking employees to make sure they do their work and comply with corporate policy. These companies get what they expect. They do indeed experience high employee turnover, low-quality work, and a poor attitude. What they do not realize is how their companies' reputations are downgraded among clients and prospective employees.

A variety of employee attitude studies done by Gallup and Yankelovich support the logic of the employee-oriented model. For example, in 1982 Yankelovich conducted an employee study that asked participants to select which of the following three statements they most agreed with:

"I have an inner need to do the very best job I can, regardless
   of pay."
"Work is a mere business transaction. I work only as much
   as I get paid."
"Working for a living is one of life's necessities. I wouldn't
   do it if I didn't have to."

The fact that 78 percent of the respondents agreed with the first
answer indicates that employees want much more out of their
jobs than pay. Further, they were willing to give more of themselves than the basic job requirements.

Management Levers

Exhibit 9-2 shows what management must do to develop motivated employees. I based the list partly on my own consulting
experience involving employee morale and turnover and partly
on various studies, such as the one presented in *The 100 Best
Companies to Work for in America.* My experience in particular
suggests that the things that cause employee dissatisfaction are
at least as important as the things that satisfy them.

As Exhibit 9-2 suggests, there are many factors that influence
employee satisfaction. However, management has four primary
levers for creating an employee-oriented company environment:

Exhibit 9-2. Factors influencing employee satisfaction.

Dissatisfiers	*Satisfiers*
• Bad managers	• Internally grown organization
• Impossible jobs	• Sense of belonging to a team
• Layoffs	• Job autonomy
• Mergers and acquisitions	• Fair compensation
• High-level external hires	• Development of skills
• No future	• Pride in company and its
• Poor quality	operations
• Disorganized processes	• Informality
• Poor company reputation	• Clear communication from top
	management
	• Attention to personal needs
	• Pleasant working conditions

1. Controlling management behavior
2. Maximizing employee involvement
3. Maintaining fairness
4. Creating an open environment

1. *Controlling management behavior.* Top management must make sure that everyone in the company who manages people has a supportive management style. Supportive styles center on coaching, counseling, and helping employees succeed in their jobs. Contrast this with an authoritarian style, which is marked by control and command rules, one-way communication, and limited job flexibility for employees.

My own personal observation is that most people who are attracted or promoted to management are poorly suited for their jobs. This is evident also from a survey conducted by *Personnel Journal* (May 1990), which found that 60 to 76 percent of workers surveyed said that the most stressful aspect of their job was their boss and that "[v]irtually every employed adult reports that he or she has spent considerable time (years) working for an intolerable boss."

The underlying problem is that not everyone can handle the power (or perceived power) of being the boss of even just a few people. The problem is compounded by a self-selection process that attracts and selects power-oriented people to management positions. As *Personnel Journal* noted in the same study:

> Within this group of confident, charming, assertive and persuasive people who fill the ranks of management are three subtypes of individuals, each of whom has a great deal of upward mobility and the potential to do some damage. They typically do well in interviews, assessment centers, and other beauty contests. ["How Charisma Cloaks Incompetence," by R. Hogan, R. Raskin, and D. Fazzini, copyright May 1990. Reprinted with the permission of *Personnel Journal*, all rights reserved.]

The first way to control this style problem is to minimize the number of management positions in the company by increasing spans of control and reducing layers of management. The next remedy is to be extremely cautious about selecting people for management positions. Be especially cautious about the seemingly attractive candidate who masquerades as a good people manager. Pick the individuals who are most likely to effect a supportive management style, people who are not motivated solely by power.

Training is another tactic for controlling management behavior. Since few people come to the management job with innate leadership skills, the company must invest substantially in management training. In fact, management training may be the most critical area for training and organizational development.

Finally, it is essential to track employee satisfaction by conducting a periodic employee survey. Topics covered should include employees' satisfaction with their boss's management style. HP routinely surveys its employees every eighteen months on a variety of topics, including opinions about their immediate supervisors. GE uses what it calls a 360-degree review, in which every employee is evaluated by his or her manager, subordinates, and peers on topics that reflect core values, such as team building.

If management uses surveys, it must take the results seriously and link them to all managers' performance evaluation, compensation, promotions—even job security. HP publishes the results of its employee surveys regardless of the outcome. It forms task forces to understand problems in more depth and to make recommendations. Given HP's strong employee orientation as part of its culture, the survey results create significant peer pressure to adhere to corporate values. And whenever peer pressure fails, HP's Alan Bickell commented, managers "get clobbered at their next review."

As self-directed teams become more popular, problems associated with management behavior may diminish. Management jobs will decrease in number, and the power granted to management over team members will disappear. For example, team leaders at Donnelly are more like facilitators whose role is to "remove barriers, take away things that get in the way," notes Maryam Komejan. Team leaders are selected with input from team members and spend most of their time on the factory floor answering questions and working alongside the team.

2. *Maximizing employee involvement.* The second management lever is employee involvement. Employees want more from their employers than a paycheck; they want to be informed and involved in the company's future and direction and consulted on day-to-day decisions. At a minimum, the company should freely share important information, go to great lengths to obtain feedback from employees, and involve them in task forces aimed at resolving key issues and problems.

GE uses a system it calls "workouts," three-day periods in which employees discuss issues of importance to them and make recommendations. They then present their findings to management, which must immediately respond in one of three ways: agree, disagree, or set up a task force to understand the problem better. Intuit's top management takes every employee to lunch and notes workers' suggestions for improving operations. In an interview with *Inc.* magazine (April 1991), one employee commented on the process, saying "It's pretty gratifying."

Another approach to employee involvement is Donnelly's equity system. Robert Levering and Milton Moskowitz, in *The 100 Best Companies to Work for in America,* say that Donnelly "may be the most democratic company in the United States. Nowhere else is fairness elevated to the plane it occupies at Donnelly. And nowhere else do rank-and-file employees have such a direct influence on company policies."

Donnelly's primary form of employee involvement is its work teams. Every employee belongs to one, and there most issues of fairness and disputes are resolved. For issues and problems that exceed the group's ability to resolve them without help, Donnelly has a decision-making system that is representative of the employee population and that operates much like a congressional system. This is called the "equity structure."

The next layer of employee decision making is what Donnelly calls its "equity committees," which consist of twenty to thirty employees elected by their work teams. The committee members in turn elect their chairpersons. Altogether, Donnelly has seven equity committees that include more than one hundred employees. The committees deal with personnel policies such as work rules, general compensation and benefit levels, recommendations for employee task forces, and conflict resolution. They resolve disagreements among employees at every level of the organization. Maryam Komejan described the system in *Glass* magazine (April 1987) as follows: "It's a true form of representative government, much like Congress. The members of a work team, who are the voters, elect a delegate to speak for them on an equity committee."

The next layer of decision making is the Donnelly committee, which consists of an elected member from each of the equity committees, the president (the only nonelected person on the committee), and a supervisor. The committee selects a chairperson, who serves a three-year term and functions as a facilitator. The committee makes all the final decisions and presents recommendations on wages and benefits to the board of directors.

All decisions must be unanimous. Donnelly believes this is important to making sure the matter has been thoroughly discussed, to get further commitment from the group, and to maintain a climate of cooperation. Each year, much like a political poll, Donnelly surveys each work team member to assess the effectiveness of the elected committee representatives.

The Donnelly committee accepts, rejects, or amends the recommendations of the equity committees. For example, in 1980 the equity committees recommended a pay raise of more than 10 percent to bring overall wages in line with key benchmark wage comparisons in the community. The Donnelly committee approved this raise, with the stipulation that employees improve productivity costs to offset the raise. Both the wage increase and the productivity goals were achieved, thus benefiting all the company's stakeholders.

3. *Maintaining fairness.* The third management lever for enhancing employee satisfaction is perceived fairness, particularly concerning job security and distribution of compensation. In the employee-oriented model, workers are expected to participate more and to be more productive and attentive to customers and quality and more loyal to the company. It is thus logical that these employees would expect the company to reciprocate and be fair with them, particularly in terms of pay and job security.

Employee-oriented companies share the company's success by paying somewhat higher than industry-average wages and provide various forms of profit sharing. In contrast to the rest of the retail industry—which is not known for its employee orientation—Home Depot hires 96 percent of its people into full-time jobs, pays higher starting salaries than its competitors, pays a 7 percent bonus in company stock, and provides health insurance. In particular, it has a strong emphasis on employee ownership of the company. Store workers wear aprons that say HI, I AM JOHN, A HOME DEPOT SHAREHOLDER.

Although it is impractical to maintain an absolute no-layoff policy in today's uncertain and cyclical environment, there is much a company can do to be fair on job security, such as promoting from within, cross-training employees from new positions when old ones get phased out, and giving extended severance pay when layoffs are inevitable. Nevertheless, having a long-term strategy, managing the company's growth, and maintaining a focused business are still the best ways to avoid situations that make layoffs essential.

Nothing erodes stakeholders' perceptions of fairness faster than the currently high levels of executive compensation, especially at a time when hundreds of thousands of workers are being laid off. In the book *The 100 Best Companies to Work for in America*, Polaroid's Owen noted that high executive compensation was "like a time bomb clicking away in the American workplace."

A *Business Week* survey indicated that that average CEO of a large company made $3.8 million in 1992, up 56 percent from the prior year and 142 times the pay of the average factory worker. In contrast, the average CEO in Japan earned thirty-two times the pay of a factory worker.

High executive compensation raises issues of fairness and efficiency for a publicly held business. For example, most stakeholders would benefit if the typical large company paid its CEO $2.8 instead of $3.8 million a year and invested the savings in the business. The company could spend the million-dollar difference on twenty extra engineers or salespeople, or it could invest in upgraded equipment or employee training to improve productivity.

At Donnelly, employees can't lose their jobs because a new technology or process improvement is introduced. This fosters an environment in which employees continually contribute new ideas to increase productivity. After five years on the job, employees have the right to bump less senior staff. If there is a layoff, Donnelly guarantees staff 90 percent of their salaries for one year. Donnelly also avoids layoffs by cutting pay during industry downturns. In the late 1980s, Donnelly avoided a layoff by reducing wages by 3 percent at the low end of the pay scale and 17 percent at the upper end. It also uses voluntary short-term layoffs during slow periods.

4. *Creating an open environment.* The fourth lever is openness—sharing information—and interpersonal dialogue. Employees want to know what is happening throughout the company, to express their views and concerns, and to access management across all levels and organizational boundaries. They want to work in an environment that is informal, where people are on a first-name basis.

Top management sets the tone for openness in the company. First and foremost, it must make sure that employees are not punished for sharing information, especially when they voice negative comments that need to be aired. The challenge for senior management is to make sure that other managers further down in the organization receive negative feedback objectively and do not punish those who express it. Management must also foster an open-door policy that guarantees anyone from any part of the company easy access to whomever they need to see—including top management. It is hard believe in openness when senior management is impossible to access. Donnelly employee Paul Prescott commented in *The 100 Best Companies to Work for in America*, "I can talk to any manager about anything, right up to the president. I always felt like I was the underdog [in his prior job], but now I feel like I can say something and it's being heard."

Top management must also minimize those privileges that visibly separate them from the rest of the organization. These barriers include executive parking and dining privileges and, in particular, special offices that are located far from the workplace. These are signals that top management is unapproachable.

HP maintains its cultural value of openness through many small things that add up. Alan Bickell commented:

Openness is the style of the company. People walk in the door from college into a very informal culture. We don't take ourselves so terribly seriously; politics and arrogance don't work at HP. We have a very open environment; we have no private offices, everyone is on a first-name basis, and we have a lot of cross-level communication. Cooperation is a natural part of what is done. If someone needs to coordinate on a particular issue that requires accessing a manager several levels up, the person just does it.

Home Depot stresses openness across all levels by making goals clear and by letting employees know what they should expect from their managers. The company values free expression, individuality, and self-reliance, but within the context of teamwork. The top two executives participate in a quarterly television broadcast with phoned-in questions so that all employees can share information on earnings, wages, and improvement opportunities.

A company's openness is inhibited by that pervasive cause of organizational ineffectiveness, excess layers of management. Each layer of management creates barriers to internal communication and builds a pseudohierarchy, classes of employees that do not communicate with each other.

Organizational Connectivity

We are all familiar with the frustrations of dealing with the "disconnected" company, whether as an employee, a customer, a supplier, or a manager. One part of the disconnected company does not know what the other parts are doing. Different divisions, departments, and geographic offices do their own thing, acting as if they were separate companies. In the disconnected company, R&D is not linked with marketing, sales, or manufacturing; each sales region has it own goals and strategies; manufacturing makes what it is efficient for it to make without considering what is salable; and the MIS department spends a fortune investing in its pet technology while users grumble about cost allocations and lack of value added. In the disconnected company, individuals pursuing their own plans and programs can cause the company to gravitate into new areas, causing the company to become unfocused and inefficient.

Members of disconnected companies can tell you that being disconnected is part of the corporate culture. It encourages entre-preneurialism, decentralization, and internal competition, which the company uses to motivate employees. These companies have a lot of autonomous profit centers that are left alone so long as they meet their bottom-line goals and have "star" systems that enthrone the top echelon of superachievers. New clients buy the individual, not the company as a whole.

The "connected" company, on the other hand, operates so that all its various elements pull together in a coordinated fash-ion. Professor David Maister, formerly of the Harvard Business School, called this type of company "the one-firm firm" in a *Sloan Management Review* (Fall 1985) article of the same name. The connected company operates on companywide coordination. It stresses group effort and identity, close teamwork, and institu-tional loyalty.

The connected company has many obvious advantages in terms of organizational efficiency and ability to focus resources on executing common initiatives; its employees are more likely to stay focused and to work towards common purposes. The collec-tive efforts of individuals are much stronger than those of a loose collection of autonomous people, regardless of their individual strengths. Furthermore, teamwork enhances employee satisfac-tion, as I have noted. From the client's perspective, buying the company as an institution with a team behind it provides more value than buying the services of an individual operating auton-omously within a company.

Management Levers

Despite the clear advantages of connectivity to both the company and the individual, it is not necessarily in human nature for employees to act in a connected way. Joseph Badaracco and Richard Ellsworth, authors of the book *Leadership and the Quest for Integrity* (1989), noted, "The most powerful splintering force that diffuses efforts within an organization is self-interest, the domi-

nant motivator of human behavior." Thus, management faces
many challenges in attempting to build a one-company company.

Despite this challenge, there are many actions that management can take to build a connected company. As Exhibit 9-3
shows, there are four levers that management can use to foster a
connected-company culture:

1. Demonstrating leadership
2. Developing a homegrown organization
3. Ensuring that behavioral drivers support connectivity
4. Using information to unite the company

1. *Leadership.* The first lever, leadership, starts with whether
top management believes in teamwork rather than internal competition as a way to manage the company and to motivate employees. Many business leaders, however, believe in motivating
managers by internal competition. Professors Clinton Longeneck
of the University of Toledo and Dennis Gioia of Penn State noted
in a study profiled in *Sloan Management Review* (Fall 1991) that
internal competition is a common business practice for attempting
to motivate employees, and they concluded, "Competition is
effective among businesses, but not necessarily within a business.
Collaboration and cooperation within the organization are de-
monstrably better strategies for improving competitiveness in the
business arena."

To create a one-company environment, management must
continually communicate, and it must act in ways that reinforce
teamwork and the pursuit of common goals. This involves minimizing political squabbles and divisive behavior at the highest
levels of the organization, because these behaviors send strong
messages and set a poor example. In particular, top management
must not tolerate lack of teamwork in the management ranks,
especially when it involves highly successful individuals.

Having a well-defined long-range plan and communicating it
throughout the organization provides a clear sense of where the
company is headed and enables employees to see more clearly
how their roles fit in the bigger picture. Connectivity is further
augmented by broad participation in the strategy development
process. For example, Donnelly has a periodic program it calls its

Exhibit 9-3. Management levers for building a connected organization.

---

1. Demonstrating Leadership Initiatives

- Develop a long-term business plan.
- Broadly communicate the strategy.
- Stick with the strategy.
- Manage steady growth.
- Be cautious about acquisitions and avoid mergers.
- Involve the sales organization in strategy development.
- Develop a mission that spells out strategy and corporate values.
- Promote an open culture.
- Develop an elite but not arrogant membership.
- Stay connected to frontline employees.
- Downplay stardom and emphasize teamwork.
- Minimize high-level turf battles.

2. Developing a Homegrown Organization

- Hire cooperative team players.
- Train employees in teamwork.
- Use corporate training to bring staff together across functions and locations.
- Employ staff rotations.
- Cautiously hire high-level lateral staff and managers.

3. Ensuring That Behavioral Drivers Support Connectivity

- Carefully design profit centers to influence the right behavior.
- Reduce layers of management.
- Never adapt the organization to fit the individual.
- Redesign processes across functions.
- Adopt standard processes.
- Replace functional managers with process owners.
- Use self-directed teams with cross-functional representation.
- Develop goals beyond budgeted profits.
- Revise the reward system to support the desired behavior.
- Employ cross-functional teams for solving specific problems.
- Adopt team selling.
- Use concurrent design teams for product development.
- Develop upward feedback systems.
- Encourage top management involvement with frontline employees.

4. Using Information

- Develop corporate databases on customer relationships and employee skills.
- Link all employees with electronic mail and network bulletin boards.

Management Forum, in which the company's top eight executives and the fifty people who report directly to them meet to discuss the long-term direction of the company. Finally, corporatewide goal setting, using processes such as management by objectives (MBO), enables management to link and integrate goals for the corporation with goals for individuals.

HP uses an integrated planning system called hoshin, which is a long-range goal-setting tool that works like a linked MBO process. The system starts with the president, who sets long-term goals. These goals are then translated into goals that the next level of management must achieve in order for the president to achieve his goals. The goal setting cascades down throughout the organization so that each operating unit or department has long-term goals that clearly fit into a greater scheme of what the company is trying to achieve. As Alan Bickell of HP commented, "The system works its way down the organization from the president's goals, reinforcing them, galvanizing the company together. Everyone is working in the same context, and even though employees have their own piece, they know how that fits into the bigger picture."

2. *The homegrown culture.* The second lever is developing a homegrown culture, which involves creating an elite—but not an arrogant—culture where membership is exclusive and the rewards great. Employing a strict promote-from-within policy is crucial for rewarding those working their way up through the organization. It also helps avoid diluting the homegrown environment with the different cultures, standards, and values that high-level hires bring with them. The company should resort to high-level hiring only to obtain new capabilities not found within the company. When done, high-level hiring should be carried out cautiously and with full participation from all levels in the interview process. When Donnelly hires externally, for instance, it uses team interviewing in a process that takes two to three days on-site.

It is important for management to start out by hiring cooperative people who, while highly motivated individually, will nevertheless make strong team players. In his article "The One-Firm Firm," Maister noted that Hewitt, a human resources consulting company, targeted hiring candidates it called SWANs, an acronym for Smart, Work hard, Ambitious, and Nice. While many of its competitors sought people with the first three characteristics, Hewitt looked for that extra quality that would make them good team players. Donnelly also looks for people who it believes will work well on teams and who are not authoritarian.

Training and development are important tactics for building a connected organization. Staff should be trained in how to work in a teamwork environment, and training staff in cross-functional areas should help them see how the pieces fit together. This helps them resolve problems that they might otherwise see as being beyond their ability or scope. Training generally brings together groups of employees from different areas and functions, which builds bonds between fellow employees. Finally, rotating staff between different functions and geographical areas lets employees understand the business better and build ties to fellow employees that otherwise would not have existed.

Developing a homegrown culture also means that management must direct the company's growth in such a way that it can hire and train new employees at a measured pace, avoiding crises that might force management to make higher-level hires to do the work. Similarly, management should avoid mergers and acquisitions, which have an impact on the company's culture greater even than that of high-level hiring.

3. *Behavioral drivers.* The third management lever ensures that the major behavioral drivers support companywide connectivity. These include profit centers, performance measures, reward systems, organizational structure, and processes.

One of the strongest drivers is profit center definitions, that is, how the company draws its profit center boundaries. In most organizations profitability is the key objective, and profit centers define who is on what team. One of the worst impediments to teamwork is having too many profit centers (whether by product or geography) in which managements are rewarded on their own profitability. Despite the CEO's speeches on cooperation, if the company has too many profit centers, it will divide into uncooperative teams that follow their own agendas.

As a spokesperson from the benefits consulting company Hewitt commented in Maister's article. "We think that having no profit centers is a great advantage to us. Other organizations don't realize how much time they waste fighting over allocations of overhead, transfer charges, and other mechanisms caused by a profit center mentality."

Management must create new performance measures to supplement financial ones and must give them equal weighting in assessing individual performance assessments. Your company should include subjective measures that identify individuals who excel in intergroup cooperation. The company should also ensure that its reward and recognition systems support teamwork, for example, by employing group bonuses to reward team, rather than individual, achievements.

Organizational structure and reporting relationships create barriers and competing teams that thwart cooperation within the company. Therefore, management must be very careful about defining the organization chart. You can foster connectivity by reducing the number of management positions, which tend to create tiny fiefdoms. In particular, you should design the organization to support the company's strategy, never to accommodate the individual.

Standardizing the company's processes is another important tactic. This gives employees a standard approach to running the business, like a common set of rules for the game, and a common language for discussing issues in a comprehensible way.

Establishing cross-functional processes, teams, and task forces are other important ways to promote connectivity. (Virtually everything that Donnelly does, including day-to-day work and task forces, is done in cross-functional teams.) A company's strategy development process, for example, should include broad functional representation from sales, operations, and other key aspects of the business.

The company should employ cross-functional task forces aimed at exploring new areas or resolving a complex problem. Team selling, mentioned in Chapter 7, is the process of drawing key resources together from multiple functions and disciplines to solve a prospective client's particular problem. Another example of cross-functional operation is concurrent design, which is a process that uses multifunctional teams throughout all stages of developing new products. Instead of a serial process, in which one function hands off to the next, concurrent design integrates a multifunctional approach along the way.

4. *Information*. The final management lever for building connectivity is information. Information covers virtually anything management needs to run a connected company, whether competitive intelligence, results of opinion surveys, or corporatewide customer databases. At the most fundamental level, databases and common information help build a cohesive, connected culture. Examples are human resources databases that indicate employee capabilities that can be useful throughout the company and customer databases that contain descriptions of the company's comprehensive relationship with customers or prospects.

All the other extreme information includes electronic mail and the client/server applications that link employees, customers, and suppliers in a new form of communication. Using Local Area Networks (LANs) and Wide Area Networks (WANs), people can share data and text, as well as messages, via bulletin boards, databases, conferences, and other mechanisms that connect disparate employees and reshape how they work. At Hewlett-Packard, for example, electronic mail connects approximately 82,000 out of 92,000 employees worldwide.

These advances in electronic connectivity facilitate organizational connectivity and promise to transform whole organizations and their cultures. In their book *Connections* (1991) Lee Sproull and Sara Kiesler describe these new electronic linkages as communications that "do not simply cross space and time; they also can cross hierarchical and departmental barriers, change standard operating procedures, and reshape organizational norms. They can create entirely new options in organizational behavior and structure."

However inspiring these new technologies may be, they are no substitute for basic managerial tools and principles. In fact, these information tools inevitably work best in companies that are already connected through their internal cultures, well-communicated strategies, and supportive organizational structures and processes.

Chapter 10
Sustaining Market Ownership

At the start of this book I described market ownership as a powerful way to compete, then explained how to achieve market ownership. It is fitting that the book end with some brief advice on how to sustain market ownership once it has been achieved and how management can avoid succumbing to its own success, which happened to once leading companies like IBM, GM, and Sears. These companies all dominated their markets for many decades and were viewed as recently as the mid-1980s as paradigms of success role models for management excellence. *Fortune* magazine (May 3, 1993), however, called them dinosaurs, big powerful companies that were so successful for so long that they failed to adapt to changing environments and were displaced by more nimble, adaptive players. Actually, the decline of these modern-day dinosaurs was evident in many ways even in the 1970s. The strength of their market ownership sustained them longer than the average company would have lasted.

The final ideas I give you, therefore, concern how to sustain market ownership—in other words, how to avoid becoming a dinosaur. Use these eight ideas for guidance.

1. *Avoid complacency.* Complacency was the key to the fall of the corporate dinosaurs; in some cases, complacency translated into complete arrogance. Success makes many executives believe they are invincible, smarter than everyone else in the business. They go down with the ship still believing it.

Peter Hawes, CEO of DPIC Companies, commented about

future success: "The thing that I fear the most is the onset of smugness; it makes it hard to stay objective. Things constantly change. You have to keep questioning everything you are doing." Maryam Komejan of Donnelly noted: "If we ever get to the point where we are satisfied, we are dead."

Do not let success go to your head! Take the attitude that there is no finish line (which is—or should be—a self-evident truth about business). On this point, a spokesperson for Bankers Trust noted: "We like to run fast even though we are ahead." Home Depot's CEO Bernard Marcus commented on complacency in *Business Atlanta* (April 1992): "You need to keep moving to stay ahead of the pack. Complacency is the root of retailers' troubles. When we start getting cookie-cutter stores that stay the same year after year, that's when we have to worry about our downfall."

Boards of directors need to pick CEOs who have sufficient humility to know that no matter how successful the company, they are not invincible. Nor are they the sole reason for the company's success. Motorola's CEO, Bob Galvin, set the tone for his company's highly regarded rise to world-class status in quality and performance by openly admitting "he did not know what he did not know." Financial Executives Research noted in a 1993 study that Galvin "led Motorola executives to the concepts of humility and listening—humility in the sense they were willing to admit they did not know or have all the answers." Companies need CEOs with balanced perspectives, CEOs whose psyches extend beyond the narrowly defined success of the company, who have the self-confidence to share the rewards of success, and who recognize that they could not (and do not) do it all by themselves. Simply put, corporate leaders must not take themselves too seriously, and they should make sure that the company's managers do likewise.

2. *Set stretch objectives.* Once the company has succeeded in attaining its goals, it should set new goals that require a quantum leap in the value of the company's products and services. This is what has kept Xerox from extinction and what separates it from IBM, GM, and Sears. Xerox's ownership of the copier market made the company complacent, and ultimately, it became vulnerable to Japanese competitors like Canon, which entered the market with higher-value, better-quality products at lower prices.

Xerox saved itself partly by setting a goal to improve the quality of its products by a factor of 10, as measured by a decrease in the number of product defects. Xerox achieved this goal, won the Malcolm Baldrige award for quality, and is one of the few American companies to regain a market share previously lost to Japanese companies.

Donnelly stretches itself by setting perfection as the goal. It has created a highly self-critical culture that, instead of relaxing with success, always finds things it could have done better.

The best time to set stretch objectives is when the company is at the pinnacle of success—before complacency sets in at all levels of the company. This is what HP did in the early 1990s: After reaching its quality goals for the 1980s, it immediately set new stretch goals for the 1990s. Motorola and Anheuser-Busch have done the same. Even though Busch sells more than its next four rivals combined and has a 44 percent market share, it has set stretch objectives of attaining 50 percent market share by the mid-1990s and of starting to penetrate foreign markets.

3. *Create a change-tolerant organization.* As the company's environment changes, so must the company. This means dropping money-losing products, merging plants, changing people's jobs, and taking any other actions necessary to adapt to a changing market and competitive forces. Either the company does this by choice, or it may be forced to take more drastic action later on.

Responding to change requires both the will to make bold moves and a change-tolerant organization that trusts management sufficiently to stick with it through periods of change and uncertainty.

In those companies with low employee loyalty, employees' first response to change is to update their résumés. Within a short time the company has lost people from all levels—and it is usually the better people who go first. They go because they do not trust management to deal with them fairly. Companies with high employee loyalty can weather enormous amounts of change and do so with the strong support of employees. Few employees leave, and those who do are often the poorer performers who know they will not be able to meet the new standards.

Donnelly, with its strong employee orientation, makes change a part of the company's culture. Change is expected and tolerated because the company has earned employees' trust. As Maryam Komejan commented, "Change is a way of life. We are always changing with our customers. We are always changing job positions and fine-tuning the organization to keep it fresh. We recently shut down a production group that displaced 250 people, yet our growth helped us reemploy all 250 of them."

4. *Block the competition.* Success, more than anything else, attracts competition. The most potent way to ward off competitors is to attack yourself before others get the chance to do it for you. This means attacking your current cash cows, high margin products, and elite lines of business with higher-value offerings that have new features, better performance, and lower pricing.

By staying way out ahead, make the game of catch-up impossible to play. Once a company owns a market, it has a powerful base from which to launch a quantum leap improvement in affinity and credibility with customers and other stakeholders.

Keep your eye on customer value. Eliminate the elements of the business that contribute little to customer value, and invest in those that do. For example, by shrinking the space devoted to its kitchen and reallocating it to create more dining room space, Taco Bell reinvigorated its chain of restaurants.

Continually restructure your business in small increments to avoid the trauma that results from a major restructuring that threatens the company and damages its internal spirit, culture, and values. Unisys is a good example. After expanding into many unrelated areas and loading up on debt, it encountered a crisis that forced it to cut its workforce 54 percent, discontinue many products, and shut several factories. Unisys's current philosophy has changed. Its CEO, James Unruh, noted in *Business Week* (November 23, 1992): "Our phrase is a little restructuring every day."

Do not give competitors any easy beachheads that could later grow into major threats. You must look carefully at your current business in terms of value provided to customers; also, scrutinize subsegments of your market that you currently overlook but that competitors could focus on to create a beachhead. You must find these subsegments before competitors do. You should learn about any subtle variations your competitors might develop in customer value and then either develop new products, services, and delivery systems or adapt existing ones to fulfill clients' needs in a more focused way.

Mercedes and BMW had enormous staying power in the luxury car market, but they failed to recognize the younger, value-oriented subsegment of the luxury car market. This gave Lexus a shot at a market that otherwise, because of the difficulty of establishing prestige as a newcomer, would have been extremely difficult to enter. As I have described, Lexus used this beachhead to become the top-selling luxury car in the United States within a few years' time.

To block the competition, your company must strive to be the leader in the competitive arenas that are pertinent to the scope of its business. Your company needs to have leading-edge clients to keep it on its toes and to enhance learning about client values and product usage. Furthermore, your company needs to play in the most competitive markets. Both Hewlett-Packard and Donnelly grew stronger by becoming highly competitive players in Japan. The Japanese market tends to have more demanding clients with higher quality and operating standards than elsewhere. If you can win in these markets, you can win anywhere.

5. *Stay focused.* Avoid letting success lure the company into unrelated business pursuits. These are distractions, resource drains that weaken the company and its continuing ability to be a leader in its core business. As part of the company's mission, create a definition of its core competencies and business scope. Use this definition as a rigorous guide to challenge all new business proposals.

In business, as in most aspects of life, the grass only *looks* greener on the other side of the fence. In evaluating new ventures, start by assuming that any new business will not necessarily be any more attractive than your current one. Honeywell learned this the hard way when it ventured outside its core instrumentation business and started making mainframe computers. Top management thought at the time that this was a "sexier" business.

Avoid the promise of synergies in considering new ventures. They almost never develop. When they do, it is because of a Herculean implementation effort to make them happen. New ventures should first be evaluated on a stand-alone basis, apart from any considerations of potential synergies.

Cut your losses early on new products, services, ventures, and declining businesses that have no future. These will drain and divert the company's resources. The earlier you start to phase out these losing elements, the less pain the organization will suffer; these problems become acute very fast, ultimately requiring quick, drastic remedies.

6. *Avoid mergers.* If management values the company's current culture and ways of doing things, then it should avoid all mergers. Mergers inevitably create radical changes in both partners. Seek growth internally instead by investing in sales, product development, and core competencies.

Do not make acquisitions for growth's sake. Acquisitions are very risky and drain resources; like mergers, they alter the company's culture. When your company needs new skills and capabilities, make selective hires, license technology, and create strategic alliances to obtain them.

7. *Avoid insularity.* While management must stay focused, it must also avoid being blindsided. It must never lack information about the business, internally or externally. Remember that myths fill the void created by an absence of factual data; they can lead people astray and keep them from taking necessary actions. Every chapter in this book outlines the need to measure things, whether it is operational performance, customer value, or employee satisfaction.

Make sure that the company's performance measurement systems track key drivers of the company's success, and make sure that the measures include leading indicators. Remember that current profitability is a lagging indicator; it reveals the results of past actions. As a guide, think, "If you can't measure it, you can't manage it."

Continually monitor the company's market share, even if it is difficult to measure. Sales performance tells you very little about the company's competitive strength in the market, because it does not take into account market growth. It is quite possible for the company's sales to increase while it is actually losing market share. Both market share and market growth are important statistics.

Continually assess whether you should modify your business model to adapt to changes in the marketplace, competitive developments, new technologies, or other environmental trends. To stay on top of changing needs and values, periodically test customer perceptions of value. Peter Hawes suggested, "Value added is very tricky; what's needed today may change tomorrow. You have to listen real carefully to the market. And, take a careful look at lost customers."

Constantly track competitors very closely. Anticipate their moves by building a competitive tracking system. In particular, keep track of noncompetitors who could spring into the market from the fringe with a new and winning market focus or value proposition. Keep track of the dynamics of distribution channels to ascertain which ones are emerging and which are languishing.

Alan Bickell of Hewlett-Packard suggests this strategy for staying informed: "Constantly look ahead to what customers expect and need. Track competitors very closely, even potential ones, not just the obvious ones. Follow things that are going on that are hard to predict."

Avoid insularity by selectively introducing new recruits into the otherwise predominantly homegrown culture. Be selective about what the needed skills are. Make sure that individuals will fit the company's culture and be accepted by existing staff, customers, and suppliers. Make these decisions slowly. Involve all levels of employees, and use team interviews to develop a consensus on the individual's fit with the organization.

8. *Sustain corporate values.* Above all, top management must preserve the company's value system across transitions in management and over the rough road of the business cycle. The board of directors and senior management must make sure that company leaders at all levels believe in and support the company's values.

Management must have the courage to promote the right people—not the loudest—to perpetuate the culture. The right people are not those drawn to power; they are those with sufficient humility to share power and rewards and to create an open environment that is so important to employee satisfaction and vital organizational productivity.

"The acid test in leadership," says Jack Welch of GE, "is whether management is willing to discipline, demote—and fire, if necessary—top salespeople, high-performing profit-center managers, and others who contribute to near-term profitability but whose beliefs, words, and actions run counter to the company's value system."

Index